MAST

RESTAURA

CW00370174

MACMILLAN MASTER SERIES

Astronomy
Australian History
Background to Business
Basic English Law
Basic Management
Biology
British Politics
Business Communication
Business Law
Business Microcomputing
Catering Science
Chemistry
COBOL Programming
Commerce
Computer Programming
Computers
Data Processing
Economic and Social History
Economics
Electrical Engineering
Electronics
English Grammar
English Language
English Literature
Financial Accounting
French
French 2
German

Hairdressing
Italian
Italian 2
Japanese
Keyboarding
Marketing
Mathematics
Modern British History
Modern European History
Modern World History
Nutrition
Office Practice
Pascal Programming
Physics
Practical Writing
Principles of Accounts
Restaurant Service
Social Welfare
Sociology
Spanish
Spanish 2
Spreadsheets
Statistics
Statistics with your Microcomputer
Study Skills
Typewriting Skills
Word Processing

MASTERING
RESTAURANT
SERVICE

H. L. CRACKNELL
and
G. NOBIS

MACMILLAN

First published 1989

Published by
MACMILLAN EDUCATION LTD
Houndmills, Basingstoke, Hampshire RG21 2XS
and London
Companies and representatives
throughout the world

Printed in Hong Kong

ISBN 0–333–42668–1
ISBN 0–333–42669–X Pbk
ISBN 0–333–42670–3 Pbk export

CONTENTS

CONTENTS

CONTENTS

CONTENTS

LIST OF FIGURES

LIST OF FIGURES

LIST OF TABLES

PREFACE

The aim of this book is to provide people newly-employed in, and those intending to enter the catering industry, with an outline of what it is like to work as a waiter and what knowledge and skills are required to carry out the job efficiently; it is also intended as an *aide-mémoire* to those already engaged as waiters. To this end it provides an outline of the whole range of activities to be undertaken and deals with the organisational requirements as found in the majority of food-service situations.

This book seeks to provide the reader with the foundations of a sound career and subsequent advancement and self-development; to do this, it takes as its basis the origins and historical background of the profession of waiter and shows how the intricate methods of food service were first introduced and subsequently developed. It gives an insight into the cultural aspects of food and beverage service from early times, and traces the course through the social changes at all those levels of society, where frequent eating away from home is a normal event in the pattern of life.

It might be felt that this book places too much emphasis on the very high-class form of restaurant service, but it does embrace all levels of food service. The authors believe strongly that the standard of food service applicable to the best restaurants should set that of all others.

The art of waiting can be defined as constant attention to small details and the anticipation of a customer's wants before he has to ask. Waiting techniques are a form of etiquette and good manners and when well carried out they add enormously to the customers' enjoyment of a meal, so enhancing the quality of life. Even such a simple chore as brushing crumbs off the table can be carried out with aplomb. Serving people and making sure that they enjoy their meal may seem alien to the British character but waiting is an honourable calling and can be the route to a very lucrative career. It is a job that requires a ready smile rather than a reluctant scowl.

Suggestions for self-teaching are given and questions are included so as to measure the degree of understanding gained at each stage. The reader should attempt to answer these questions before proceeding to the next chapter or section.

Reference is made throughout to the food-service operator or waiter but it must not be thought that this book is for men only; it is equally applicable to female staff who excel at this career.

H. L. CRACKNELL
G. NOBIS

THE EVOLUTION OF

RESTAURANT SERVICE

1.1 INTRODUCTION

A study of history helps to identify the traditions of a nation's customs, and a knowledge of the evolution of food and beverage service will not only assist in discerning the trends that have led to present-day standards but produce a sense of pride in an employee in being part of an ancient and honourable calling. An understanding of table manners and etiquette, the changing fashions in food presentation and the influence of foreign travel, all help in gaining a better knowledge of the job of being a waiter and so make it more than merely a means of earning a living.

To be a waiter was once looked upon as being a domestic servant and many who chose it as their job viewed it as being an undignified calling because they had to serve their better-off fellow-human-beings who could order them about and treat them with disdain. The 'upstairs–downstairs' distinctions between master and servant no longer apply and the work of serving food and drink to customers in a correct manner is not in the least demeaning.

1.2 EARLY INFLUENCES

How man first discovered that cooking food made it fit for consumption is open to speculation but bronze cooking vessels dating from 2000 BC have been discovered in China. In 450 BC the Greek historian Herodotus wrote an account of the way in which the Persians celebrated an important event or a festive occasion by spit-roasting a whole beast such as a camel, horse or ox. Spit-roasting was also done in ancient Egypt and when the beast was cooked it was portioned into baskets and served to the celebrants who were seated on the ground. Chairs for sitting up to table were not in common use until about 650 BC, the first recorded being those at the palace of the King of Assyria.

By the fifth century BC cooking methods had reached such an advanced stage with food being cooked by baking, boiling, grilling and frying as well as spit-roasting, that chefs were employed by wealthy Greeks to create the exotic dishes that were in demand and again, Herodotus (c. 485 – 425 BC) has recorded the meal he had at the house of a merchant named Micias who lived at Corinth. The family plate was on display with the wine served in solid silver goblets. The waiters came marching into the dining room bearing aloft great silver dishes of food which they then presented to each guest before placing them on the service table. Guests then rose from their sofas and went to select what they wanted from the array of thirty or more magnificently garnished dishes of food. From Greece, these practices of food preparation and service were adopted by Rome, the newly-risen Mediterranean power, where they were further elaborated and elevated to even greater heights.

As the military and economic power of the ancient world, Rome adopted the role of Greece and proceeded to make the art of eating even more ostentatious. The Romans ate in a reclining position, each person on a divan or sofa and attended by an acolyte who washed the guest's feet and hands in scented water and garbed him in a banqueting toga. The meal was preceded by a burnt offering to the gods, then waiters bore in the first of the three-course meal and proceeded to offer the dishes to guests, in order of precedence. The event ended with entertainment in the form of declamations and music.

1.3 FOOD SERVICE IN MEDIEVAL TIMES

As their zest for conquest was replaced by love of the good things of life so the defence of the Roman Empire was left in the hands of mercenary forces with the result that towards the end of the fifth century AD Rome was overrun by a succession of foreign invaders and the once-great Empire expired. But records of the Roman Empire survived and when cities were built and rose to prominence in Italy, many of the Empire's practices were revived, especially those of the table.

Although these cities were founded on democratic ideals, political intrigues amongst the powerful families brought about the rigid class-system that soon spread across Europe. The hierarchical structure of princely households meant that noblemen assumed responsibility for the various activities not only of the armies but of the domestic aspects of the castle or palace. Sons of gentlemen did not consider it demeaning to serve their lord in the bedchamber or at table, any more than they did when called to take up arms.

The pattern of service was the responsibility of the major domo, a nobleman who was master of the household staff and who directed the work of the next most important members, the *trinciante* or carver, the *echanson* or cupbearer, and the *pantler* or *panetrere* or bread-keeper, all of whom were men of great importance. The hierarchy of these staff later became the basis of the system of restaurant operation as carried out today in all the great hotels and restaurants of the world.

1.4 INTRODUCTION OF TABLEWARE

The shaping of various materials into serving and eating utensils helped considerably towards the improvement of service techniques. The Chinese started to use chopsticks as long ago as 500 BC. They prepared food by chopping it into small pieces and serving it in small bowls which could be brought close to the mouth making it much easier to eat. Glass was first made by the ancient Egyptians and silver, gold and ivory dishes were in use in Roman times.

The fork was first introduced to Britain in 1708 from Venice where it had been in use for several centuries. Before this the carving knife had always been used for cutting meat and bread, and for conveying it to the mouth, but with the introduction of the fork the standard of table manners was advanced considerably. Porcelain had been made in China from about the year 1350 AD and in Italy from 1575; its manufacture in France which started in 1693 was followed by its manufacture in Germany in 1704 when the Meissen factory started to produce hard-paste porcelain articles.

Table decorations began to assume importance and Benevenuto Cellini (1500–71) produced the most beautiful dishes in gold – cups, vases, spoon-warmers, salt-cellars, bowls and tureens and other serving utensils. England became the world's foremost producer of fine silverware and Paul Storr was a notable silversmith who adapted classical Grecian themes for many beautiful table utensils including sauce-boats, tea-urns, coffee-pots and salvers.

1.5 DEVELOPMENT OF TECHNIQUES

For many hundred years until the latter part of the nineteenth century, a formal meal had consisted of two courses, each composed of a large number of dishes that were a meal in themselves, as each course had several dishes of each of the courses of the menu as we know it today.

This form of presentation provided an extensive selection of dishes that showed the affluence of the householder, whilst assuaging the gigantic appetites of the diners. Great care was taken in the arrangement of dishes on the table and guests helped themselves, mainly from those nearest to them, in any order. The neat and orderly table arrangement was enhanced by the artistry of the dishes of food which were garnished and embellished to a marked degree. The practice of artistic presentation reached its apogee in late Regency and early Victorian times, in particular by a great French chef named Marie-Antoine Carême (1784–1833). He worked for kings, princes and very wealthy families who were able to afford his extravagant methods of decoration that converted every dish into a masterpiece of architectural beauty.

The word 'service' then meant one group of dishes as a course or part of a meal. The first service was called the *entrée*, a French word meaning the meal that was on the table when the diners entered the dining room. The remains of this course were then removed whilst guests stretched their legs and they came and sat down again to the remove course, called the *relevé* in French. Each course was carefully arranged on the table under the watchful eye of the cook or butler, in accordance with the symmetrical pattern previously planned, but not such as to make the table look overcrowded. The names of these two courses are still used but nowadays indicate main meat courses, an entrée being a fairly simple dish of meat with little or no garnish or potatoes or vegetables, the relevé being a more substantial piece of meat, poultry or game with a sauce and a fairly elaborate garnish, and vegetables and potatoes. As Byron wrote, 'The mind is lost in nightly contemplation of intellect expended on two courses.'

As the years went by, the two courses were expanded to four or six as the logical sequence of courses was introduced, in accordance with the order of the menu, with a choice of at least two dishes on each course, one at each end of the table to be carved and served out by the host and hostess or by the head butler, and taken by a butler to each guest. This method of service was known as *service à la française* because it had been brought to this country by French chefs who started coming to work in the houses of rich people, after the French Revolution in 1793.

It was in 1856 that a new and better method of serving food was introduced to this country from Russia. In the 1888 edition of her *Book of Household Management*, Mrs Beeton says 'dinners *à la russe* as they used to be called, are now so anglicised and so common that we find them even in the houses of people of very moderate incomes'. Credit for the introduction of this form of service is given to Félix Urbain-Dubois (1818–1902) a French chef who had worked in Russia for the Czar.

Whereas previously large joints, whole roast birds and big fish on the bone were borne into the room, carved and served at table, the carving was now done in the kitchen by the cook who arranged it in portions on a silver flat or in an entrée dish, together with the garnish. The dishful of food with enough for four to ten people was carried into the dining-room and profferred to each guest in turn to help him or herself to as much as required, using the serving spoon and fork poised on the rim of the dish. The advantage of this was that guests received the food in better condition because it was carved and presented by a professional person, and was still hot because it came directly from the kitchen. But some chefs did not welcome service à la russe because it denied them the opportunity of creating the great displays that had been developed earlier in the century.

This new form of service was ideal for all kinds of restaurants, the only drawback being that some guests found using the serving-spoon and fork to be a clumsy operation. This led to the waiter giving the customer some assistance by asking him what he wanted and proceeding to transfer it to the plate. It could have been that banquet service caused waiters to begin to take the initiative of serving so as to quicken the rate of service but this slight adaptation became the accepted method and is still in wide use, known as *silver service*.

1.6 EFFECTS OF SERVICE

In addition to silver service, there are several other methods of food service and the full list with explanations is given in Chapter 2. A caterer can choose which particular method of service he will use in his restaurant and this will indicate how he will equip and staff it to suit the purpose. As most of the methods of food service originated in private service, they had to be modified so as to be implemented on a commercial basis. This was all right for the two main meals of lunch and dinner but there were problems with breakfast service because by tradition it has always been an informal meal. The difficulty was overcome by making breakfast a semi-formal meal by getting the guest to choose his first course from a counter and having a waiter to serve the main course and beverage. For a continental breakfast all the items can be laid out on a counter and waiters need only to bring round the hot beverage.

In some resort hotel restaurants, particularly those where a large number of people have to be served at once, the luncheon meal is made semi-formal and is served from a buffet counter containing a selection of cold and hot dishes, salads and sweets. The buffet may be staffed so as to ensure strict portion control, or may be run on help-yourself lines.

Another form of semi-formal service is the carvery as originally conceived by Ellsworth Statler in the restaurants of his chain of hotels in the USA. In these, customers could carve as much meat as they liked, cover it with gravy, vegetables and potatoes and pay 25 cents. Nowadays it is advisable to have an expert carver to serve the customer with meat and let him help himself to the vegetables and adjuncts only.

Serving methods are as important as cooking methods as each affects the other in a mutual fashion. Many of the principles of menu planning concern the dining-room as much as the kitchen and the ability of the waiters must match that of the chefs so that the entire meal experience stems evenly from the two sides of the operation.

1.7 CAREER PROSPECTS

This subject has been placed here first because there is something to be learned from the change in the pattern of employment over the past fifty years, and second, because of the present-day job situation. Details about courses and examinations are given in Appendix 3 and information on working conditions in Chapter 4.

A major shift in the pattern of employment occurred earlier this century when men left their jobs on the land to go to work in the manufacturing industries. This was because increased mechanisation required fewer farmhands, and factories offered much higher wages. Over the past twenty years there has been a trend away from the manufacturing to the service industries. This is because many of the heavy industrial operations are now done by robots, and there is increased competition from other countries. Whereas most women got married to spend the rest of their lives as housewives and mothers, the pattern now is for both husband and wife to be in employment, thus there is a higher amount of disposable income which enables them to eat out fairly frequently.

In this country, some 16 per cent of meals are eaten in catering establishments whereas in the USA the figure is 30 per cent. It would appear that as the standard of living of a country, or of a section of its population, increases, so more use is made of commercial eating places. But this does not necessarily mean that there will be an immediate demand for high-class restaurants. In fact the pattern is that newcomers to eating out start in the modestly priced restaurants and gradually work their way up through the various levels until they reach the kind of place they enjoy most at their level of expenditure.

Fast-food establishments are very useful to people who live their lives at a fast pace and for those who do not wish to spend a lot on food. As their amount of time and money permits, so such people will probably move up one category of restaurant, as the desire to improve on experience expands.

There are over 2 million people employed in the catering industry in the UK. Some 60 per cent of the jobs are in the commercial sector with 15 per cent being in hotels, 23 per cent in public houses and clubs, 5 per cent in contract catering and 13 per cent or 156 000 persons in restaurants. The number of establishments increases all the time and it is estimated that approximately 120 000 jobs become available each year because of the expansion of the industry and job turnover.

The value of a career as a waiter has been that promotion is quite rapid for the right type of person and that the rewards are very good.

QUESTIONS

1. Suggest how the word 'service' came into being in restaurant terminology.

2. Define the meaning of the terms *entrée* and *relevé* in early forms of food service.

3. Estimate the time when the high-class table presentation of food reached its peak, discuss the reasons for it.

CHAPTER 2

THE ORIGINS

OF

RESTAURANTS

2.1 THE ORIGINS AND DEVELOPMENT OF EATING PLACES

The history of the hotel and catering industry spans more than 2000 years and embraces a wide range of different kinds of places that offer food and lodgings to travellers. The need for places where pilgrims could stay overnight had existed since shrines were first established and even before the beginning of the Christian age we know that in the days of the Druids there were the equivalent of today's motorway service areas, where travellers could find refreshment and rest. In ancient Rome there were drinking-places, eating-rooms, lodging-houses and inns, and the inhabitants of Pompeii used to frequent the equivalent of our snack bars.

In the sixth century BC monks welcomed pilgrims into their monasteries by providing food, drink and accommodation, but as the number of travellers increased the monks had to find additional accommodation so they built lodgings which eventually developed into inns, the first of these being at Assisi in 1337. The inn soon became the centre of the town's social life and provided facilities for dinners, meetings, lectures, auctions, plays and other entertainments, as well as providing food and accommodation for travellers.

When stage-coaches first started to link towns and cities in the mid-eighteenth century, inns added a further dimension by offering facilities to travellers who wished only to eat and refresh themselves along the route, whilst the horses were fed and watered. The inns of this country provided a very high standard of hospitality and writers such as Goldsmith and Smollett have given us glimpses of 'mine host' as a genial and bucolic person, ordering the duties of his workers so as to provide an enjoyable stay for all his guests.

The word hotel gradually came into use instead of inn as it gave a connotation of better facilities than those available at an ordinary inn or post-house. From 1826 when the first railway trains ran, the railway companies built hotels at all the main-line stations on their routes and these provided service in the best traditions of the inn. The railway companies also provided refreshment-rooms at every major station and put dining-cars on long-distance trains so that travellers could enjoy breakfast, luncheon or dinner during their journey. Grand hotels were built everywhere that people of wealth or rank foregathered – at the notable spas and seaside resorts, in the mountains, and in most towns of any importance. Among the earliest were the Regent Hotel at Leamington Spa which opened in 1819, the Royal Danieli at Venice in 1882, the Bayerischer Hof at Munich in 1841, and many others right on through the 1930s, and then again in the 1960s.

The reputation of many hotels often rests on its restaurant and it is actually the quality of the food and service that can bring fame to the whole establishment. This was evidenced by the appointment of César Ritz as manager of the Savoy Hotel soon after it opened in 1889. He brought Escoffier to run the kitchen and Echenard to direct the restaurant and among them, they made the Savoy Restaurant the most fashionable place in the whole of London. Ritz had served nearly every person of rank and note at the hotels in which he had worked across Europe and such was his reputation as the perfect host that when he came to the Savoy, they flocked to be served by him in the sumptuous surroundings of the great hotel.

2.2 THE RISE OF THE CLASSICAL RESTAURANT

The name restaurant comes from the word 'restorative' and at first these places offered only revitalising and health-giving soups. They then extended the menu to include invalid food such as boiled chicken, calf's foot jelly and beef tea, but the invalids had to come to eat on the premises because it was only the *traiteurs* who were allowed to sell take-away food. The first restaurant as we know it today was opened in Paris in 1782 by Monsieur Beauvilliers who had been chef to the Comte de Provence. His establishment was a high-class place and quickly achieved a fine reputation, not just because the food was good, but because Beauvilliers had a strong but pleasant personality, and also a good memory that enabled him to greet his customers by their names and to remember their likes and dislikes.

By 1820 there were hundreds of restaurants all over France and they became part of the social pattern of French people's lives because they saw the advantages of eating meals prepared by professional chefs and served by experienced waiters; thus eating out became a normal way of life and the French now spend more of their income on meals away from home than any other nation.

The history of restaurants reminds us of the names of well-known restaurateurs who, after working as head waiters for many years, opened a restaurant of their own, often with the backing, financial and otherwise, of some of their customers. César Ritz spent most of his working life as a waiter before becoming the director of his own group of hotels, which was named after him. There are many other famous names including Oddenino, Romano, the Quaglino brothers, Mario Gallati of the Ivy and the Caprice, Gatti, and Contarini of the Savoy.

2.3 THE AMBIENCE OF THE RESTAURANT

Apart from the provision of food and drink there are several other factors that contribute to the enjoyment of a meal in a restaurant; these include the atmosphere within the room, the colour of the decorations, the layout, and the furniture.

Each establishment is designed to satisfy the demands of a particular class of customer and the overall impression first gained on entrance should reflect the particular consumer need. However consumer needs can vary according to given situations or occasions and account has to be taken of possible changes as otherwise the meal experience will not be completely satisfactory to all comers. By the meal experience is meant the pleasure, both mental and physical that can be derived from a meal partaken under perfect conditions that satisfy the physiological and psychological requirements; it is the interaction of good food with man's senses and the environment in which it is eaten. The following are factors that affect the ambience.

The food is undoubtedly the focus of the entire proceedings and the selection, cooking and service of the meal must be perfect in every way. The menu must be suitable for the occasion, the food of the best quality and cooked by skilled chefs, and the standard of service must be impeccable. But equally important are the physiological requirements; the complex mechanism that keeps the body functioning requires a balanced diet that provides the requisite amounts of the five nutrients which are protein, carbohydrate, fat, minerals, and vitamins. Recommended amounts of these nutrients are laid down by national authorities to inform people what they should eat, according to age, sex, job of work, body weight, etc., and it is the job of the caterer to see that these nutrients are present in the food he serves.

The caterer also has to be aware of all the religious and cultural laws that affect what foods people of various sects and nationalities are allowed to eat, and whether they may partake of alcoholic drinks.

The people's food habits and preferences are developed during childhood and are brought about by the availability of certain foodstuffs, geographical and cultural influences, and the religious persuasion of the family. At a more personal level, individual predilections can vary according to personal experiences and pre-dispositions and these can be influenced by the five senses of sight, hearing, touch, smell and taste. An understanding of the effect of these senses is of use to food-service personnel since they contribute to the enjoyment of a meal and have to be taken into account when a new restaurant is being planned.

2.4 THE SENSES AND FOOD ACCEPTANCE

The sight of a dish of food is usually the first impact on the senses and it can create a positive or negative reaction according to how appetising it looks. The visual sense notices the colours, shapes and arrangements of foodstuffs on a dish and will register a positive reaction if these are natural and compatible, or a negative response if the dish presentation is untidy, the colours unnatural and the shape unrecognisable.

The sense of hearing can arouse the appetite by detecting sounds of cooking and eating, but loud background noise in a restaurant may heighten nervous tension which adversely affects the digestion, thus detracting from the enjoyment of the meal experience.

The touch of food is sensed by the mouth and tongue which are extremely susceptible to the viscosity, texture, moisture, and temperature of foods. The sense of taste is also in the mouth and the tongue perceives the four basic tastes which are sour, bitter, saline and sweet. The temperature of food conveyed to the mouth can limit or intensify sensitivity of taste, which is why it is important for it to be served hot or cold rather than lukewarm or frozen.

The sense of smell enables us to recognise good and bad odours so the nose elicits food acceptance or rejection. When a person is hungry the olfactory cells in the nose are very sensitive to food aromas but as hunger is diminished during the eating of a meal, the smells of the food need to be intensified in order to maintain interest in what is being served.

All five senses are exposed to continuous stimuli but will lose interest in food if confronted with too much of the same colour, smell and texture; thus in order to maintain interest it is necessary to offer variety in these aspects.

2.5 THE ENVIRONMENT AND THE SETTING

The food itself is only one part of the full meal experience because the senses are affected by the surroundings, which also have an effect upon the state of mental alertness. The starting-point of acceptance or rejection of the eating environment can be as distant as the external facade and the entrance to the restaurant. The more inviting it is, the easier it will be for a customer to decide to go inside. Once within the restaurant the first consideration is its size and shape.

The restaurant

The shape of the room and its features, including different floor levels, any chandeliers or ornate columns, the reception area and so on, all contribute to the frame of mind of the customer and how he will accept the food and drink.

Décor

The colours used in decorating the room must harmonise and aesthetic colour combinations that help to accentuate the features and create a lively or relaxing atmosphere, according to type of restaurant, must be used. Strong primary colours in the warm spectrum, such as red, create a sense of excitement and exhilaration whereas diffuse pastel colours in the cold spectrum are more conducive to a feeling of relaxation. Haphazard use of colour schemes will create a mood of restlessness and dissonance.

Lighting

Good lighting plays an important part in the meal experience as it assists in modifying colours and can convey a feeling to the guest that he looks his best in the surroundings. It has an effect upon the presentation of food and can enhance its appetising appearance. It is possible to install lighting fitments that can be changed in a moment to suit a particular situation, or to provide a special effect which is sometimes necessary at a dinner-dance or presentation ceremony.

Normal lighting which gives a daylight effect will prevent customers lingering too long over their meal and will thus make it possible to increase turnover. An intimate restaurant will use very little light, possibly only a few candelabra.

Acoustics

Although excessive noise can cause stress, a completely silent room would be totally unacceptable to most customers therefore some background sounds are required. The sound of chatter by customers, the music of an orchestra or a pianist, can be harmonious, but the clatter of dishes is not. The tempo of activities within the room may not be immediately apparent to a newly-arrived customer but he will adapt himself to the pace and the mood of the restaurant, once seated in the midst of it. Discreet manipulation of the background environment, including the music and the pace of the waiters, can affect the rate at which customers eat their meal. It should be realised that curtains, drapes and thick carpets are noise-absorbent and can diminish overall sound levels.

The temperature

Air conditioning is necessary to keep a restaurant at the best temperature and should be set at 18°C for optimum comfort. This will contribute to the feeling of well-being that customers expect, whatever the weather outside may be like.

The human element

The good behaviour of waiting-staff on duty needs to be taught, as staff interaction with customers can be crucial to the good name of the restaurant. Staff must be adaptable to the various roles adopted by customers; each member of staff must put on a smiling face to customers no matter how sad he may be feeling at heart, or how irascible the customer. The smile must not be too broad and must be tailored to the customer's response which could be friendly but might be hostile; the waiter must learn to adopt the requisite social interaction for each encounter.

According to the kind of restaurant so must waiters adopt a different role; for example in a good-class conventional restaurant his pace of work should demonstrate suave efficiency, his uniform will add to the formality of the situation and his behaviour will need to be very deferential. Customers also affect the atmosphere of a restaurant; for example, those who patronise the conventional type will be likely to be all of a certain age group which means they will also be dressed in a certain style thus presenting a harmonious image. Too great a contrast of age and dress in the same restaurant may cause dissonance with the result that the minority group, who may be good spenders, will leave for a less conformist place, only a very proficient restaurant manager will be able to prevent any conflict, so enabling all groups to enjoy the common surroundings.

The language of the menu

The style, layout and content of the menu needs to be compatible with the entire meal experience. Too great a choice tends to bewilder customers whereas too limited a list usually causes habituation. Whilst the use of French is absolutely right for top-class restaurants frequented by an international clientele, it is wrong at many other levels and a translation needs to be included. Nothing can be done to help customers with the wine list apart from giving verbal or written outlines of what the wines taste like.

Price

The higher the prices charged by a restaurant the higher a customer's expectations are likely to be, which means that the pricing policy is an indication of food quality. Customers' choice of restaurants is largely influenced by the prices charged and value for money received, some places use price as a discrimination against certain types of customers and keep it artificially high so as to bar unwanted or undesirable persons. It is possible to operate a flexible pricing policy whereby a popular dish on a menu is increased in price during the course of a meal according to demand, while on the other hand a slow-moving dish is reduced in price in an attempt to sell out.

2.6 THE METHODS AND LEVELS OF SERVICE

The environment of a place in which food is served to the public varies according to the needs of the customer and the purpose of the establishment. This means that waiting-staff, as they move from job to job, may find themselves in a variety of situations where there are different operational requirements and therefore, a need for different skills.

Food Service can be classified into seven separate levels ascending from the utilitarian to the classic or hedonistic, as it is sometimes described; each level can be outlined as follows:

1. The basic and most utilitarian method is the *self-service* or buffet style which was brought into popularity because of a shortage of labour during the Second World War. It is now the most widely used method because it suits the requirements of industrial and institutional catering establishments where large numbers are served.

2. The second level is known as *counter service*; here the customer sits on a high stool at the serving counter and is handed his plate of food by the food service operative who may also have cooked it. This form of service was used in cinemas and theatres and in supermarkets that serve meals; it now meets the requirements of catering in many public houses and – with small adaptations – a buttery in an hotel, club or college.

3. The third level is called plate service and it originated in the home and is widely used in most cafes, snack bars, bistros and cheap restaurants where its simplicity avoids any pretensions and keeps labour costs down. Plate service has recently come very up-market and is widely used in first-class restaurants that offer nouvelle cuisine. Food is put onto the expensive plate by the chefs, in a decorative and artistic fashion so as to look like a still-life painting; it is then covered by a silver dome. But even at its most basic level, plate service must not be ranked as inferior since it can be exactly the right method for many restaurants, especially those which employ unskilled waiting staff, for it leaves no opportunity for a waiter to show any ability other than to carry half a dozen full plates. Plate service became popular in many good-class restaurants in the USA more than sixty years ago; this was because it removed some of the pretentiousness that exists with other forms of service.

4. *Buffet service* is the fourth level; it is connected with receptions and balls but is also applicable to carveries. It is the best form of service to use if it is desirable for guests to mingle and if the room is not large enough for them all to be seated formally. It also helps to reduce staff numbers since only carvers and clearers are needed. A formal buffet should be operated if there are no tables and chairs; this means having all the food in bite-size pieces and only serving items that may be eaten without the need for a knife.

5. The fifth level of service is silver service, occasionally referred to as *English service*. Food is placed on serving dishes by the chefs

in the kitchen and transferred by the waiter onto a plate in front of the customer. Soup may be ladled from a tureen into the soup plate or poured from an individual tureen, in front of the customer. The waiter, having been given food sufficient for a number of people, makes a decision as to how much each person will be given; in this way he is fulfilling the role of the host at the head of the table which is why it is often referred to as English service.

6. The sixth level of food service is known as *family service* and is sometimes called *French service*. In it the dish of food for a given number of people is held by the waiter so as to enable the guest to help himself to as much as he wants. Vegetables may be served in the same way but sometimes the dish is placed on the table for the guest to help himself and pass the dish on to his neighbour. This is the form of service still used today in clubs, at high table in college, and in royal households.

7. The highest level is *guéridon service*; the word *guéridon* means a mobile table or trolley which is brought close to the guests' table, and any carving or finishing of the food is done there. Only skilled or well-trained staff are allowed to do this form of service as there is the risk of spoiling food by overcooking it, and of the lamp causing a fire on the premises.

QUESTIONS

1. In your own words write a brief but clear outline of each of the levels of food service described in this section.

2. State which you consider to be one of the major contributory departments to the reputation of an hotel.

3. Define the origins of the word 'restorative'.

4. Describe the main contributory factors to the ambience of a restaurant.

5. Why is good food presentation of such great importance?

RESTAURANT LAYOUT, FURNITURE AND EQUIPMENT

3.1 ALLOCATION OF SPACE

The layout of a restaurant must be in keeping with its circumstances as the way the furniture and fittings are installed has much influence on the environment, which in turn has an effect upon the type of customer who will patronise the place.

The size and shape of a restaurant is often decided by structural limitations which in turn govern the number of persons that can be accommodated at any one time; the kind of furniture chosen has a bearing on this as does the style of service, because this dictates how many sideboards need to be installed. Table 3.1 shows optimum space allowance per person for different styles of service.

Table 3.1   *allocation of space*

Level of service	Allowance per person in m^2
1 self-service	0.8
2 counter service	1.4
3 plate	1.2
4 buffet style (help-yourself)	0.5
5 silver	1.5
6 family	1.5
7 guéridon	1.8

Note: The allowance does not include facilities such as reception area, bar, toilets, etc.

Table 3.2 details the amount of space taken by various shapes and sizes of tables. Most restaurants find it necessary to provide various sizes of tables for two to six persons, but it is possible to achieve this by fixing various sizes and shapes of table top to one basic table frame, covering it with a cloth of the correct size, over a baize liner. Round tables provide a family feeling but require more overall surrounding space than square or oblong ones. As a rough guide to space allocation, a restaurant that measures 15 m by 11.5 m or approximately 172.5 m^2, with gangways 1 metre wide, can accommodate 100 customers at three tables for six each, sixteen for four and nine for two, or similar combinations. The overall plan would show the dining room as being at least three times the size of the kitchen and ensure that they are next to each other rather than on different levels, and that the cellar and bar are adjacent.

Table 3.2   *table sizes*

Square	Rectangular	Round (diam)	Number of persons
0.75×0.75	0.6×0.75	0.85	2
0.90×0.90	1.2×0.75	1.05	4
1.00×1.00	1.8×0.75	1.20	6
—	2.5×1.50	1.80	10
—	3.25×1.50	2.10	12
—	4.25×1.50	2.40	14

The use of an extension will enable a larger number of people in a party to be seated together, rather than at adjoining tables.

3.2   RESTAURANT LAYOUT

The physical layout of a restaurant is dictated by (i) the boundaries of the building; (ii) the demands of the customer; (iii) the type and extent of the menu; and (iv) the organisation and policy of the company that is in charge. The demands of the customer are identified to some extent by the location of the restaurant, as to what kind of district it is in, and what socioeconomic class of customer is likely to patronise it, or be attracted to it by the marketing strategy.

According to the likely type of customer, so are the layout and environment planned and the facilities provided; the pricing policy is reflected in the furniture and fittings and the amount of space per customer – the better these are, the higher the prices on the menu.

The menu is the blueprint of the operation and governs the entire proceedings; its effect upon the layout is according to whether it is à la carte or table d'hôte and the kind of service needed. If it is a nouvelle cuisine menu with each portion being individually plated, there must be sufficient kitchen servery space to lay out the plates for filling; if flambé dishes are included on the menu, adequate space must be made available in the restaurant for the movement and accommodation of the trolleys.

Customer amenity areas such as foyer, bar and cloakrooms are in addition to the allocation of space for tables, chairs, sideboards, buffet and trolleys, plus an area for spare furniture storage; there may be semi-permanent divisions with floral decorations or similar artistic decorative features that assist in providing colour and atmosphere. If there is a dance floor or cabaret show, additional space will be required, bearing in mind also the need for an orchestra.

The way in which tables and chairs are laid out in a restaurant has a subconscious effect upon a customer entering it and so has the way that the tables are laid and the stance of the waiters at their stations. It is necessary to have uncluttered gangways from each sideboard to the service entrance and exit, as well as to the dispense bar. Chairs and tables can be placed in straight lines down the room or in echelon fashion, according to which makes the most economical use of available space. Figures 3.1 and 3.2 show space allocations on these layouts in a restaurant that measures 15.0×11.5m.

Many restaurants install bench or banquette seating, mainly around the walls of the room, finding it makes greater use of available space than having only movable chairs, but it usually means shifting the table to let customers take their place against the wall. In Figure 3.3 the use of round tables is illustrated; it demonstrates that not quite as many people can be seated as when the restaurant is equipped with square tables.

A restaurant is apportioned into stations which are work-centres based on a sideboard, and each consisting of a number of tables. Figure 3.4 shows how a restaurant seating 76 persons can be divided into four stations.

Fig 3.1   *table lay-out in straight lines – number of places 96*

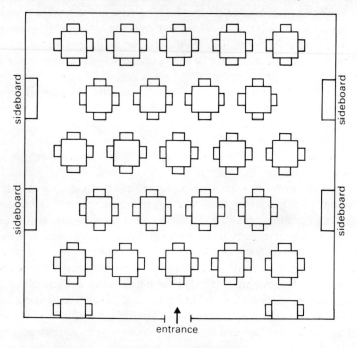

Fig 3.2   *table lay-out on the echelon system – number of places 100*

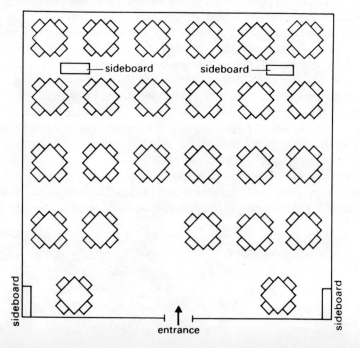

Fig 3.3   *table lay-out using round tables – number of places 96*

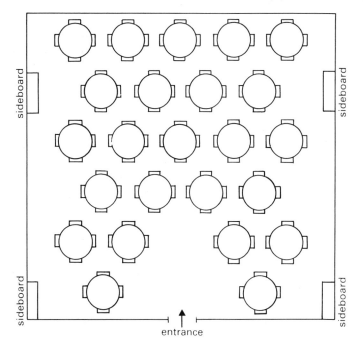

Fig 3.4   *division of stations*

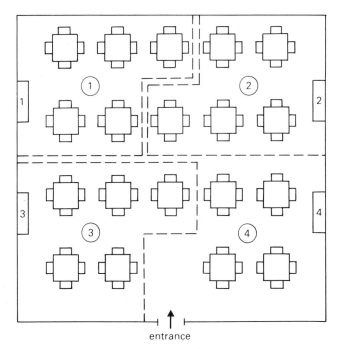

3.3 PURCHASE OF FURNITURE

Restaurant tables normally covered with tablecloths are not seen by the customer so they can be utilitarian rather than elegant, but the chairs are seen and felt so these must be of good quality. The actual size, colour and design will be in accordance with the standard of the restaurant and chairs with arm rests are provided in high-class places. It is usually necessary to keep some in reserve and it is useful if they can be stacked as storage space is usually at a premium.

The height of the seat from the floor is usually 46 cm which should be ideal for persons of average height to be at the right level with the table top. The back of a chair is usually 40–50 cm high and the size of the seat 40 × 45 cm, which should provide comfort during a meal. If the legs are not straight there should be only a slight curvature of the back legs as waiters may trip over them if too splayed out.

Tables should not be so heavy that it takes two people to move them when allowing customers to get into banquette seating. It is usual to cover tables with a baize underfelt to prevent anything on top from slipping and to tie this underfelt to the legs. Table extensions must be strong but lightweight, and readily stackable. Some restaurants feature polished wooden tables and table mats.

3.4 USE OF THE SIDEBOARD

Sideboards are the work-bench for waiters and act as the central point of a station. They must be functional but good to look at since they can be seen by customers. They are available as mobile sideboards but as it is usual to connect the hotplate to an electrical point they need to be situated close to a double-plug socket. In some restaurants the computerised ordering and billing machine may be housed on the sideboard.

The normal layout and equipping of a sideboard is shown in Figure 3.5 and the pattern should be standardised in order that waiters can put their hand on anything they require without having to look or fumble. The upper part at the back can have a panel for affixing the copy order for each table and the top shelf accommodates the hotplate or réchaud on which hot foods are placed as soon as they are brought from the kitchen. There are several designs of these and various kinds of apparatus, including rechargeable metal hotplates and the table cooking lamp normally used for flambé work. The open section is for general items of *mise en place* such as sauces, casters, sideplates, finger bowls, etc., and the bottom is for table napkins and slipcloths.

Fig 3.5 *the lay-out of a sideboard*

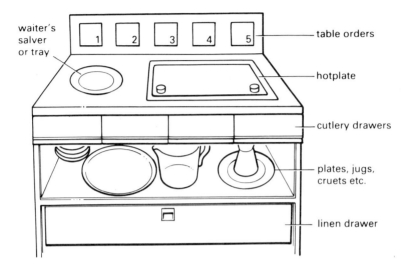

3.5 EQUIPMENT – LINEN

Linen is the name given to all the napery used in a restaurant even though it may be made of cotton or other material. Linen is the best material because of its quality and appearance and the starched creaselines of tablecloths add symmetry to the way the table is laid. It is possible to purchase linen of a suitable colour to match the décor of the room, or to have cloths and napkins of contrasting colours.

Tablecloths are made in several sizes to fit all sizes of table and it is usual to purchase them with a drop of at least 30 cm all round. Measurements range from 120 cm square for a table for two to four persons to banquet-cloths of 50 metres in length. Slipcloths of approximately 1 metre square are sometimes used to make a table-cloth last longer before having to be laundered, or to cover a stain; they can be in shades of colour to contrast with the white of the tablecloth. Table napkins are made in several sizes, small ones of approximately 20 cm for afternoon tea and bigger ones from 40 to 55 cm square for main meals. Paper serviettes are not used in good-class restaurants but there are many other kinds of disposable ones that look and feel like real linen; they can have the restaurant's name or logo design printed on. Suggestions for folding table napkins attractively will be found in Figure 3.6.

Fig 3.6 *folding table napkins*

the candle

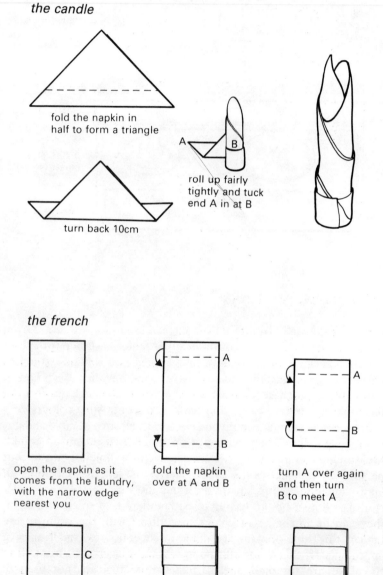

fold the napkin in
half to form a triangle

turn back 10cm

roll up fairly
tightly and tuck
end A in at B

the french

open the napkin as it
comes from the laundry,
with the narrow edge
nearest you

fold the napkin
over at A and B

turn A over again
and then turn
B to meet A

turn C
under

there will now
be three folds
overlapping

turn the
napkin around

wings

fold into four

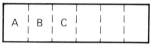

divide into six;
fold A on top of B
and B on top of C,
and then do the same
from the other end

fold A and B
under the roll
back C and D

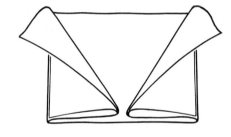

the rabbit

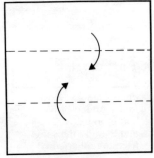

1 fold the napkin into three

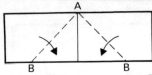

2 fold each side over from A to B

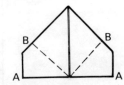

3 fold corners A to B

4 turn napkin over and other way up

5 turn corner up

6 bring A and B round and slot A inside the base of C

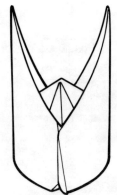

7 stand upright and pull out the ears

the rosebud

open out the napkin, fold the
four corners to the centre; do
this three times

turn it over
and fold the four
corners to the centre

hold the points at centre
A and pull out the twelve
points from underneath

place in goblet

the pointed cap

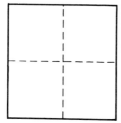

fold the napkin into four

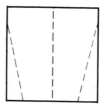

turn the two
sides underneath

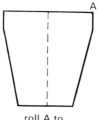

roll A to
the centre

roll B to
the centre

press the rolled
part to keep in
place and stand it up

the butler

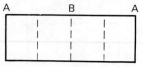

open the napkin as
it comes folded in three
from the laundry; fold
edges A to B

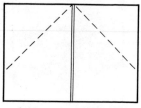

fold corners to centre

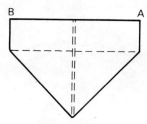

turn pointed end
downwards and plain
side upwards;
roll from A right across

tuck B
into A

the princess

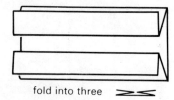

fold into three

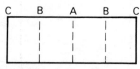

fold in half; keep
the four open edges
to the front; fold
B to A and C back
to B

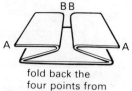

fold back the
four points from
A to B on both
sides

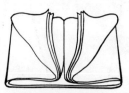

turn the napkin
around so that
the points are at
top centre

the arum lily

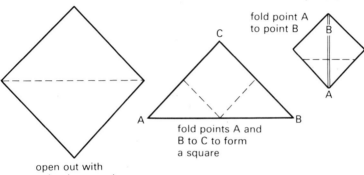

fold point A
to point B

C

A   B

fold points A and
B to C to form
a square

open out with
point downwards
and fold in half

turn point
B back on
itself twice

turn it over
and turn the two
ends A and B
inwards and tuck
them in

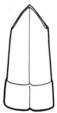

stand upright and pull
down the two sides

the water lily

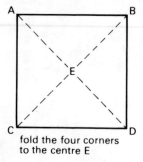

fold the four corners
to the centre E

again fold
the four corners
to the centre

turn it over
and again fold
the four corners
to the centre

place the fist in
the centre and
pull out the eight
points one at a
time

For a more elaborate water lily, use a large square table napkin, open it
out and fold the four points to the centre. Do this three times, then turn it
over and again fold the four points to the centre. Hold down the centre
whilst pulling out the twelve points from underneath. The napkin will
hold together, especially when a bowl is placed inside it for display
purposes.

the cone

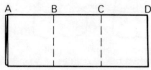

open out the napkin
as it comes from the
laundry
already folded
in three and fold over
a third; D to B

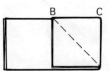

fold corner C
over towards B
and continue to
roll

have these
join at the
back and
fold point
A up to
hold it

stand it
upright

the cockscomb

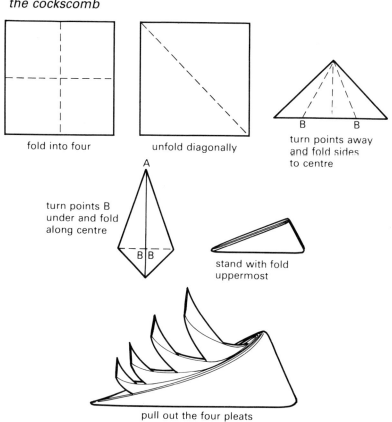

fold into four

unfold diagonally

turn points away
and fold sides
to centre

turn points B
under and fold
along centre

stand with fold
uppermost

pull out the four pleats

32

the mitre

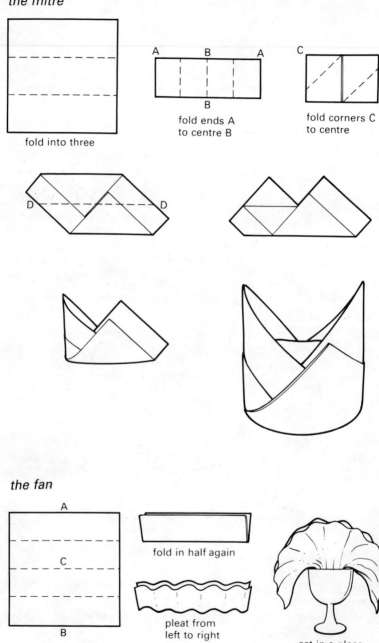

fold into three

A   B   A

B

fold ends A
to centre B

C

C

fold corners C
to centre

D   D

the fan

A

C

B

fold edges A and
B to C

fold in half again

pleat from
left to right

set in a glass
and open
the folds

3.6   EQUIPMENT – CROCKERY AND GLASSWARE

These items add considerably to the good looks of a restaurant as seen by a customer immediately he enters it, and its quality must be in accordance with the class of restaurant. It must be elegant and look expensive, yet be functional so that it withstands harsh washing-up procedures and careless handling. A single plate as used for serving a nouvelle cuisine meal costs as much as £10 and a cut-glass goblet is equally expensive, so waiting-staff should take reasonable care in handling them so as to avoid breakages and damages.

Crockery is made in several qualities with bone china and porcelain being reckoned as the best; it can be coloured, plain or decorated, elegant to look at, yet functional and easy to obtain future stocks. If it is to be badged with the name or logo design of the restaurant it will be necessary to place a large initial order and to order replacements well in advance. It may be necessary to limit the number of items of crockery and glassware by making one size and shape serve several purposes.

Glasses are made in many shapes and sizes as shown in Figure 3.7 and waiting-staff need to familiarise themselves with all these so as to be able to select the correct one for a particular drink; various manufacturers make these in several sizes and capacities but in order to limit the range in stock it may be necessary to have a general-purpose goblet that is suitable for serving water, mixed drinks, etc. Some glasses are marked to show that an exact amount is dispensed, in order to conform with the Weights and Measures Act.

3.7   EQUIPMENT – CUTLERY

Cutlery is made in several kinds of metal and in many shapes and patterns, each pattern or decoration having its own name. The best quality and most expensive cutlery is known as e.p.n.s. which is an abbreviation for electro-plated nickel silver which means that the blank shapes of nickel have been coated with a plating of silver, the thickness of this plating being according to quality, A1 grade being the best. This kind of cutlery has a good appearance when laid on a starched and ironed tablecloth and adds greatly to the overall perception of the room. It does however require constant cleaning because it stains easily, especially when it comes into contact with egg and a special polishing or *burnishing* machine is necessary.

Stainless steel is widely used for making cutlery because it does not need as much care as e.p.n.s. ware as it does not become stained. The

Fig 3.7 *shapes and sizes of glasses*

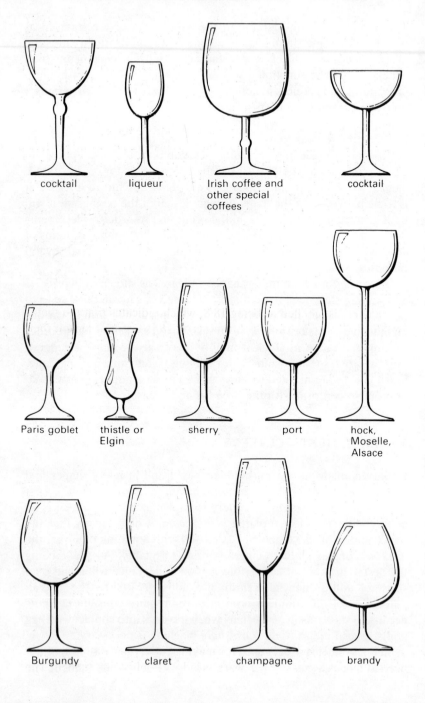

cocktail

liqueur

Irish coffee and
other special
coffees

cocktail

Paris goblet

thistle or
Elgin

sherry

port

hock,
Moselle,
Alsace

Burgundy

claret

champagne

brandy

Fig 3.8 *shapes of bottles*

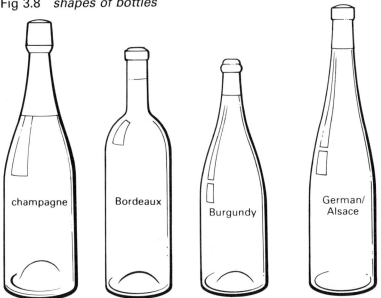

champagne | Bordeaux | Burgundy | German/Alsace

Each wine producing district appears to have established a distinct preference for bottling its wine in specific bottle shapes which are easily recognisable, as the examples given here.

best quality is labelled as being 18/8, which indicates that the metals used includes 18 per cent of chromium and 8 per cent of nickel; there are many styles and patterns and in some forms of cutlery the handle can be of e.p.n.s. and the blade of stainless steel.

The list of cutlery in constant use includes knives – table, fish and side; forks – table, fish and dessert; spoons – soup, dessert, tea, and coffee. The term 'cover' is used to denote the items of cutlery together with a side-plate, glass, and table-napkin required for a normal three-course meal for one person. To the kitchen, a cover means one customer's order for food.

3.8 SPECIAL EQUIPMENT

These are the larger items of equipment that are used only for exemplary dishes or forms of service; they are mainly trolleys and the adjuncts used in conjunction with them. They include an hors-d'oeuvre trolley, a heated carving trolley, salad trolley, sweet trolley, liqueur and cigar trolley and possibly a Turkish or other special coffee trolley; sometimes a cheese trolley is put into service. In addition there is what is known as a guéridon which is actually a mobile table which can be used for flambé dishes and any personalised service done in close contact with the customer. Figure 3.9 shows two of

Fig 3.9

heated meat-carving trolley

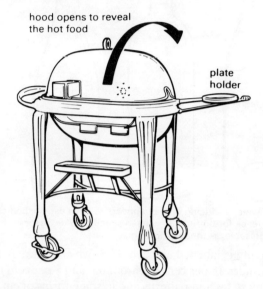

hood opens to reveal
the hot food

plate
holder

*refrigerated trolley (for cold buffet, for making salads
and for serving cold sweets, chilled drinks, etc.)*

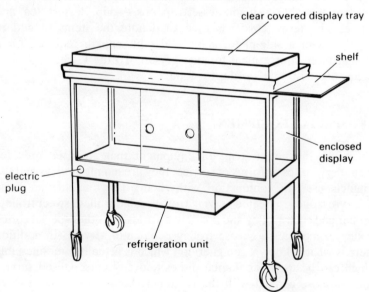

clear covered display tray

shelf

enclosed
display

electric
plug

refrigeration unit

Fig 3.10

spirit lamp

duck press

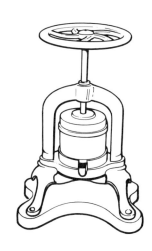

Parma ham holder

ham stand

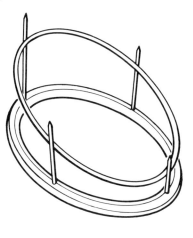

these trolleys, which are usually made of steel and wood. Figure 3.10 shows some of the articles used on trolleys.

The carving trolley is used only in restaurants that feature whole roasted or braised joints to be carved in front of the customer at his table. The domed e.p.n.s. lid is opened to let the customer see the joint which is kept hot by means of a container of very hot water housed underneath it. The gravy and any accompaniments are inside the trolley and an expert carver slices the meat to order. An hors-d'oeuvre trolley is made to hold a number of dishes of hors-d'oeuvre for serving to the customer's choice. A sweet trolley usually has several tiers on which a variety of cold sweets are displayed to advantage; there is a shelf for plates, cutlery and cream.

A spirit or gas lamp is used in conjunction with a guéridon to provide a flame for flambé work, to reheat food and to keep food hot whilst it is being prepared. A skilled waiter will make good use of his lamp to ensure that customers' meals are served hot but not spoiled by being dried up. The lamp is of metal with a container of methylated spirit and a wick, or it can hold a cylinder of butane gas; both are capable of being regulated to provide the required flame.

A duck press is used in the preparation of Canard Sauvage à la Presse which is a complicated procedure that demands skill and expertise. After slicing the meat, the carcase is placed in the press and squeezed to extract the juice which is then used in making the accompanying sauce. Wild ducks are in season from August to March which means that the press is out of use for four months of the year.

Parma ham must be sliced as thinly as possible otherwise it can be tough to eat since it is cured but not cooked. By clamping the whole ham in a press it is held firmly thus facilitating the carving process. A whole York ham is easier to carve if it is impaled upon a ham stand which holds it at exactly the correct angle for cutting into fairly thin slices.

3.9 SPECIAL UTENSILS

There are a number of small items of restaurant equipment that are used only for specific dishes and therefore kept out of general use and the number available restricted; they include:

A lobster pick which helps a customer eating a lobster in the half shell to extract the flesh from the crevices;

a caviar knife which has a short, wide blade for spreading the caviar on the blinis or toast; the handle may be of ivory;

an oyster fork which is a short two- or three-pronged fork with a nitch on one prong that is used to detach the beard from the oyster after which it is then conveyed whole to the mouth to be swallowed, rather than being sucked from the half shell;

a corn-on-the-cob holder which is comprised of two identical pieces with pointed ends which are inserted into the cob at each end so the customer may hold it whilst turning and eating the cob;

a cheese knife which is kept on the cheese board or trolley to assist in portioning and serving most firm cheeses;

a Stilton cheese scoop which was mainly for use in gentlemen's clubs where it was the custom to serve it from the centre into which some port had been poured; it is now more usual to cut the cheese into portions and serve the port in a glass;

a pair of lobster crackers which is used for a customer or waiter to break the claw so as to extract the flesh, but this is normally done by the larder chef;

a pair of asparagus tongs which is used to pick up a stick of asparagus and eat it in a slightly more decorous manner than by picking it up with the fingers;

a pair of grape scissors which is placed in a basket of fruit that contains a bunch of hothouse grapes, to cut off a small branch and convey it to the plate;

the snail set which consists of a round silver dish with six indentations into which the prepared snails are placed for reheating in the oven; the customers picks up one in the prongs of the server, takes out the snail with the fork and eats it then drinks the hot snail butter from inside the shell;

an ice cream spade which is like a teaspoon with a flattened bowl;

a grapefruit spoon which is like a teaspoon with an elongated bowl and pointed tip.

Figure 3.11 shows some of the special utensils in use.

Fig 3.11 *special restaurant utensils*

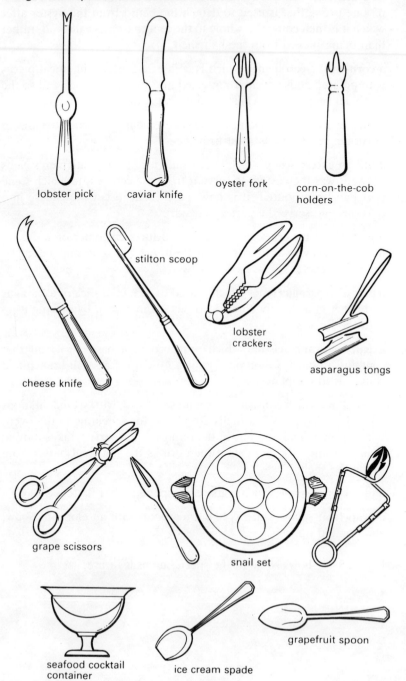

lobster pick   caviar knife   oyster fork   corn-on-the-cob holders

stilton scoop

cheese knife

lobster crackers

asparagus tongs

grape scissors

snail set

seafood cocktail container

ice cream spade

grapefruit spoon

Other items of silverware include salt- and pepper-pots, mustard container and spoon, peppermill, salt mill, butter-dish and knife, finger-bowl, toast-rack, bread basket, table-number- and menu-holder, posy vase, Parmesan-cheese container, shellfish cocktail holder, and avocado pear dish; these last two may be made of glass.

Some items of silverware are kept in the still-room – these include tea- and coffee-pots, milk-jugs and sugar-basins. For receptions, large urns are used to dispense hot beverages, kept hot by means of a small methylated spirit lamp in the base. Some items are kept in the dispense bar – these are ice-buckets and stands and cradles for wine bottles as well as bar tools.

The kitchen keeps the round and oval silver flats of various sizes on which food is served; the lids for these are usually made of aluminium rather than silverware since they are not normally seen by customers. Entrée dishes are shallow oval or round dishes with lids. Vegetable dishes are usually oval in shape with a division across to separate two different kinds of vegetables. Sauceboats and underdishes are made in several sizes according to the amounts being served. Silver dishes retain the heat and waiters should always handle them with the protective waiters' cloth which is issued to him. A salver is used for carrying a number of dishes by piling them on top of each other, holding them in place tightly by means of the folded waiters' cloth wrapped around them.

A gadroon tray is a richly ornamented oval, round or square tray with a raised, chased, or perforated rim all around the edge. It is used for displaying cold-buffet items or, if it has handles, for handing drinks at a cocktail party or reception.

For nouvelle cuisine service where the meal is arranged artistically on the plate by the cooks in the kitchen, a silver-plated dome-shape lid is used; it is the custom to place the covered plate in front of the customer and to whip off the lid with a flourish.

The cost of equipping a restaurant is very high and in addition there will be maintenance costs to keep it looking good by re-silvering or re-shaping. It is usual to have all silverware badged with the name or design logo of the establishment, as this may deter pilferage, although losses, especially of small items of cutlery are inevitable. Regular stocktaking can help in preventing continual losses as discrepancies on the stock sheet will be investigated to find the possible cause.

QUESTIONS

1. What effect, if any, does price have on customer expectations, when eating out?

2. Give the restaurant space requirements for each level of service, as defined at the beginning of this chapter.

3. Suggest reasons why such a wide variation exists between the various methods of service.

4. Describe the role of the menu in any catering operation, with specific reference to the taking of an à la carte order.

RESTAURANT STAFF

4.1 PROFILE OF THE IDEAL RESTAURATEUR

There are few other jobs in which a pleasant disposition is of such importance as that of being a waiter in a restaurant. Each member of staff must be chosen carefully for his or her personal attributes, which include certain inborn social graces that cannot be instilled by training. The higher each person progresses up the career ladder, the more cultivated must he become because he is then totally exposed to personal contact with customers and has to be perfectly acceptable to all classes.

Not everyone can be an Adonis of graceful and dignified bearing but a person who aspires to the rank of head waiter needs to overcome any lack of physical attributes and to cultivate those social traits which facilitate human interaction. The characteristics of the ideal person in overall charge of a restaurant should include personal charm by which to influence people, a vast professional knowledge of the job, a ready smile, the necessary skills to demonstrate his expertise, and great strength of character. It is he who sets the standard of service and obtains a reputation for the establishment and he who must motivate his staff and set them an example by his personal conduct, his deportment, and even his mannerisms.

4.2 SOCIAL SKILLS

Body language is a way by which a person can convey a variety of feelings and create certain impressions in given situations and as such is an attribute that every waiter should try to acquire. The adoption of a deferential stance and the giving of a slight bow to customers as they enter the room, helps to put them at ease and relieves any apprehensiveness they may feel. The approach to a customer with the hands clasped behind the back can project an intimation of respect on the part of the waiter. A superior stance with hands high on the hips and the right foot forward can be adopted when necessary to control any undue commotion or over-enthusiasm on the part of a number of high-spirited customers who might annoy others.

Facial expressions can be used as an influence in a variety of situations, such as giving a smile of welcome that helps to put a customer at ease, or raising an eyebrow quickly to indicate an acknowledgement of intent to give service. Persistent eye contact can mean the maintenance of careful attention to a customer's wants.

Intonation of voice can convey differences of feeling and is a useful aid in many situations in the restaurant.

4.3 MENTAL ATTRIBUTES

Good memory is of great importance to a waiter and should he not be born with it he should endeavour to cultivate or improve it. Waiting at table includes attention to many small details that combine to make the customer's experience more pleasant and the waiter's job easier. It is by paying attention to the way things should be done and going over them in a quick chronological order at the end of the day that helps to memorise the correct methods of service.

Good memory can help to improve work performance brought about by being better organised because small but important details are not forgotten. Customer satisfaction can be increased by a waiter being able to put a name to a face because of having served him on a previous occasion. This can be taken further by placing the customer at his preferred table and in his favourite seat and, better still, remembering his likes and dislikes regarding food and wine.

An inquiring mind is an asset for a waiter and the desire for knowledge should be encouraged. Life is a continuity of learning experiences and the broader the accumulated knowledge, even though not totally relevant to the job, the easier it becomes to converse with a customer on a wide range of topics. At one time, the waiter's maxim was the same as for a freemason '*Audi, vide, tace*' or 'Hear, see, keep silent', which meant to listen carefully and to observe what customers do, but not to speak to them except to answer a question. Such a social barrier no longer exists in most restaurants and if a customer wishes to converse with a waiter, the waiter must respond; but he should not initiate it unless encouraged by the customer to do so, and he must not gossip. The power of observation as a means of getting to understand the needs of customers comes with experience, but a waiter can use that power to classify customers, so being able to treat them in the way they would wish and to address them in the most appropriate manner. Some customers encourage a degree of intimacy or familiarity whereas others hold themselves at a distance, so it is important for a waiter to treat each customer accordingly.

4.4 PHYSICAL QUALITIES

All the time a waiter is on duty he is continuously under observation by a customer who is watching how he holds himself, how quickly he moves around, and what his general demeanour is. This is in addition to his proficiency as a server. A waiter should be chosen on the basis of his average height and weight, his presence and demeanour, his ease of movement and robustness. He must be taught to take care of his appearance, especially his hair, hands and uniform. Hair should be kept neatly trimmed and be well brushed so that it never looks untidy nor falls over the forehead. Hands must be kept clean and the nails neatly manicured; continual handling of hot dishes can cause dehydration of the skin and nasty-looking crevices so it is advisable to protect hands with a non-greasy hand-cream.

A waiter spends all his time on his feet and covers a lot of ground in fetching and carrying, much of it on tiled floors and soft carpeting. It is therefore imperative to wear comfortable but smart-looking shoes and socks that give support to the arches, so as to prevent long-term complications. It is said that César Ritz wore shoes that were a size smaller than they should have been so as to keep himself literally on his toes and be always on the move when on duty. This hyperactivity led to a nervous breakdown and Ritz passed the last fifteen years of his life in a nursing home.

4.5 STAFF UNIFORMS

Dress sense is a factor that takes shape gradually rather than occurring at a certain moment in time. A person who cultivates his appearance in mufti usually looks smart when he puts on his working garments. Pride in one's job leads to pride in appearance from head to foot and a well-groomed member of staff conveys an air of cleanliness and hygiene. Hygiene of the person and of the uniform is imperative for all who work with food, and legislation can be enforced by Environmental Health Officers who are strict in their demands for the highest standards. This includes good changing-room with shower for the use of staff before or after each tour of duty, and the regular dry-cleaning or laundering of uniform and waiters' cloths.

Uniforms must be kept well-pressed, missing buttons sewn back on, badges and epaulettes properly attached. Shoes must be brushed regularly and staff must combat perspiration not so much by the use of an antiperspirant, as by frequent bathing and a change of socks and underclothes. The olfactory senses of customers must not be upset by staff who have sprayed themselves with perfume to overcome body odour. The head waiter usually inspects waiters before each service period to ensure they reach the desired standard and will send away those whose appearance fails to reach it. He will also look to see that pendants, necklaces, bracelets, rings, earrings, badges and stickers are neither obtrusive nor in bad taste.

Uniform is often the property of the employee and it is his responsibility to keep it in good repair and to pay for laundering. Some establishments supply staff with house garments of a particular design and colour and launder them free of charge, but most staff have to supply their own white shirt, bow-tie and black shoes and socks. Some restaurants dress their staff in a colourful regional or historical costume, in a lightweight garment, or else allow them to work in their ordinary clothes; but mostly the traditional uniform is worn as this helps to show the structure of the hierarchy. The normal uniform is:

Restaurant manager – lunchtime: striped trousers, grey tie and waist-coat, black jacket; dinnertime: evening dress with black bow-tie and waistcoat, starched cuffs;

Head waiter: black bow-tie, black tail-coat, waistcoat and trousers similar to formal evening dress;

Chef de rang: black bow-tie on white shirt with turn-down collar, black trousers, white jacket with black or gold epaulettes; at dinner time, evening dress (tails) and white bow-tie;

Commis waiter: black Eton jacket, long white apron, black bow-tie; sometimes a commis dresses in the same way as a chef de rang but with a white bow-tie to match the white jacket;

Commise waitress: black dress, white collar and apron and white headband; or black skirt, white blouse, black bow-tie, beige or black tights and black plain shoes; the dress may also be dark blue or grey;

Sommelier: small black alpaca jacket left open on a black waistcoat, long black serge or leather apron with a pocket, black bow-tie, badge depicting a bunch of grapes pinned to left lapel.

4.6   ADDITIONAL ESSENTIAL PERSONAL ATTRIBUTES

Waiting-staff must be honest and sober and able to maintain a calm composure in the face of outbursts of temper by customers and chefs. This means the ability to provide a service to others in an altruistic fashion that benefits both the proprietor and his customers. These moral qualities indicate a liking for the job of waiter, and the cultivation of a polite, pleasant and courteous manner helps a lot. Willingness and perseverance are virtues that can assist in progressing from commis to chef de rang, to station head waiter, then upwards to head waiter.

These qualities are recognised by employers who are also aware of the temptations that beset some of their staff in obtaining food and drink illicitly, taking advantage of customers by making unwarranted additions to the bill, or withholding monies received. Some companies have a rule that any shortfall of cash takings be made up by the member of staff responsible. On the other hand, should a customer feel that he has been given exceptional service by a waiter, he can feel free to reward that person accordingly.

4.7   THE REQUIREMENTS OF SOCIAL AND TECHNICAL SKILLS

In most occupations there is a need for only one sort of ability, either social or technical, and such jobs are that much more simple because they demand the skilful use of only one of these attributes. An insurance agent, for example, has to obtain the trust of the client from the outset and present a tailor-made proposal backed by a reliable company and by means of obtaining a personal rapport which gives the impression that he, the client, is in control of his choices, whereas it is really the agent who is. By means of his bodily posture and eye contact the agent is able to clinch the deal, doing it without exerting any undue pressure. This is an example of the use of a social skill. On the other hand, good mechanical skills are almost totally technical such as when a motor engineer quickly diagnoses a fault in a car and can rectify it without any unnecessary dismantling and so get the car back on the road in a short space of time, at small cost.

Although the social skills of personal interaction are of value to every individual, it is clear from this second example that a manipulative and persuasive personality is of greater significance than in the example of the insurance agent.

To carry out his duties to the full, a waiter needs both social and technical skills and has to be prepared to have and adapt them both, according to the nature of the operation and in relation to the class of customer, whose requirements can alter according to the time of day. For example, a busy executive will need quick service for a business luncheon and the waiter must serve the main course immediately the first course is cleared. The same executive may be patronising that restaurant for dinner but will expect a more relaxed service and would wish to make it a social rather than a business occasion. The waiter must be aware of the changed situation and adopt a different style of service with changed social, but not necessarily changed technical, skills.

An important part of the social skills required of a waiter is that of being confident when having to talk to important people who are patronising the restaurant.

Methods of addressing people

A waiter should know how to reply, if addressed by a person of titled or noble rank, in the course of his duties. He may reply, only if asked questions by such a person, and in order to respond correctly, needs to know what rank the person holds.

The way to address personages of title is as follows:

The Queen is 'Your Majesty', then afterwards 'Ma'am';

the Duke of Edinburgh is 'Your Royal Highness', then afterwards 'Sir';

a Royal Princess is addressed as 'Your Royal Highness', then as 'Ma'am';

a Prince is addressed as 'Your Royal Highness', then as 'Sir';

a Duchess and a Duke are addressed as 'Your Grace';

a Marchioness, a Countess, a Viscountess, a Baroness and a Life Peeress are all addressed as 'My Lady' and their male counter-parts as 'My Lord';

an Archbishop is addressed either as 'Your Grace' or 'My Lord';

a Cardinal as 'Your Eminence';

a Baronet is called by his title and Christian name.

All others are addressed as either 'Sir' or 'Madam'.

Normal rules of etiquette and the demonstration of social skills help to make it easy to serve such personages and staff are proud to say they have served royalty and the nobility.

In some establishments, waiters have to wear white gloves when serving these people, not for any hygienic reasons or to cover cigarette-stained fingers, but to show respect. A deferential but not abject demeanour is required; for example, it is customary to bow or curtsy, according to sex, but not to have to walk backwards away from them.

4.8 POTENTIALITY FOR ADVANCEMENT

There are few other occupations which afford such potential for rapid progression as that of waiting at table. The technical skills can be learned quickly by practice and if the required social skills have not been acquired in a previous environment, they can be quickly assimilated by observing all that goes on whilst at work. There has always been a shortage of Britons for jobs as waiters and the reason may be because the idea of waiting at table has been considered somehow demeaning. It is unfortunate that this impression should exist as the human rapport that is often established at the table between the provider and the receiver of food can result in a sense of achievement that, coupled with the opportunity for advancement, makes waiting a very worthwhile job.

4.9 KNOWLEDGE OF FOOD AND BEVERAGES

A waiter does not need to learn how to cook; it is true that some dishes are cooked in the restaurant by a waiter but the only method used, as shown in Chapter 12, is that of sautéing. The knowledge required by a waiter is of the basic methods of cooking and the kinds of foods cooked by each method, of those special commodities which are seasonal in use and how they taste; and a basic knowledge of nutrition and the nutritional value of a range of foods. If specialisation as a sommelier is envisaged then an understanding of the link between food and wine is necessary. Information on nutrition can be found in the Master Series Book, *Mastering Nutrition* by O. E. Kilgour. Among the many good books on wine is the *Encyclopaedia of Wines and Spirits* by Alexis Lichine, and *A Caterer's Guide to Drinks* by Conal Gregory; *Mastering Cookery* by J. and E. Taylor will provide the necessary culinary knowledge. Information on courses and examinations in these subjects is included in Appendix 3. A recommended book list is given in the Bibliography.

The job of being a waiter demands an intellectual dilettantism that embraces general knowledge kept up to date by constant reading, which coupled with a good communicative facility, enables him to discourse on a wide range of topics. It also demands a knowledge of the theory of cooking so as to be able to describe the making of any dish and to memorise most of the classical terms used on a menu. A knowledge of French is of importance as it is the language of the culinary arts of the Western world. A waiter must master the technical and manipulative skills of his job and be strong enough to carry heavy loads of dishes for a considerable distance.

The menu is the schematised schedule of the dishes a waiter has to serve and an understanding of the different kinds of menus is basic to everything a waiter does. A knowledge of how menus are written and what menu composition means is of great help in being able to guide a customer in selecting a well-balanced meal and of interpreting the culinary jargon used in the naming of dishes on the menu. Closely associated with a knowledge of the menu is that of international food habits and customs and a waiter should make a conscientious effort to learn something about the food and drink of different nations and religions. A failure to recognise these may lead to misunderstandings and consequent loss of business. This is why working abroad is invaluable as part of a waiter's early training.

4.10 COMMUNICATION SKILLS

In his everyday life a waiter must be confident of his ability to read, write, listen and speak effectively and accurately, and learn how to interpret and explain all aspects of his craft. Practice in choosing the right words and in listening carefully helps to improve human relations in the daily routine of the workplace. A sense of humour helps to oil the wheels of communication should the atmosphere become strained because of pressure of work.

There are two sides to communication – the receptive side which involves receiving written and oral information, including memos, notices, instruction manuals, telephone messages, radio announcements, etc., and the productive side which involves writing letters and reports and speaking to people by word of mouth directly or over the telephone. A good waiter must be able to receive and take action on any form of message, be able to understand duty rotas, charts and codes, recognise the value of signs and instructions, analyse an argument and be able to support or reject it. In some restaurants the waiter will have his own computer terminal for ordering and billing meals which is part of the food and beverage control system.

As a waiter mounts the ladder of promotion he may become involved in the training process and be responsible for writing food-service training aids and manuals, or act as training director for his department. If he becomes staff head waiter he will have the task of developing an effective brigade and increasing the productivity of his department through proper communications. Each member of the waiting-staff acts as a sales promoter by helping to market what the restaurant has to offer. The staff head waiter requires great communication ability since he interviews, counsels and disciplines employees as a means of influencing their performance.

4.11 ACQUISITION OF MANIPULATIVE SKILLS

Throughout this book the main emphasis is on demonstrating the manipulative practical skills of serving food and drink, skills which must be observed and practised from the very first day at work. The art of waiting stems from observing the many traditions and customs that have been in use for centuries and are still relevant today, for it is these that make the job such an interesting one, especially those lovable touches of bravura, craft and ceremony that add much to the mysticism of the activities. The young recruit should observe how senior members of staff perform various tasks and take note of how efficiently they are carried out, or if an improvement could be made. The catering industry has been accused of being hidebound by tradition and resistant to change but it is always willing to try new ideas and to adopt new gadgets, even though it may entail de-skilling some aspects of service, such as giving waiters pairs of tongs instead of a serving-spoon and fork, or not folding table napkins into any of the wonderful shapes that are so fascinating to customers. There are nearly 100 different items of equipment on the inventory of a restaurant, covering crockery, silverware, glassware and linen, and some restaurateurs have attempted to reduce this to a smaller and less expensive list by, say, eliminating fish knives and forks, having only two sizes and shapes of glasses, not using water jugs, etc., but unfortunately customers notice such attempts at streamlining and vote with their feet to go where the service is still completely authentic and where staff still excel in all the little nuances that are an integral part of the waiter's art.

Details of the technical skills required for the service of dishes on each of the courses of the menu are given in Chapters 8 to 13.

4.12 THE RESTAURANT BRIGADE

A brigade is the total complement of staff employed in a restaurant to serve meals to customers; it includes waiters of all ranks plus ancillary staff of restaurant porters, dispense-bar workers, and in some establishments the washing-up department, still-room staff and cellarmen.

In its present form the brigade structure dates from 1889 when César Ritz took over at the Savoy Hotel in London and made its restaurants the most famous in the world. He refined the eating-out experience to its highest apogee by employing a team of skilled staff whom he trained to his own standard, as practised by his staff in the many places he had directed in Europe. He had been accustomed to serving persons of the highest rank and had become a confidant of royalty, the aristocracy and members of high society, to whom he gave complete satisfaction through excellence of service. He insisted that his staff cultivate those social and technical skills which were the very foundation of first-class service and gave them a strong sense of loyalty and purpose, thus creating a highly efficient and stable restaurant brigade. Ritz was able to employ a large brigade because staff costs were low and waiters lived on their share of the *tronc* or pool of tips as distributed by the staff head waiter on a percentage, according to rank. Working under Ritz guaranteed a very-well-paid job; the prestige of using his name as an employer, and of having worked at the Savoy, was all the recommendation required by a subsequent master.

Ritz had owned and run his own establishments and many of his waiting-staff went on to open their own restaurant where they could emulate him, often by obtaining financial aid from the customers they had come to know by serving under Ritz at these establishments.

The organisational chart of this kind of restaurant is shown in Figure 4.1, which illustrates a first-class establishment capable of seating approximately 100 diners. The staff–customer ratio is high at four to one but it should be understood that at lunch the turnover

Fig 4.1 *organisational chart – the restaurant brigade*

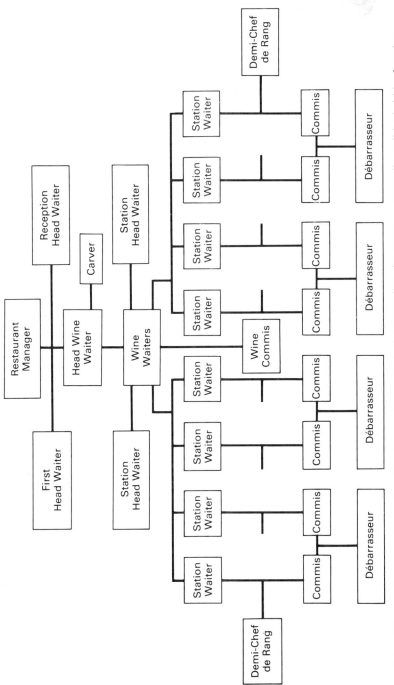

Note: Although for convenience, the titles are all given here in the masculine, the posts may equally well be held by females.

could be double that number because most customers will opt for the traditional three-course table d'hôte meal and only a few for à la carte dishes. The chart gives the names in English but the French names are still very much used, especially when advertising for staff as the French titles convey a more exact job description; for example a *commis débarrasseur* is the waiter who does the fetching and carrying and as such is not permitted to serve anything, yet to advertise for a clearer would probably attract the wrong person. It might be thought that as the chart shows an all-male brigade there is no place for a girl at this rarified level but this is an incorrect impression and girls are every bit as good at this work. Profiles of the restaurant brigade are given, together with their French titles.

Restaurant manager (directeur du restaurant) is the person in overall charge of the restaurant and the team of staff who are the front-of-house people. As one of the important heads of department he should have an office and secretary. The manager is always a person who has had wide experience and risen through the ranks; very often, the next step is to that of hotel manager or owner/ proprietor. A knowledge of food preparation, serving techniques, eating habits, social customs and languages, and the ability to be a good conversationalist, are some of the necessary attributes. Qualities of deportment and presence are required, to convey a feeling of suave efficiency to both customers and staff, and the manager must have the ability to put on a performance according to the different situations that arise, appearing in humble guise to a reserved person who is in need of comfort or encouragement, or as an authoritarian to a boisterous one who needs to be subdued.

First head waiter (premier maître d'hôtel) is the one who is in direct charge of the brigade and is deputy to the manager. He is sometimes known as the Chef de Brigade or the Staff Head Waiter. He needs considerable experience of service techniques and powers of leadership and motivation. He is the one who interviews, trains, counsels and disciplines employees rather than a personnel officer who may be lacking in sound hotel or restaurant experience. As the first head waiter is more closely associated with the daily routine of service it is he who ensures that the standards set by the manager are carried out in practice and he is the one who acts as the catalyst in keeping staff morale high so that it operates at optimum efficiency, thus ensuring maximum customer satisfaction.

The responsibilities of first head waiter include assisting the restaurant manager in his duties, organising the staff and rotating them between the stations (see table 4.1), carving and doing flambé work, and acting as relief to the manager. The first head waiter draws

Table 4.1 *allocation of stations*

Station 1	Station 2	Station 3	Station 4	Station 5
Ramirez	Conty	Smith	Sullivan	Green
Brown	Diore	Koch	Ross	Fearn

This shows members of staff the number of the station they will be on duty.

up staff duty rotas as shown in Table 4.2, which ensure that staff are present at peak periods of service and that the preparation work is fairly allocated. He will keep the register of attendance, showing days off, hours worked, etc., as shown in Table 4.3 which is sent to the Wages Office as the basis of remuneration.

The *second head waiter (chef de réception)* is the person who takes reservations for tables and discusses any special requirements of guests. He may also be required to look after the service to customers who are deemed to merit special attention. He should have a good memory for names and be able to recognise faces so as to greet guests by their title and to remember their requirements. His duties in the taking of bookings requires diplomacy as it is sometimes necessary to refuse because of pressure of business, or to obtain a deposit before guaranteeing a table to an unknown customer – and to do so without causing offence.

Regular customers like to be greeted by name and the second head waiter normally takes his stand at the entrance or goes to the foyer to welcome – by name – and then to conduct guests to their favourite

Table 4.2 *staff duties rota*

vacuum cleaner	linen	ménages	sideboard	hotplate
Brown	Ramirez	Diore	Koch	Ross

cold buffet	trollies	menus	plates	glasses
Conti	Smith	Sullivan	Green	Fearn

Table 4.3 *register of attendance*

name	Monday	Tuesday	Wednesday	Thursday	Friday	Saturday	Sunday	total hours	overtime	observations
Abdullah, I.	Ab	✓	✓	✓	✓	✓	DO	40	—	
McIntosh, J.	✓	DO	✓	✓	✓	✓	✓	48	—	
Oneteme, E.	✓	✓	DO	✓	✓	✓	✓	48	—	
Peake, R.	✓	✓	✓	DO	✓	✓	✓	48	—	
Ransom, F.	✓	✓	✓	✓	DO	✓	✓	48	—	
Short, B.	✓	✓	✓	✓	✓	DO	S	40	—	
Thompson, J.	✓	✓	✓	✓	✓	Ab	DO	40	—	
Wood, C.	AL	AL	✓	✓	✓	✓	✓	40	—	
Young, T.	✓	✓	✓	✓	✓	✓	DO	48	—	

Note: shifts = 10.00–14.30   less 2 × ½ hour meal breaks
                    18.00–22.30

DO = day off
Ab = absent
AL = Annual leave
S = Sick

Table 4.4 *weekly staff timetable*

name	Monday B L D	Tuesday B L D	Wednesday B L D	Thursday B L D	Friday B L D	Saturday B L D	Sunday B L D
Brown	B L	off	off	L D	L D	L D	L D
Ramirez	B L	off	off	L D	L D	L D	L D
Diore	off	L D	L D	L D	L D	B L	off
Kock	off	L D	L D	L D	L D	B L	off
Ross	L D	L D	L D	B L	off	off	L D
Conti	L D	L D	L D	B L	off	off	L D
Smith	L D	L D	B L	off	off	L D	L D
Sullivan	L D	L D	B L	off	off	L D	L D
Green	L D	L D	L D	L D	B L	off	off
Fearn	L D	B L	off	off	L D	L D	L D
total	2 8 6	1 8 7	2 7 5	2 7 5	1 6 5	2 7 5	7 7

Breakfast brigade

name	Monday	Tuesday	Wednesday	Thursday	Friday	Saturday	Sunday
Agnes		B	B			B	B
Josie		B			B		B
Lynn				B	B		B

Note: breakfast (B)   7.00–10.30
lunch (L)   10.30–14.30
dinner (D)   18.30–23.00

table. As the greeter, he must make them feel most welcome and of importance to the establishment as this kind of attention helps to generate repeat business. The second head waiter is responsible for organising an efficient booking system, a customer profile index, and a record for the purpose of mailing promotional material, seasonal goodwill messages, etc.

The *wine waiter (sommelier)* is the head wine butler in charge of the service of all alcoholic drinks in the restaurant and often has charge of the dispense barmen and cellar staff. He should have a large say in the purchase of wines and the production of the wine list and have a flair for salesmanship so that he maximises sales. A good knowledge of cooking will enable him to make recommendations as to the choice of wine when asked by a customer. Visits to vineyards to see wine being made will assist in this, as would a stint in the kitchen to learn about flavour and aroma of dishes.

Wine is a popular subject amongst lay people who, on gaining an empirical knowledge, love to show their expertise. The sommelier must therefore be much more knowledgeable than any customer and convey the impression that he is an expert because he studies the subject in a professional capacity. It is not enough to read popular books on the subject; he must taste so that he can describe and recommend. Rare wines are extremely expensive and in a high-class restaurant the sommelier will handle wines that sell at anything from £150 per bottle upwards, which is quite a common occurrence in such places.

The sommelier's responsibilities include organising his team of wine waiters, ensuring that they know each wine on the list and which foods they complement and that they can serve aperitifs, wines, spirits and liqueurs, with particular attention to correct serving temperatures. He is also responsible for the sale of cigarettes and cigars and the storage and control of these items; control of the dispense bar; training staff in the service of drinks, especially new additions to the wine list, and new items on the market, and liaison with the head waiter and the head cellar man.

The *station head waiter (maître d'hôtel de carré)* is in charge of a section of the restaurant consisting of three stations, each of three to five tables for two to ten people each. It is his job to greet customers as they are escorted to his area by the head waiter, to assist them to be seated and to take their order, which he then gives to the chef de rang to carry out. The station head waiter must possess linguistic skills so as to give succinct descriptions of the dishes on the menu, and to make customers feel at home in his part of the restaurant. He must be seen to be in charge by giving orders to his staff, constantly moving around to check that they are doing the job properly, assisting where necessary, and by carrying out any carving or filleting, and doing flambé dishes, or instructing his staff when there is this kind of work to be done. A station head waiter should be charming, courteous and reassuring and be able to keep calm under pressure; his responsibilities are the supervision of his section during the service, its preparation prior to service, and supervising clearing it afterwards.

The *carver (trancheur*, or *chef du buffet froid)* is the person of head-waiter rank who takes charge of the carving done on the buffet table and carving trolley. He is employed only in those restaurants that feature a large cold-buffet table for lunch daily in the dining room; in the evening he would be a third head waiter. He takes control of all the items on the buffet table and serves them against checks made out by the waiters; he must be an expert carver and know which viandes should be carved thinly and those that must be cut into thick slices. He knows the size of portions and keeps strict control to ensure that the stated number of portions per kilogram are obtained.

If a carved joint is featured as a *plat du jour* he does the carving from the heated trolley, serving it neatly onto a plate in front of the customer. He may be assigned a chef from the kitchen to assist with this duty but normally he has only a commis waiter to do the fetching and carrying of additional supplies or special orders.

The *station waiter (chef de rang)* is responsible for the service at from five to nine tables, seating from two to ten people each or twenty-five to thirty customers, in his section of the restaurant. He is under the orders of the station head waiter and is assisted by a number of commis waiters. He sees to the actual service of the food ordered and must know the rules governing the order of service and correct plate layout. He must be competent at organising the work of his station so that it operates efficiently and the sequence of service runs smoothly on each table, without favouring or neglecting any one of them. He must be pleasant but not obsequious and have a nature that enables him to establish an amiable rapport with customers. He must ensure that every item consumed is charged to customers, present the bill when requested and take the cash.

The *assistant station waiter (demi chef de rang)* is an aspiring chef de rang who is given charge of from three to five tables for two or three people each, which is part of a station. He will be a fairly well-experienced commis who is being groomed for promotion and can work on his own, given the guidance and help of his chef de rang and the assistance of a commis waiter.

The *commis waiter (garçon de restaurant,* or *commis de suite)* is an assistant waiter who takes orders to the kitchen and brings the food for the chef de rang to serve; he may assist by serving the vegetables, sauces and accompaniments and by clearing the empty plates from the table. The commis or commise (assistant waitress) prepares the station in readiness for the meal, cleaning and dusting before laying up the tables and putting the *mise en place* on the sideboard. The distribution of these preparatory jobs is as shown in Table 4.3. A commis should realise that this mundane job could be the first step to a lucrative career and endeavour to make his way through the ranks rapidly, absorbing all he can of the finer points of service, the protocol, and the routine.

The *clearer (commis débarrasseur)* is a young waiter who is starting his career by doing all the menial chores whilst becoming adapted to the hours of duty and the environment. He must keep the sideboard stocked with items of equipment and remove the dirty dishes and cutlery from it so as to ensure that no delays occur during the service. Although this is the lowest rank of waiter and the rate of pay is poor, the new recruit will find the luxurious surroundings so congenial as to give a certain cachet to the work, raising it from being a menial below-stairs kind of job to one of dignity.

Catering is a service industry and serving at table is where the cycle that began with the purchase of food and its conversion into a magnificent repast by skilled chefs, reaches its zenith and ends as the waiter presents it to the customer. If the waiter serves it correctly the entire endeavour has succeeded; if he serves it badly, drops dishes, knocks over glasses, and fails to come to terms with the customer, or allows anything else to go wrong, the enterprise has failed.

4.13 WORKING CONDITIONS

Having extolled the merits of a career as a waiter it is necessary to point out some of what may be said to be the drawbacks of this kind of job. Although the work is mainly carried out in a pleasant environment, the atmosphere of the back of the house may not be so salubrious; this can include changing-rooms, rest and recreation facilities, on-the-job training, correct payment of overtime, meal breaks, regular days off, and other important matters.

Any person entering the catering industry must realise that the job entails working unsocial hours. This means early and late shifts and, in the case of a waiter, split shifts which entail being on duty for both main meals of the day, at lunch and at dinner. A restaurant in an hotel may open at 7.00 a.m. for breakfast and not close until 2.00 a.m. the next morning, with only a brief interlude between the service periods.

Some companies look after their staff by means of a grievance procedure for use in matters of discipline; by encouraging membership of a trade union whose aim is to advance the interests of its members; by offering four or more weeks paid holiday a year, a pension scheme, life assurance, service awards, staff discount scheme, loans, and even company shares; others may not be so generous.

To walk across a deep-pile carpet as he enters a restaurant may give a customer the feeling of luxury and good living, but to the waiter who has to tread upon it for eight hours each day it can become intolerable and harmful to his feet, no matter how good the pair of shoes he wears. Thus a waiter in order to keep himself in a fit state of health, has to condition himself to the working environment.

QUESTIONS

1. Without referring to the text, list the names and state the responsibilities of each member of the brigade of a luxury restaurant.

2. Summarise the differences between social skills and technical skills.

3. Define the main attributes of a food-service worker.

4. Say what is meant by personal care and hygiene.

THE MENU

5.1   THE RULES OF MENU PLANNING

A menu is the means of informing customers what food a restaurant has to sell and as such it becomes the outward expression of the aim of the establishment. The dishes that are listed on the menu are the blueprint of instructions that outline the chef's and waiter's duties, which means that the quality of the menu controls the scope of operation and also helps to make the waiter's job more pleasant by listing good dishes to sell.

Menus are written by the head chef, or by the catering manager and he has many rules to bear in mind when composing the list. Amongst these rules are:

1. the class of restaurant;
2. the type of menu;
3. the ability of the staff to cook and serve the dishes;
4. the cooking and serving equipment available on site;
5. the language in which the menu is to be written (see 5.10);
6. profile of the customers;
7. time and season of the year;
8. any nutritional requirements;
9. combinations of food; and
10. the price to be charged for the meal.

These are the bare outlines of the rules to be observed and each needs to be discussed, but as space does not allow, reference should be made to *Practical Professional Catering* or *Practical Professional Gastronomy* (both published by Macmillan) which have large chapters on the subject of menus.

It is not just the list of dishes that has to be considered but their combination into a meal which has good eye appeal, avoids repetition and satisfies the customer. For example, it is considered wrong to allow him to select a meal that turns out to be of one colour, such as cauliflower soup, blanquette of veal and vanilla bavarois, which are all white, or to select goulash of beef and have stuffed tomatoes and marquise potatoes which would be too red and without a contrasting colour. Yet the possible combinations on a table d'hôte menu can allow this to happen and the waiter should diplomatically point it out and suggest some better alternatives.

A menu is written in accordance with the accepted sequence of courses that constitute a meal, starting with hors-d'oeuvre, then soup, egg or farinaceous dish, fish, meat, sweet and cheese, followed by coffee. This sequence is universal except that French people prefer to eat cheese before the sweet. Sometimes a menu will have two lists of meat dishes, one headed 'Entrées' and one 'Relevés'; there may be another list of meats headed 'Grills', but the main difference between an entrée and a relevé is that the former consists of small cuts of meat such as noisettes, suprêmes, sweetbreads, vols-au-vent, stews, etc., whereas a relevé is always a joint or bird cooked whole by braising or poêléing with an elaborate garnish. An entrée is served with little or no garnish and usually without accompanying vegetables, if it is being followed by a relevé. Dinner meals are more elaborate and leisurely than are lunches and the menus used reflect this difference.

5.2   TABLE D'HÔTE MENUS

This kind of menu is the one most widely used, and although at one time it was a fixed menu with no choices, nowadays it usually includes at least three alternative dishes on each course for lunch, and up to five at dinner. These dishes should be the most popular ones in the culinary repertoire and of fairly equal appeal to most people's taste so that if one item runs out, the alternatives are equally acceptable. All the dishes except green vegetables are normally cooked in advance so that customers can be served quickly; it is usual to include seasonal commodities in the choices.

A table d'hôte menu is sold at a fixed price which may be inclusive of VAT and service charge, or this may be additional. In some establishments the price charged is according to that of the main course. The service charge is usually from 10 to 15 per cent of the basic price and the total sum of service charges received during the week is distributed to staff according to status. (At one time it was shared among the waiters only but is now distributed to most grades of staff. Many customers wish to reward waiters by leaving a tip as well as paying the service charge; in some restaurants the gratuity is kept by the waiter who receives it but more usually it is put into the *tronc* and shared out weekly by the staff head waiter.)

A *prix fixe menu* is the same as a table d'hôte menu except that in some smaller establishments no choice is offered and the customer has to take what is listed. Most prix fixe and table d'hôte menus give a semblance of an à la carte menu because of the flexibility of choice on every course. An example of a table d'hôte menu is given in Table 5.1.

5.3   A LA CARTE MENUS

As may be seen in the example in Table 5.2, this kind of menu is much more complete than the table d'hôte kind, although the extent will vary according to the type of restaurant. As may be seen, this menu shows the complete choice of dishes that are available from the kitchen at all times. It lists the dishes in the normal menu sequence, with each dish priced separately. The customer bears the onus of responsibility as regards his choice in building a well-balanced meal but is free to order as many courses as he wishes – just one course or ten courses, although there may well be a minimum charge. The great benefit of this menu is that every dish is freshly cooked to order with only a minimum of basic preparation such as previously chopped onion, diced tomato, stock or sauce, to cut cooking time.

The service of an à la carte meal demands a lot of thought from the waiter so as to maintain the even flow of service without lengthy pauses between courses. Some of the main dishes on this kind of menu have a time printed next to them showing how long each will take to cook; for example a roast duck requires 45 minutes from the time of placing the order so the waiter must time the service of the first courses to coincide. He must not waste time standing at the hotplate when he should be present in the restaurant.

An à la carte menu is printed to last for several months until it is felt necessary to change prices or dishes, as it costs a lot to print menus and waiters are expected to take good care of them and to prevent them becoming too soiled for continued use; they must also deter customers from taking them away. Some restaurants add stickers to an à la carte menu to publicise special dishes of the day which may feature a seasonal item or a chef's speciality. The à la carte menu is used for both lunch and dinner and the waiter must be able to give guidance as to those dishes that are suitable for lunch as against those that are more suitable for dinner, as shown in Table 5.3.

Table 5.1   *example of a table d'hôte menu*

HÔTEL AMBASSADOR

MENU
TABLE D'HÔTE

Hors-d'Oeuvre Variés
ou
Avocat au Crabe
ou
Pâté Maison
ou
Crème Dubarry
———

Omelette à l'Espagnole
ou
Filet de Merlan à la Meunière
ou
Fricassée de Veau Printinière
ou
Poulet Sauté Bourguignonne
ou
Pièce de Boeuf Braisée à la Mode
Haricots Verts au Beurre   Ratatouille Niçoise
Chou-fleur Mornay   Choux de Bruxelles Sautés
Pommes Croquettes, Delmonico, Frites, Lyonnaise, Purée
———

Ananas Créole   Savarin aux Fruits   Flan aux Pommes
———

Café
———

Service $12\frac{1}{2}$%

Lundi le 26 juin 1988

Table 5.2 *example of an á la carte menu*

HÔTEL AMBASSADOR

MENU

A LA CARTE

Hors-d'oeuvre	Jambon de Parme £3.50 Parfait de foie gras au Porto £12.00 Melon Frappé £3.00 Saumon Fumé £6.50 Caviar de Beluga £30.00 Terrine Truffée £5.00 Crevettes Roses £6.00
Potages	Consommé Madrilène £2.25 Tortue Claire au Xérès £3.00 Petite Marmite £3.00 Crème Solferino £2.50 Vichyssoise £3.00 Bisque de Homard £4.50 Germiny en Tasse £4.00
Oeufs et Farinages	Oeufs en Cocotte (2 piéce) £3.00 Oeufs plat Bercy £3.00 Omelette Arnold Bennett £5.00 Omelette aux Queues d'Ecrevisses £4.00 Rigatoni al Sugo £4.00 Raviolis £4.25
Poissons	Quenelles de Sole Nantua £5.50 Brochet Meunière £6.00 Escalope de Saumon à l'Oseille £7.50 Suprême de Turbot Walewska £8.00 Homard Newburg £16.50 Douzaine d'Escargots de Bourgogne £7.00 Vol-au-Vent de Fruits de Mer £4.25 Mayonnaise de Saumon £6.50
Entrées	Ris de Veau Florentine £8.75 Rognons Sautés au Madère £7.50 Entrecôte Marchand de Vin £9.75 Tournedos Forestière £9.00 Trois Filets sautés aux Trois Poivres £12.00 Côtelettes d'Agneau Vert-Pré £7.50 Noisette de Chevreuil Grand-Veneur £9.50 Râble de Lièvre à la Crème £8.75 Filet de Boeuf Strogonoff £8.75 Côte de Veau en Papillote £8.50 Suprême de Volaille Normande £7.25 Poulet Sauté Provençale £7.50 (20 mins) Poulet Poêlé £15.00 for 2 (40 mins) Cailles aux Kiwis £12.50 (20 mins) Pintade Rôtie £15.00 2cvts (35 mins) Canard à l'Orange £17.00 for 2 (40 mins)
Buffet Froid	Côte de Boeuf £5.25 Langue Ecarlate £4.75 Jambon de York £4.50 Assiette Anglaise £6.50 Suprême de Volaille Jeannette £5.75 Salades Variées £3.00
Légumes	Asperges Fraîches £6.50 Fonds d'Artichauts Farcis £4.00 Aubergines Frites £4.00 Epinards en Branches £2.25 Choufleur Polonaise £2.00 Endive Meunière £2.00 Pommes: Croquettes, Frites, Lorette, Nouvelles, Parmentier, Soufflées £2.00
Desserts	Poire Belle-Hélène £2.10 Pouding au Riz £1.50 Beignets de Banane £1.50 Crème Caramel £3.00 Flan aux Pommes £2.50 Pêche Melba £3.50 Ananas au Kirsch £3.50 Fruit Exotiques £4.50 Crêpes Créole £3.50 Soufflé au Grand Marnier £10.00 for 2 (30 mins) Omelette Norvégienne £8.50 for 2 (20 mins) Sabayon au Marsala £4.00 (20 mins)
Savouries	Buck Rarebit £3.00 Canapé Diane £2.15 Champignons sous Cloche £3.00 Croûte Windsor £2.15 Diables à Cheval £2.15 Scotch Woodcock £2.15 Welsh Rarebit £2.15

Table 5.3 *comparable suitability of dishes*

course	lunch	dinner
Hors d'oeuvre	grapefruit, pâté, charcuterie, hors-d'oeuvre variés, smoked mackerel	shellfish cocktail, melon, oysters, caviar, foie gras, smoked salmon, asparagus, globe artichoke
Soup	broth, purée of vegetable	consommé, velouté, crème, bisque
Farinaceous	lasagne, macaroni, rice, spaghetti, etc.	not applicable
Egg	poached, scrambled, en cocotte, omelette	not applicable
Fish	crab, scampi, cod, herring, whiting, skate – plainly poached or fried	lobster, salmon, sole, turbot – in a rich sauce
Meat	stew, pie, pudding, rechauffé, hot-pot, offal, hamburger, cutlet, chop, steak	tournedos, escalope, noisette, sweetbread; poêléd or braised saddle of lamb, fillet of beef, chicken, duck, pheasant
Vegetable	cabbage, carrot, parsnip, swede, turnip, leek, onion, marrow	cauliflower, French beans, endive, asparagus, seakale, lettuce, courgette
Sweet	milk pudding, jelly, pie, pudding, flan, mousse, fruit salad, ice cream	soufflé, pancake, coupe, bombe, flambé fruit
Cheese	all varieties	more expensive cheeses
Savoury	not applicable	angels on horseback, canapé-Diane, Ivanhoe, quo-vadis; croûte-Derby, baron, Windsor

5.4 SPECIALITY MENUS

These are of fairly recent introduction and are used in those restaurants that offer only one basic item to which a limited number of variations may be added. The speciality can be chicken, pizza, hamburger, fish, steak, pancake, baked potato, etc., usually sold under a brand name for which there is probably a trade mark. The main item is usually a snack type of meal but with one of the appetisers and a dessert from the limited range available, a reasonable collation may be formed. The kind of service in operation can be either take-away or self-service, with waiters doing plate service in the more expensive places such as steak houses. In the cheaper places the meals are served in a paper bag or on a cardboard plate and the customer is expected to dispose of his used dishes in the waste bin. This type of catering is often referred to as the fast-food business because production is geared to the volume of customers expected so that they are not kept waiting for long, but food is not cooked so far in advance that it starts to deteriorate. The food is so simple that it can be consumed quickly and seats are used over and over again during peak periods.

5.5 THE COMPOSITION OF DISHES

As may be seen from the menu examples given throughout this book there is a kind of culinary shorthand in use for naming dishes which serves to describe the make-up of each. There are thousands of such names and nobody has yet claimed to memorise them all so as to declare what each one means. Yet a waiter must know the several hundred most popular ones in order that he can describe the make-up of the dish according to its name. It is true that most of the restaurants that have menus written in French give a brief translation of the main dishes but the professional waiter will know them all and will be pleased to give customers more information than can be written on the menu.

The classical names have been conferred on dishes conceived by chefs over the centuries to commemorate special events, notable places, the lives of famous people, the restaurant where the dish was created, names of plays, operas, books etc., and new names are still being created for new dishes. Customers are interested in these dish titles and often endeavour to learn their meaning so as to prove their knowledge of the culinary arts, to astonish their friends, or even to confound waiters.

The classical name codifies the method of cooking and the ingredients of the garnish; it is left to the chef to decide on actual presentation but the formula should be the same wherever the dish has been adopted so that customers will receive the exact item wherever they dine. Some garnish names are peculiar to a particular restaurant because first conceived there but in most cases customers are assured of receiving the authentic dish. Books that record these names are the *Repertoire de la Cuisine*, and *New Professional Kitchen Repertoire* and *Hering's Dictionary*.

French is the technical language of the catering industry and it is not possible to work as a waiter without a knowledge of the jargon. With so many French terms included in every menu no caterer worthy of the name dare confess his ignorance of the vast number of technical titles. A chef in the kitchen may pronounce these terms rather badly but with only his colleagues listening it does not matter. A waiter has to use them in the presence of customers so it is imperative that he pronounces them absolutely correctly so that a knowledgeable customer can understand. The waiter who pronounces the word blanquette as 'blankwetty' immediately reveals his lack of professional knowledge. Definitions of some of the classic names and menu terms in everyday use are listed in Table 5.4.

5.6 THE ORGANISATION OF THE KITCHEN

Waiters spend much of their time at the hotplate or service counter of the kitchen and have time to see what goes on in that department. A knowledge of the way a kitchen works and of its routine of operation will help a waiter to understand the work of his opposite number – the cook. There should be a close relationship between restaurant and kitchen staff since each relies on the other in providing well-cooked and well-served food for customers; chefs want their dishes to be properly served and waiters want foods they are proud to serve; therefore in order to obtain job satisfaction, chefs and waiters should cooperate and be aware of the problems that can arise in the course of their work on each side of the hotplate as in many hotels and restaurants there is antagonism and rivalry between the cooking and serving sides with the hotplate as a barrier to harmonious relationships. Often there is no valid reason for this lack of cooperation and it may be historical but it should be remembered that chefs work in a hot environment, often against the clock, and they can become extremely temperamental. The atmosphere is noisy, the work is strenuous and the pace is rapid, all of which can account for

Table 5.4 *examples of dish names*

Name on menu	Definition
Artichaut Vinaigrette	cold boiled globe artichoke served with vinegar and oil dressing
Asperges Hollandaise	hot asparagus with warm butter and egg sauce
Assiette Anglaise	sliced ham, ox tongue, pressed beef, etc.
Avocat Pasadena	half avocado pear filled with diced tomato, chopped olive and crabmeat
Bavarois Réligieuse	chocolate and vanilla bavarois in layers
Boeuf Strogonoff	strips of beef fillet cooked in butter with onion, paprika, lemon juice and cream
Boeuf Wellington	fillet of beef, covered with duxelles or pâté, encased in pastry and baked
Canapés Russe	selection of about ten different cocktail savoury titbits
Canard Sévillaise	cold duck with orange segments and mousse of foie gras in aspic
Caviar de Beluga	brined sturgeon roe from Russia or Iran, of large black grains
Choux à la Crème	small cream buns filled with whipped cream
Crème Dubarry	cream of cauliflower soup
Darne de Saumon Grillée	grilled round slice of fresh salmon
Escalope de Veau au Madère	sautéd thin slice of veal covered with Madeira sauce
Escargots Bourguignonne	snails cooked in the oven with herb butter
Filet de Plie Caprice	grilled crumbed fillet of plaice with grilled banana and Robert sauce
Fraises Melba	strawberries on a layer of vanilla ice cream, covered with raspberry purée
Gâteau St-Honoré	elaborate puff and chou pastry cake filled with cream

Haricots Verts Tourangelle	cooked French beans mixed with cream sauce
Homard Thermidor	half a lobster in bercy sauce flavoured with mustard, served in the shell
Jugged Hare	pieces of hare stewed in red wine
Kedgeree	flaked smoked haddock, diced hard-boiled egg and rice, served with curry sauce
Langue de Chat	thin finger biscuits for serving with ice cream
Moules Marinière	boiled mussels served in the half shell, covered with creamy sauce
Noix de Veau Poêlé	pot-roasted cushion of veal served in slices, covered with sauce
Oeuf Moscovite	hard-boiled egg filled with caviar and anchovy fillet
Omelette Soufflé Milord	ice cream and pears on a layer of sponge-cake, covered with meringue and quickly baked
Pommes Anna	thinly sliced potato arranged overlapping in a mould and baked
Quenelle de Veau	veal pounded with egg white and cream, moulded into ovals and poached
Quiche Lorraine	flan filled with savoury egg custard, pieces of bacon and Gruyère cheese
Rouget Niçoise	grilled red mullet with cooked diced tomato, anchovy and black olives
Scotch Woodcock	scrambled egg with anchovies and capers on toast, served as a savoury
Seafood Cocktail	crab, lobster and shrimps on shredded lettuce, covered with tomato and mayonnaise sauce
Terrine de Gibier	pâté made of hare, venison, etc., flavoured with brandy and spices

frayed tempers which are often vented onto waiters, especially when they bring back food and say it is not what was ordered, or that the customer has made a complaint about it.

The traditional routine of food service is as follows:

1. the waiter gives the top copy of the order to the kitchen clerk at the hotplate;
2. it is time-stamped in a machine and read in a loud voice to the chefs at large who are constantly on the alert and have to memorise every order appertaining to their section, as shown in Figure 5.1 the traditional kitchen brigade;
3. orders are usually given in French;
4. when a course is required by the waiter he tells the clerk the table number who then shouts 'Envoyez (e.g.) les quatres Tournedos Rossini, quatres pommes et légumes!' which the chefs have been busy preparing;
5. the chefs bring the order to the hotplate where it is checked against the order, covered with lids, crossed through on the check and passed across to the waiter;
6. the waiter piles the dishes on his tray using his waiter's cloth because he knows they will be very hot; he has already taken four hot meat-plates from the hot cupboard, makes sure all is evenly balanced and hastens to his sideboard;
7. the dishes are placed on the heater element on the sideboard, the plates wiped and placed in front of each customer;
8. the food is served, the meat first and then the vegetables and potatoes;
9. the sauce is ladled either on or around the meat, according to what dish it is.

Some of the items on an à la carte menu have a time stated next to them to inform customers that these are cooked only when the order is received in the kitchen so there may be a delay between the courses. The timed items are large ones that take twenty minutes or more to cook, as shown in Table 5.5. Ordinarily, grilled steaks and chops, fried fish, pasta dishes, soufflés, etc., can be cooked in readiness by the time the customer has reached that particular course and there need be no delay if the waiter times the pace of service accordingly, so no time is printed next to them on the menu.

Fig 5.1 *the traditional kitchen brigade*

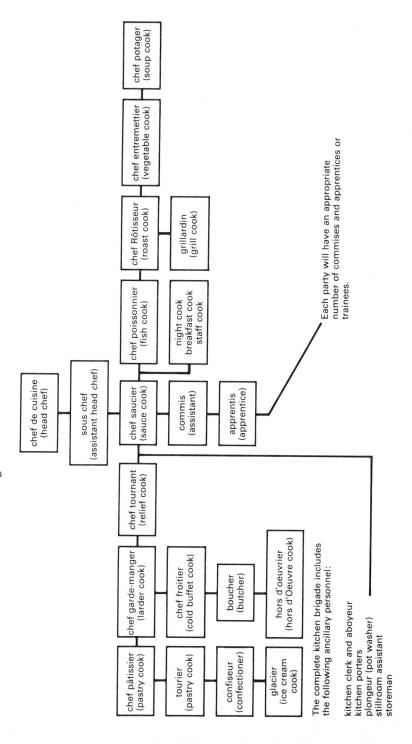

chef de cuisine
(head chef)

sous chef
(assistant head chef)

chef potager
(soup cook)

chef entremettier
(vegetable cook)

chef Rôtisseur
(roast cook)

grillardin
(grill cook)

chef poissonnier
(fish cook)

night cook
breakfast cook
staff cook

chef saucier
(sauce cook)

commis
(assistant)

apprentis
(apprentice)

Each party will have an appropriate number of commises and apprentices or trainees.

chef tournant
(relief cook)

chef garde-manger
(larder cook)

chef froitier
(cold buffet cook)

boucher
(butcher)

hors d'oeuvrier
(hors d'Oeuvre cook)

chef pâtissier
(pastry cook)

tourier
(pastry cook)

confiseur
(confectioner)

glacier
(ice cream cook)

The complete kitchen brigade includes the following ancillary personnel:

kitchen clerk and aboyeur
kitchen porters
plongeur (pot washer)
stillroom assistant
storeman

Table 5.5   *average cooking times for à la carte dishes*

Item	Minutes	Item	Minutes
Chateaubriand for 2 persons	20	Roast poussin (double) for 2 persons	20
Chateaubriand for 4 persons	30	Roast best end of lamb for 4 persons	35
Roast chicken for 4 persons	45	Roast saddle of milk lamb for 2 persons	30
Roast duck for 2 persons	45	Fillet of Beef Wellington for 2 persons	30
Roast grouse for 2 persons	20	Grilled Spatchcock chicken for 2 persons	25
Roast partridge for 1 person	15	Omelette soufflé Norvégienne	30
Roast pheasant for 2 persons	35	Crêpes Normande	20

5.7 EXAMPLES OF MENUS

The following are examples of the many kinds of menus that are written each day in the wide variety of establishments that go to make up the catering industry. There are sample menus from the famous gourmet restaurants of France where the chef-patron is internationally known, as well as those in daily use in our hospitals and nursing homes. Waiting-staff need a good knowledge of the art of menu composition as they are often consulted by customers wanting to organise a very special meal at a table in the restaurant, often of dishes that are not on any of the menus in use in the establishment. The waiter must be able to advise on suitable dishes and appropriate wines for all kinds of occasions.

CHRISTMAS DINNER

La Coupe des Trois Mages

——

Le Berceau d'Aiglefin aux Crevettes

——

La Dinde de Norfolk Rôtie
La Farce aux Chatâignes
La Chipolata Grillée
La Sauce aux Airelles
Les Choux de Bruxelles Rissolés au Beurre
Les Pommes Château

——

Le Pouding de Noël aux Feux Follets
La Sauce Anglaise à l'Armagnac
Le Délice Feuilletté Pastorale

La Bonbonnière Fleurie de Friandises
Les Fruits et Noix à Volonté

——

Le Demi-Tasse Mocha

* * *

NOUVELLE CUISINE MENU

Salade Tiède de Foie de Canard aux Artichauts

———

Etuvée de Turbot aux Epinards, pulpe
de Tomate fraîche à l'Estragon

———

Cervelle de Veau aux Ecrevisses, Spaghettis
Frais, au Jus de Veau au Porto

———

Tartelette Sablée aux Fruits Rouges et Ananas

———

ENGLISH MENU

Smoked Mackerel Mousse with Oatcake

Roast Rib of Beef, Madeira Sauce
Brussels Sprouts with Chestnuts
Parsley Potatoes

Iced Cherry Soufflé with Hot Cherry Sauce and
Sponge Fingers

Coffee and Mints

BANQUET MENU

Coupe de Melon à l'Orange

Vol-au-vent aux Fruits de Mer

Noisettes d'Agneau Chasseur
Bouquetière de Légumes

Vacherin Belle de Fontenay

Café
Petits Fours

MENU GASTRONOMIQUE

La Ballotine de Canard Truffée et Pistachée
____

Le Foie Gras Frais Chapon Fin
____

Le Suprême de Turbot Soufflé Curnonsky
____

La Gigue de Chevreuil Grand-Veneur
La Mousseline de Marrons
Les Pommes Hérisson
____

Les Pêches et Fraises
Les Petits Fours
____

La Tasse de Café
____

GOURMET DINNER

Le Zéphyr de Foie Gras à la Gelée au Porto
Les Petites Brioches Chaudes

Le Suprème de Turbot Braisé Amphytrion

La Caille Fourrée à la Façon du Grand-Vatel

La Neige au Champagne

Le Coeur de Contrefilet de Boeuf Epicurienne

Le Turban de Comices Lucullus
Le Coffret Fleuri de Frivolités

L'Extrait de Mocha

* * *

AFTERNOON TEA MENU

Brown or white bread and butter, jam, honey

Sandwiches – fish paste, cucumber, tomato, egg and cress,
meat paste

French pastries – coffee eclairs, choux buns, fruit tartlets,
sponge fancies, madeleines, frangipane
barquettes, macaroons, mirlitons, meringues

Sliced fruit cake, chocolate gateau, millefeuilles

Toasted tea cakes, muffins, Sally Lunns, Chelsea buns

Pot of Tea – Indian or China

NEW YEAR'S EVE DINNER

Les Huîtres Royales Perlées au Citron
———

Le Foie Gras en Croûte Strasbourgeoise
———

Le Rosé d'Ecosse au Pain Bis
———

Le Bisque de Homard à l'Armagnac
———

La Tasse de Consommé Madrilène
———

La Paupiette de Sole Grand-Duc

Le Coeur de Filet Reveillon
Le Fond d'Artichaut Marie-Louise
Les Pommes Lorette
———

Le Parfait Grand Marnier
La Tranche d'Ananas Bonne Année
La Corbeille de Friandises
———

Le Café
———

MENU FOR A COCKTAIL PARTY

Cocktail canapés

Assorted sandwiches

Filled bridge rolls

Sausage rolls – Chipolatas

Chicken bouchées – Quichelettes

Celery filled with Rocquefort cheese

5.8 SEASONAL MENUS AND FOODS

Modern technology and air transportation have revolutionised the pattern of foods in season so that it is possible to use the same à la carte menu throughout the year without needing to say that a particular food is unavailable. When the home season has ended there is bound to be some other country where the food is ready to be air-lifted to the UK or to any other country where there are people prepared to pay the price.

It is still nice to taste the first new potatoes from Jersey, locally grown strawberries, Norfolk asparagus, Avon salmon, or a fresh grouse from Scotland on 12 August, and customers expect to be offered these and the many other new season's foods as they become available during the course of the months. This means printing a new menu for the main seasons of the year, or having space to attach details to the current menu to announce seasonal availability. Foods in season from local sources not only taste better but once the novelty has worn off, are usually cheaper to purchase, but such is their appeal on the grounds of freshness, food value and tenderness that initially they command a premium price on the menu.

5.9 BASIC DIETETICS

People are becoming ever more health-conscious and therefore want to eat intelligently so as to avoid various kinds of illnesses, and also to lose weight. It might be thought that the only places where customers are likely to request a light diet is in a convalescent or nursing home but nowadays such requirements have to be met in all classes of restaurants and a waiter needs a basic knowledge of nutrition so as to be able to make sensible statements about the value of foods and drinks he serves.

Clients who eat out in restaurants are not likely to suffer from malnutrition because they have a wide variety of foods made available to them. Food promotes growth, repair and energy for the body and different foods contribute to these by providing various nutrients. The essential nutrients are proteins – contained in fish, meat, eggs and milk; carbohydrates – in breakfast cereals, pasta, biscuits, cakes, puddings, bread, and sugar; fats – in butter, margarine, oil, cheese and meat; vitamins, with letters to distinguish the eight which are essential to good health – A, B_1, B_2, B_6, C, D, E, K, each having a different function and found in various foodstuffs; mineral salts, the main ones being calcium, iodine, iron, fluorine and zinc, which fulfil various functions in the diet and are found in several foods.

The energy value of the foods we eat is measured in kilocalories and an average adult needs approximately 2500 per day, with each gram of the nutrients contributing a number of kilocalories. In a balanced diet the calories will be contributed by the mixture of foods, including fish or meat, fruit and vegetables, milk, butter and cheese, bread and cereals, that we normally eat and drink. When a person regularly exceeds the recommended number of calories he may start to put on weight and become obese, the most common dietetic problem. Table 5.6 shows the recommended calorie figures for different persons.

It is easier to follow a diet than to go without food entirely and fast for a few days. Jogging or other exercises helps to prevent weight gain but the only way to keep to the desired weight is by always eating intelligently and being a gourmet rather than a gourmand.

Many customers ask for low-calorie foods and are able to count the calories contained in many daily items so the waiter has to respond to such persons and assist in their requests for light diets. A waiter, however, is not expected to know what foods are suitable for, as example, a diabetic person or somebody suffering from dyspepsia.

Table 5.6   *recommended daily nutritional requirements*

		kcal	Protein g	Vit C mg	Calcium mg	Iron mg
boys	9–11	2280	57	25	700	12
	12–14	2640	66	25	725	12
	15–17	2880	72	30	600	12
girls	9–11	2050	51	25	700	12
	12–17	2150	53	30	600	12
women	18–54	2150	54	30	500	12
	55–74	1900	47	50	500	10
	pregnant	2400	60	60	1200	13
Men	18–34	2900	72	30	500	10
	35–64	2750*	69	30	500	10
	65+	2400	60	30	500	10

* additional 900 kcal if doing hard manual work

Table 5.7 gives details of foods suitable for a so-called light diet. A book on *Nutrition* is included in the Macmillan Master Series.

5.10   WRITING A MENU IN FRENCH

This is a difficult task, even for people who write and speak French fluently because not only has culinary French its own intricate technical terms but also its own way of abbreviation so as to keep menu titles short. Many of the problems are caused by misuse of language, i.e. participles, lack of agreement, no recognition of genders or numbers, difficulties in the use of definite, indefinite and partitive articles, the way adjectives are formed into feminine, and how verbs are formed; also the use of prepositions, and single or plural nouns and adjectives. Other common mistakes include forgetting to use a capital letter for proper nouns, use of the article on some but not all of the entries, attempting to translate local or national dishes into French, use of vague terms that have no accepted meaning, not knowing when or when not to include 'à la'.

Table 5.7 *list of low-calorie dishes*

Item	approximate number of calories	Item	approximate number of calories
Consommé Brunoise (2dl)	60	Melon aux crevettes roses	130
Crème Argenteuil (3dl)	90	Artichaut nature	15
Oeufs pochés (2)	160	Asperges nature (120g)	10
Omelette nature (2 egg)	200	Champignons grillés (100g)	200
Darne de cabillaud à l'Anglaise (150g)	130	Ratatouille (350g)	200
Bouillabaisse (150g)	260	Endives braisés	105
Dinde rôti (150g)	200	Riz pilaff (35g raw)	200
Poulet rôti (meat only) (150g)	260	Compote de pruneaux	80
Kari de Volaille	200	Crème renversée (180g)	230
Salade de Volaille	190	Fraises nature (150g)	35
Steak grillé (240g)	440	Macédoine de Fruits Chantilly (120g)	208
Faisan rôti (350g)	330	Sorbet au Citron (150g)	190
Ris de Veau sauté (150g)	330	Yoghurt, natural (150g)	90
Moussaka	390	Yoghurt, Fruit (150g)	150
Carbonnade de Boeuf	420	Skimmed milk (2dl)	500
Salade d'Endive	80	Red wine (1.5dl)	100
Huîtres au pain bis (6)	150	White wine (medium) (1.5dl)	100

French cookery has given much pleasure to the whole of the world and is a central part of French culture. The language therefore deserves to be spoken and written correctly by all who earn their living from it. As Brillat–Savarin, the great French philosopher said, *'menu mal fait, repas perdu'*.

QUESTIONS

1. Compare an à la carte and a table d'hôte menu.

2. Outline all the factors that govern the composition of menus.

3. Discuss the subject of nutrition and suggest what knowledge a waiter should have of it.

4. Suggest the effect which the seasonal supply of foods, has on dishes featured on a menu.

RESTAURANT ORGANISATION

6.1 INTRODUCTION

A restaurant should be run in an efficient and businesslike manner so that it gives satisfaction to customers and staff alike. An airtight control over the entire operation covering every detail, will result in a smooth, relaxed working atmosphere conducive to good staff relations, which in turn should ensure satisfaction on the part of the customers. A restaurant is only as good as its head waiter and it is essential that he commands the respect of the brigade by his competence, and the loyalty of customers by his integrity.

6.2 THE MISE EN PLACE OF THE RESTAURANT

The term *mise en place* means having everything in readiness for the commencement of service at the stated time of opening of the restaurant. Staff will have been on duty beforehand, engaged in the many aspects of preparation that are necessary to ensure the smooth running of the service immediately customers start to arrive. The work that has to be carried out includes dusting and cleaning the room, filling cruets, stocking sideboards with necessary equipment, laying the tables with linen, cutlery, crockery and glassware, so that all the paraphernalia of the room is in position when the doors are opened, and each member of staff knows exactly what he has got to do.

The way this is usually done is that last thing at night, chairs are placed on tables so that cleaners can do their work efficiently, or in an hotel where the restaurant is used at breakfast time, cleaning is done either before or after this meal. Commis waiters carry out basic cleaning duties whilst chefs de rang do less arduous and more

advanced work; these duties are done in accordance with a duty rota to ensure they are shared evenly. (Table 4.3 illustrates such a rota.)
The preparation of the restaurant includes the following:

1. Cleaning the carpet with a vacuum cleaner.
2. Dusting chairs and other furniture and putting them in place.
3. Counting items of soiled linen, entering totals in the laundry book and wheeling the basket to the linen room to exchange for clean items, then distributing them to the stations.
4. Equipping each sideboard with (a) spare cutlery; (b) extra crockery; (c) waiter's silver salver; (d) large service plate with a folded napkin for conveying clean cutlery; (e) sauce and soup ladles; (f) waiter's cloth.
5. Filling the spirit lamp and trimming the wick, or checking gas cylinder lamps for safe and efficient use.
6. Filling the waiter's hotplate with the necessary amount of crockery for use with hot meals, including coffee cups.
7. Laying tables in an orderly manner with one chef de rang placing a particular item on every table, commencing with the side or entrée plate as the centre of the cover, followed by a waiter placing the large knife in its exact position, then one placing the large fork on the other side, followed by the other accoutrements until the cover is completed; the side plate is then moved to the left hand side. Reserved signs will be placed on booked tables.
8. The linen waiter places a folded table napkin in the centre of each cover; the elaborateness of the fold will be according to the policy of the head waiter, ranging from a simple cone to an elaborate fan, mitre, coronet or fleur de lys (see Figure 3.6 on how to fold napkins).
9. The wine commis places glasses upside down on the table allowing a 1.5 dl and a 2 dl glass per cover; these are turned right way up just as the restaurant opens.
10. An ashtray may be placed in the centre of each table but is more likely to be kept in the sideboard until towards the end of the meal; a table number, menu holder and any floral arrangement are placed in position.
11. A basket of rolls, plateful of melba toast, dish of grissini and dish of butter pats are placed on the table last of all.
12. A briefing of the menu to include descriptions of dishes, chef's recommendations, etc.

6.3 PREPARATION OF TROLLEYS AND BUFFETS

Certain members are detailed to get hors-d'oeuvre, sweet, cheese and any other trolleys ready for the service, take them to the appropriate section to be filled, then into the restaurant with serving utensils and plates ready on the shelves. It may be necessary to obtain replenishments during the service period. The carver prepares the heated trolley for the joint.

Many restaurants display a cold buffet for customers to admire as they enter the room. It will have several joints for carving and dishes of cut fish, meat, poultry and game as well as salads and baskets of fruit. An attractive display of fresh fish, meat or vegetables may also be arranged to tempt customers with the quality of the day's market produce. A carver may serve portions of food to the waiter, or direct to customers who may go up to make their choice.

A refrigerated display cabinet helps to keep dishes fresh and appetising to look at and a few selected bottles of wine may be placed here and there. The person in charge must be an expert at carving and must know appropriate portion sizes.

6.4 MEAL SERVICE ROUTINE

When the restaurant is fully prepared for service and waiters have had a break for lunch, the head waiter will be in his place at opening time near to the entrance, ready to greet customers as they arrive. The reception head waiter will decide where to place customers according to the number in a party and conduct them to their table where the station head waiter greets them and assists in seating them. Then it is in order to unfold the table napkin and drape it across the customer's lap, doing this from the left-hand side.

If he knows that guests have arrived without going to the bar, the station head waiter will enquire if they would like to order aperitifs, if so he will call a wine waiter to take the order while he gives a menu to each member of the party. Depending upon the size of the menu and wine list it can take five to ten minutes for customers to decide what to order in the way of food and wine. In the meantime the waiter will place butter and bread on the table, if this had not been done prior to the opening of the restaurant. Water should be offered.

When serving a party of several guests the waiter must ascertain who is the host as he is the one who will take any overall decisions and to whom the bill will be presented. He is also the person who will indicate if speedy service is required.

6.5 TAKING THE ORDER

Taking the order is possibly the most important part of the waiter's
job; he must be ready to explain the nature of dishes, advise on
suitable meal combinations, use his ability as salesman to recommend
a dish that the chef may have asked the head waiter to 'push', note
which guest has ordered what dish so as to know to whom to serve it
without having to ask again, and pay close attention to what
customers say to him. It is at this time that a waiter exerts all his social
skills so that guests are impressed by his ability to communicate in a
serious manner and so that he interprets their requests correctly and
avoids mistakes.

Waiters should bear in mind that regular customers may resent
being pressurised by a pushy member of staff into making a certain
choice, also that a host often likes to act as the mouthpiece for his
guests and expects them to inform him of their choice of dish so that
he alone may instruct the waiter. The experienced waiter can sum up
any kind of situation by interpreting the cues arising while he takes
the order. One party may wish to be left alone to discuss business or
other personal affairs and may not want the waiter to obtrude too
often; another party may be in a happy mood to celebrate an occasion
and will make its presence felt by a display of high spirits – a waiter's
conduct should satisfy all classes of customer.

6.6 RECORDING THE ORDER

A customer expects to be served with the exact dish he ordered, in a
style commensurate with the establishment; he should have no cause
to complain about being served with a dish he did not ask for. The
order as taken and written down by the waiter acts as a firm link
between the client and the establishment and can be considered as a
form of contract. It is also the authorisation for obtaining food from
the kitchen as the head chef has to rely on the salesmanship of waiters
in order to sell his dishes. A good salesman will adopt the soft-sell
approach, acting as informant as well as advisor and consultant; the
waiter has to convey these traits and make each customer feel he is
important as an individual. One way of doing this is for the waiter to
try to remember what each person ordered, so that he does not need
to interrupt an intimate conversation by asking 'did you order the
fish/duck?' etc. A system of mnemonics can help in guest identification: as each person states his order the waiter adds a coded sign that

shows that person's position at table, or uses a personal outline such as *y.l.* (young lady).

An experienced waiter will recognise if a customer is feeling insecure in the eating environment and afraid of showing his ignorance of the conventions, and he should do all he can to diminish that fear and make the customer feel more at ease. The full panoply of a high-class restaurant with its brigade of dignified waiters and a background lighting of flambé lamps can cause a customer to feel ill at ease so the waiter should try to allay these fears by offering a warm welcome.

There are many different ways of taking down an order, ranging from a notepad to electronic and computer devices that cost thousands of pounds to install, but the cheapest and most popular at many levels is the triplicate checking system as shown in Figure 6.1. The operation is as shown in Figure 6.2.

It is customary to complete the check only as far as the main course and vegetables because the first parts of the menu come mainly from the kitchen; the menu is then presented for a second time so that customers may choose their sweet and the waiter then makes out

Fig 6.1 *the triplicate checking system pad and the method of recording information on it*

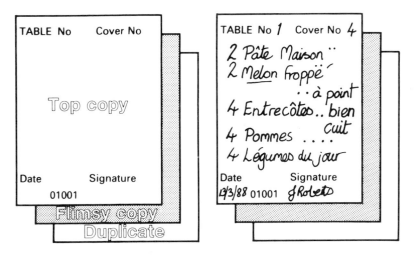

note: The purpose of the dots is to assist in keeping the check tidy by writing the name of the item requested followed by one dot for each portion ordered.
When all the guests have ordered the dots are transferred to the left in a total numerical form.

Fig 6.2 *triplicate checking system operation*

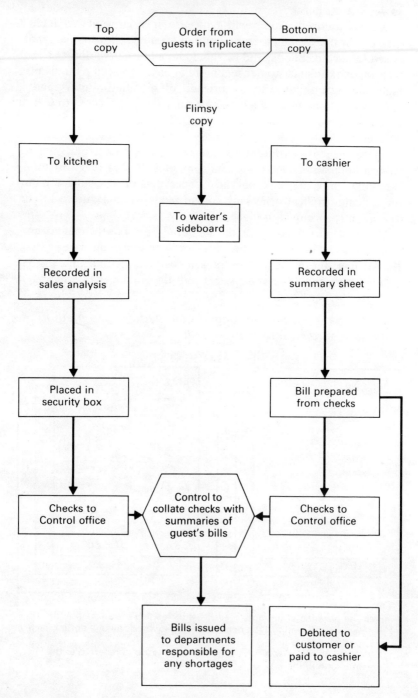

another order under the same table number, sending this to the pastry department to obtain the items ordered. Yet another order is made to obtain coffee from the still-room. Checks are collated in the control office, together with a copy of the bill as paid by the customer, any discrepancy being referred to the waiter for an explanation of errors.

As an example of how the order is taken, the waiter initially writes down the table number, number of covers and the date, then he writes down the name of each item ordered. For a table of five persons, three of whom order Cream of Mushroom soup and two want Oeuf en Cocotte: as one guest asks for the soup its name is written with a dot after it and when all have given their order for the first course, the number of dots is added up and the total entered in front of the title. The order for the main course is recorded similarly, making allowance for any special requirements, e.g. Entrecôte Marchand de Vins which one person wants well done, one underdone, and one medium rare, again using dots to distinguish requirements. The selected vegetables are written in and the check is signed by the waiter and taken to the kitchen by the commis where it authorises the issue of the food as ordered.

6.7 RESTAURANT BILLING MACHINES

These are nothing new as machines have been used as means of control in food service since the 1930s, more especially in Austria, Germany, Italy and Switzerland. A simple machine is like an unsophisticated cash register operated by each waiter who works it single-handed with his own number and key but without putting the takings in it. The waiter takes the customer's order on a check pad and rings up the price of each dish by pressing his number and turning his key. The machine issues a duplicate receipt which is both the waiter's authorisation for obtaining meals from the kitchen and the bill to present to the customer for payment.

At the end of service the duty manager rings out the total cash value of meals issued to each waiter under his number and the waiter pays in that amount. The machine can handle food, drink, cigarettes, service charge, VAT, etc., thus providing management with a complete breakdown of the day's business. Waiter are given a receipt for monies paid in and at the end of the week their earnings are calculated from these sums, as waiters often operate on a commission basis. Waiters' checks act as an additional control.

There are many modern developments in checking systems which operate electronically on microchips. A billing machine connects the restaurant with the kitchen by pressing the appropriate buttons that signify the items required. These are shown in the kitchen and when the order is ready for collection the waiter's number or the station number is flashed to inform him that he should go and collect. The same machine will print out the customer's bill in an easy-to-read form listing the actual dishes, wine, spirits, VAT, and service charge. At the end of the day's business the duty manager can obtain full details of every transaction and the total value. Other devices include a form of remote control like those used to change channels on a television set, where the waiter can press dish-code buttons which appear on screen in the kitchen. Another is a walkie-talkie gadget for 'intercom' ordering.

6.8   PROCESSING THE ORDER IN THE KITCHEN

The waiter hands the check to the aboyeur who acts as the kitchen control clerk; the aboyeur time-stamps it and then shouts out the name of each item. Each partie or section of the kitchen is on constant alert to receive the shouted orders and responds by shouting 'Yes' or 'Good', in French; it acknowledges that the order will be prepared and sent to the hotplate as quickly as possible. If one of the items ordered is from the à la carte menu the partie responsible for its cooking has to order it from the larder, doing this over the intercom system. Needless to say, this shouting plus the noise made by the pans being tossed on the stove and the clash of silver dishes, all add to the excitement of the proceedings and is one of the reasons why it is necessary to have two sets of 'in' and 'out' doors between kitchen and restaurant.

It is necessary for the waiter to remain at the hotplate while his order is announced and accepted as it is possible that an ordered item may have been sold out in which case he has to go back and tell his superior to inform the customer of this, then return with a revised order. Depending on what is required the commis may be able to collect the first course immediately and the aboyeur in handing it over will cross it off the check as having been served. When the whole order has been fulfilled the check is placed in a locked box for control purposes, being compared with the bill paid by the customer; any underpayment may have to be made up by the person responsible. There will be several service-points along the kitchen hotplate, some of which may be manned by sous-chefs so as to speed up the rate of service; these chefs also inspect every item brought to them for service in the restaurant to ensure that it is properly cooked and served, is hot and of the correct quantity. They act as quality controllers thus pre-empting possible complaints.

Wine or other drink as selected by the customer for consumption with the meal is obtained from the dispense bar by the sommelier who will write out a check similar to that used by waiters and that follows a similar course as shown in Figure 6.1 and is collated with the food check by the cashier.

6.9 PROTOCOLS OF SERVICE

There are many time-honoured rules of table service that are worthy of observance by waiting-staff at whatever level they are working. Many of these rules are also points of etiquette and good table manners. Accepted rules of service, attention to detail, stance, politeness and diplomacy, are required as part of the social skills to ensure that customers feel they are being properly served. The waiter must be in charge of the situation and carry it out in his own professional way, taking into account the desires of the customers. The service must be unassuming but confident and by attending to all small details there will be no need for the host to have to keep calling the waiter's attention. By serving bread and water as soon as a customer is seated, a waiter can help him to feel at ease because this pre-eating activity will keep him occupied and he knows that the waiter is aware of his presence.

The importance of rearranging the cutlery to suit a particular dish must be recognised and a customer should not be perplexed by having either too much or too little cutlery in front of him. The basic cover is as shown in Figure 6.3. The word cover comes from the French *couvert* which indicates a place setting at table. Since the choice of dishes may differ from the normal soup, fish, meat and sweet the waiter may have to remove or add some items of cutlery which must be done using a plate covered with a folded napkin so that there is no unnecessary clatter. The cover plate is held in the left hand and cutlery added or removed with the right hand, from the right-hand side of the customer. Most customers are aware that cutlery is used from the outside in sequence until it is all used, or changed.

The protocol of serving people in descending order according to age, sex and importance is still rigidly observed on all formal occasions and sex-discrimination has not affected these unwritten

Fig 6.3 *basic cover for a table d'hôte meal*

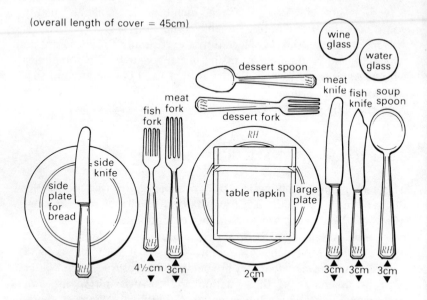

(overall length of cover = 45cm)

rules so far. As previously remarked, the waiter should identify the host in a group of customers, as the one who made the booking, or will be paying the bill. As an example, for a party of four consisting of the host and his wife with a lady and gentleman guest, the order of serving is (1) the female guest; (2) the host's wife; (3) the male guest, and lastly, the host. At a table of six the order is (1) the lady on the host's right-hand side, (2) the lady on the host's left-hand side, (3) the host's wife (4) the man on the right of the host's wife, (5) the man on the left of the host's wife, and (6) the host himself, as shown in Figure 6.4. If a waiter has difficulty in identifying who is who, he should ask his superior or the host, otherwise he should remember that females are served before males and older-looking persons before younger ones.

For a large number of persons at a table of more than eight, it is usual for two waiters to share the service, one commencing at the lady to the right of the host, the second at the lady to his left and so on to all the ladies around the table, then in a similar way with the men, one starting from the right of the host, the other from his left. At a private party of twelve and more, the service should start simultaneously from the right- and left-hand sides of the host and continue around the table regardless of sex and age. If the meal has

Fig 6.4 *sequence of serving customers*

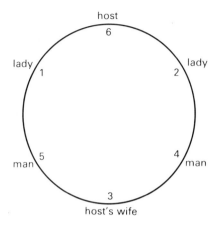

an important guest or chairperson that individual must be served first then the person to the right and then around the table. A guest of honour is seated on the right-hand side of the host and is the person to be served first. This rather starchy order of service is most important when arranging the seating plan of a formal banquet or wedding breakfast, details for which are given in Chapter 14.

The waiter must not start to clear away the used plates until everybody at table has finished eating, even though there may be a person present who adheres to the principle of chewing each mouthful of food several hundred times before swallowing it, so causing the others to wait before the next course can be served. A waiter must be able to distinguish between when a customer puts down his knife and fork for a short pause and when he has eaten sufficient. The way he lays down the cutlery gives an indication since in this country we are taught to place the knife and fork close together down the centre line of the plate, fork concave side uppermost. When pausing, the customer usually lays the cutlery across the plate in the form of an inverted V, but it should be borne in mind that other nationalities have different table manners and on the Continent the knife placed between the prongs of the fork is the sign that the meal is ended, whilst many Americans use only a fork to eat a main meal.

As much skill and protocol is required in clearing a table of used crockery and cutlery as when serving it. Plates are removed from the right of each guest, commencing with those of the ladies in the same sequence as they were served, then on to the men in the same order, using one plate held by the fingers of the left hand as the receptacle for debris and cutlery, inserting the knife blades neatly under the bend of the forks whilst piling the cleared plates on the forearm. A skilful waiter should be capable of clearing as many as ten soup plates with underplates and spoons, or the same number of meat plates, knives and forks and even all the sideplates, according to the weight of each item of crockery.

6.10 THE ROLE OF ACCOMPANIMENTS

Accompaniments to dishes are those things which complement a meal, many of which are kept in the restaurant as part of the general mise en place; an accompaniment should not be confused with a garnish which in most cases is an inherent part of a dish and is always served from the kitchen.

The role of an accompaniment is to:

1. keep the senses alert by continuous stimulation of the palate, such as English mustard which is normally put on the table as one of the condiments but may be offered by the waiter when serving roasted or grilled red meat;
2. tone down or neutralise the predominant flavour of a certain item such as when lemon is served with fish, because the citric acid helps to modify the salt content;
3. add variety to the texture and flavour of an item, e.g. sambals with curry;
4. add piquancy or smoothness to very delicate flavours, such as salad dressing with lettuce or hollandaise sauce with hot asparagus;
5. assist digestive processes, as apple sauce with pork;
6. detract from the fatty nature of a dish such as mint sauce with roast mutton;
7. add a slight sweet and sour effect, as redcurrant jelly with venison;
8. add sharpness such as Worcester sauce with a stew;
9. add colour as when tomato ketchup is poured over anything, and
10. add intensive flavour, such as Tabasco sauce.

Many accompaniments are purely traditional although they were soundly based when first introduced, but nowadays the nature of the item with which they are served has changed to such an extent that the accompaniment is superfluous. Nevertheless, customers expect to be offered them even though they know they are not obligatory.

Some accompaniments are a part of a cultural tradition, others – such as grated Parmesan cheese in Italy – are a national habit, this cheese being served indiscriminately with all broth soups, every pasta dish, with fried and boiled vegetables and even over tripe. Mustard is very popular in Germany and is served with all grilled meats, with sauerkraut and sausages, and with boiled meat and offals.

Waiters should learn how and where to serve accompaniments because they have to serve most of them on the edge of the customer's plate, others should be offered, whilst yet others are placed on the table or handed around. The list of accompaniments that should be offered with individual dishes is given in the chapters on the various courses of the menu.

6.11 CONDIMENTS

Although a cruet was originally an ornamental stand for bottles of vinegar and oil and cellars for salt and pepper, nowadays it usually consists of a container for only each of these last two, placed in the centre of every table for customers to use or not, as they decide. However there are now many versions of these and they are very much a feature of restaurants. Some customers ask for sea salt, others for rock salt, and flavoured salt such as celery salt may be requested; those who fear the effects of salt request demi-salt which is a low sodium mixture, and various models of salt-grinders for coarse salt are made. There are even more varieties of pepper, including many shapes and sizes of pepper-mills for grinding white, black, green or red peppercorns, which may need to be wielded by the waiter because of their length. Pepper is now made in various flavours by the addition of a spice, and there are cayenne pepper, chilli pepper, paprika pepper, and Tabasco which is a fiery liquid pepper distilled from chillies.

Red peppercorns are not true peppercorns but are the berries of a very common shrub found in South America and in many tropical and sub-tropical regions but mostly imported from Reunion Island, via France. Real pepper grows on a vine.

Not so long ago when a customer asked for vinegar he was presented with a bottle of malt vinegar; nowadays he will be asked which he wants of a dozen or more different vinegars including, chilli, cider, lemon, malt, distilled, raspberry, sherry, tarragon and wine vinegars. Oil for making into a dressing can be almond, corn, hazelnut, olive, peanut, sesame seed, sunflower or walnut – each with its own distinctive characteristics. Mustard used to be either English or French but now includes beer, cider, Dijon, herb, honey, peppercorn, tarragon and many others, for various uses. Waiters should also be aware of the many different kinds of sugar that are used in hot beverages, including the substitutes. Thus, in many respects the job of being a waiter is becoming more complicated, requiring greater knowledge and skills.

6.12 THE IMPORTANCE OF A KNOWLEDGE OF WINE

Although all high-class restaurants employ sommeliers who deal only with wine and other drinks, every waiter must acquire a working knowledge of wines and have the means to taste the quality and be able to discuss the characteristics of the main wines of the world.

Wine is the most appropriate beverage to serve with food for it stimulates the appetite, aids digestion and is a nutritious food. Its qualities combine most naturally with food and it contributes much to the enjoyment of a meal. It is worthwhile noting that as much as one third of the takings of the average licenced restaurant is derived from the sale of drink and that drink yields more profit than food. Thus it is important that staff try to influence customers to drink wine with their food and are able to recommend and comment on the wines on the list. The following brief outline of wine is given to introduce waiting-staff to the subject of wine; as interest in this fascinating subject grows, readers may wish to study wine in greater detail than is possible here so fuller details of wine and other drinks are given in Chapter 15; only a brief outline of the subject is given below.

The quality and characteristics of wine stem from:

1. the vines and grapes which produce it;
2. the geographical location of the vineyard, which is generally within the temperate zones 35° to 50° parallel north and south of the equator with the best coming from the 41° to 43° parallel in the northern hemisphere;
3. the soil in which the vines are grown has a big effect on the wine produced;
4. the climate, which if too cold and rainy, causes acid wine and if too hot, flaccid wine;
5. the method of pruning the vine which controls the quantity produced and therefore its quality;
6. the method of vinification or manufacture of the wine.

Wine is made by pressing the juice from grapes and the sugar in the juice is exposed to the natural yeast of the skins converting it into alcohol. A mixture of red and white grapes is used for most wines and the red colour is obtained naturally by leaving the red skins in the grape juice, or '*must*', during the fermentation process. It is usual to use a number of different varieties of grapes to make a wine though some of the great ones are from a single variety. A wine expert is able to identify the kinds of grapes used in making a wine and this helps him to name it without looking at the label. Waiting-staff will find it useful to familiarise themselves with the names of the grapes in wide use for wine making as this helps in describing it to a customer.

There are three main kinds of wine:

1. still or table wine;
2. fortified wine including Madeira, port and sherry;
3. sparkling wine such as champagne where the second fermentation is induced within the bottle thus giving the typical sparkling effervescence. Other sparkling wines are brought to the second fermentation in a large tank and then bottled, while cheap ones are made by adding carbon dioxide gas to very ordinary still wines.

Most people drink a still wine with food, and the rules they follow are:

> white before red,
> dry before sweet,
> young before old.

White and rosé must be served chilled; sparkling wine cold, and red at room temperature. Individual wines are named in the chapters on the service of foods, given under the title of the actual course. The wine that is ultimately chosen by a customer will depend on the wine list of an individual establishment.

QUESTIONS

1. Say why an ordinary waiter should have a basic knowledge of wines and wine service.

2. Discuss the provision of accompaniments and condiments as supplied in the restaurant.

3. Write an account of all the preparatory work (mise en place) that has to be done before a restaurant can be opened for service.

4. Outline the full treatment that should be afforded to customers from the time they arrive at the restaurant, until their departure.

SERVICE PROCEDURES

7.1   INTRODUCTION

There is a generally accepted method of food and beverage service that follows a prescribed procedure and becomes a ritual which is recognised by discerning customers. There may be a few divergencies from the methods discussed below but they are likely to be the house rules of particular establishments rather than an improved system of food service.

Silver service has been accepted as the highest level of food service since it was introduced in the 1860s. It was Félix Urbain-Dubois, a well-known chef, who introduced what was then known as service *à la Russe*, when he came to work in this country after some years in Russia. It replaced service *à la Française* whereby all the foods were placed on the table at once for customers to help themselves, by having waiters bring in each course in its proper sequence and offer the dish for each guest in turn to help himself.

7.2   GENERAL RULES OF SERVICE

A dish of food that has been elaborately and skilfully prepared by a chef, whether for one or more people, deserves to be shown to the host or customer prior to being served onto the plate and this should be done as soon as it is brought from the kitchen, being displayed at a slight angle across the table from the best vantage-point. A waiter should carry out his duties in accordance with the following rules:

1.   Carry a salver, tray, etc., with the left hand, balancing it in the centre, underneath, on the outstretched hand, or on the levelled thumb and three fingers.

2. Arrange all the items on the tray so it is balanced evenly and is not overweighted at any edge.

3. Go through a swing-door by pushing with the left shoulder or pressing with the left foot, turning the body straight on going through.

4. When loading several dishes on top of one another on the salver, drape the folded waiter's cloth over and tuck it underneath; by holding it in place it will prevent the dishes from slipping off.

5. When carrying a tall item such as a bottle, lay it flat (provided it is stoppered!) on the salver between other items thus preventing it from toppling over or rolling around.

6. When serving vegetables and potatoes from two separate dishes, place both on the salver or silver flat with a serving-spoon and fork for each item, and serve all at one and the same time rather than going round with each dish separately.

7. To carry glasses or cutlery, line the salver with a neatly folded table-napkin so as to prevent them slipping about or making a clatter; to carry a small number, a large plate may be used instead of the salver.

8. Serve all food at the customer's left-hand side and try to carry out all necessary duties such as removing crumbs from the table, from this side.

9. Clear from the right-hand side of the customer. When a customer has finished a meal take the plates and cutlery from the right-hand side removing them from the table with the right hand and passing them to the left hand.

10. Serve all *drinks* on the right-hand side; the natural place for a glass on the table is at the top right just above the plate, and the waiter should not stretch across from the left to reach it.

11. Serve *coffee* from the right-hand side of the customer; when placing the coffee cup on the table do it at the right-hand side (see Chapter 11 for full details of coffee service).

12. Use a graceful style of movement serving at table; to do this stand about 15 cm away from the customer's chair, put the left foot forward so as to achieve perfect balance, rotate the body from the hip to turn it slightly to the left then lower the left shoulder slightly so as to bring the service dish of food just above the plate on the table as shown in Figure 7.1(a) and (b).

13. If the crockery and cutlery bears the name or logo of the establishment, always lay them so that this is directly in line with the customer, which means putting plates, etc., with the badge

Fig 7.1   *position for service*

(a)   *(b)*

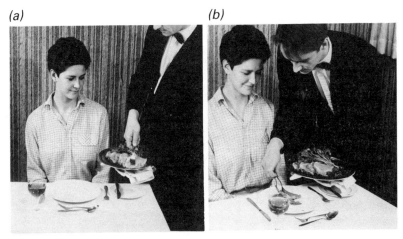

Fig 7.2   *correct position for badged plate on table*

at 12 o'clock with the badge uppermost, as shown in Figure 7.2.

14. When placing hot plates in front of customers hold the required number in the left hand with the waiter's cloth and rub it over the surface of each one before placing on the table, using the end of the cloth to put it in front of the customer. Always use the cloth to avoid burning the fingers on hot plates or dishes, as shown in Figure 7.3.

15. When placing cold plates in position get hold of each one with

Fig 7.3 *carrying hot plates*

the palm of the hand underneath and the thumb just on the edge; see Figure 7.4, and note that the thumb must never be placed on the rim of the plate.

Fig 7.4 *placing a cold plate on the table*

note: thumb must not touch
upper rim of plate

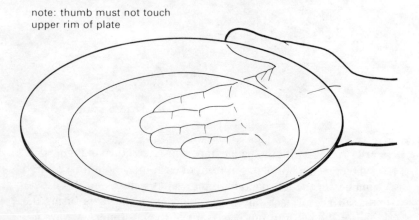

16. To carry a number of hot plates and food together into the restaurant, wrap the waiter's cloth around them, as shown in Figure 7.5.

Fig 7.5   *carrying food and hot plates together*

17.   Serve rolls and bread from the left-hand side by offering the basket for the customer to help himself, or by taking one from the basket with a serving spoon and fork and placing it on the side plate. See Figure 7.6.

Fig 7.6   *serving bread rolls*

18.   To clear the table when customers have eaten the main course, having waited until the last person of the party has placed his knife and fork in the vertical position, go to the right-hand side of the first lady, lower the left hand level with the hips, palm uppermost and pass the plate from the right hand to the left hand, holding it between the thumb and middle finger

next dirty plate and place it above the first plate on the tips of the small and ring fingers and the thumb. Place the fork on the first plate and use the knife to scrape any debris from the second onto the first plate then put the knife under the handle of the fork on what is now the clearing plate; the curve of the fork handle keeps the knives in place. Continue around the table in the same way until all the used dishes and cutlery are cleared, then put the plate of debris and cutlery on top of the others and take to the sideboard; see Figure 7.7.

19. If desired the sideplates can be removed in the same operation by going round the table once more, piling each one on top of the large plates, inserting the knives under the forks, putting the first plate of debris and cutlery on top of the whole. When clearing each plate, turn the body away from the table so that the customer cannot see what is being done and does not see the plateful of debris. It is not feasible to clear a table of more than six people by this method.

20. To clear soup plates, take the empty plates from the first person, remove the soup plate onto the forearm then take the second and place it on the outstretched hand; take the spoon from the first soup plate, place it in the second soup plate then place that in the first one, repeat this with each guest, turning away from the table whilst doing the movement. When all are cleared place the pile of soup plates on the underplates and take to the sideboard.

21. When serving a group of people at a table some of whom have ordered cold dishes while the others have chosen hot, serve the cold items first then the hot ones.

22. Use a sauce ladle or spoon to serve a sauce rather than pouring it onto the plate.

23. Offer to pour each customer a glass of water as soon as they are seated. People go into a restaurant because they are hungry and thirsty, but some head waiters are of the opinion that to provide drinking water dissuades customers from ordering wine. However this is a shortsighted view that is not borne out in fact. me restaurants bottled water is sold rather than providing ap water.

ractice is necessary before attempting to carry a the upstretched left arm; a skilled waiter makes it difficult to keep it level, especially when going s.

been used by several people at a table it clean one which is put upside down on

Fig 7.7 *clearing used plates and cutlery*

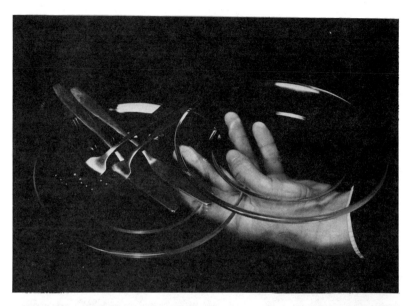

the full one then removed to the salver and the clean one placed on the table right way up.

26.   A box of matches is part of a waiter's personal equipment so that he can offer a light when he sees a customer taking out a cigarette (see also under Cigars in Chapter 12).

27.   To serve a packet of cigarettes ordered by a customer, peel back the cellophane, open the lid and pull a cigarette forward before offering the pack on the salver or on the side-plate to the guest.

28.   A finger-bowl must be provided for a customer who has to eat something messy such as asparagus, globe artichoke or lobster with his fingers. This is a specially made glass or silver bowl half-filled with warm water and with a thin slice of lemon or some rose petals floating in it. It is placed just above the plate of food and must be removed as soon as the item has been consumed.

29.   When serving fresh fruit from a basket, a finger-bowl of cold water is placed on the table for the customer who has chosen grapes, cherries, plums, etc. to dip the fruit in so as to cleanse it (see also Chapter 11).

30.   Always remove the condiments from the table when clearing after the main course; if a savoury is ordered the salt and pepper must be replaced.

31.   It is necessary to brush the crumbs from the table after clearing the plates from the main course, using the folded waiter's cloth to brush them into a plate held in the left hand, going in between each customer.

32.   While removing crumbs from the table it is possible to bring the dessert-spoon and fork into position for eating the sweet by bringing the spoon down whilst standing to the right of the customer, then going to the left and after brushing, bringing the fork into position.

33.   The waiter's cloth must be kept clean and tidy and used only for handling equipment, removing crumbs from the table, etc., it should not be flicked about like a duster nor kept on the shoulder or around the neck but neatly folded over the left forearm when not in use.

34.   A waiter should not disappear from the room unnecessarily and when not busy, should stay by his sideboard in an upright position so that he can keep his station under surveillance.

35.   A waiter may not eat or drink while on duty and should resist even tasting something left on the serving dish after the customers have been given all they want.

36. Equally a waiter should never consume alcoholic beverages whilst he is on duty, as his breath may smell offensive to the guest.
37. A waiter should refrain from smoking during the food service and remember that it is an offence for food-handlers to smoke whilst handling food.

7.3   USE OF THE SERVING-SPOON AND FORK

A serving-spoon is bigger than a dessert-spoon and a serving-fork is the same as that normally used for a main meat course; they should be of a similar size and pattern. These are used together to serve all kinds of foods and can do the work of a pair of serving tongs in a much more elegant way. To achieve full control place the handles in the palm of the right hand so that they lie over the little finger, and the two next to it, as shown in Figure 7.8a. Now insert the index finger between the spoon and fork and grip the top with the thumb. This makes the fork an independent instrument that will grip onto anything picked up in the bowl of the spoon, as shown in Figure 7.8b. The fork can now be reversed as shown in Figure 7.8c to make it possible to grip even larger items more firmly whilst transferring them from the dish to the plate. The pressure of the fork against spoon must be adjusted according to the density of the item of food, for example, a crème caramel will break under very slight pressure so must be served cupped in the spoon and lightly held in place with the fork when being served.

When serving a sauce or stew some of it may seep over the edge of the serving spoon and fall onto the tablecloth or customer unless it is drawn against the edge of the serving dish or removed by manoeuvring the fork under the spoon.

Flat kinds of food – for example, a whole trout, fillet of sole or omelette – are best served with two serving-forks as shown in Figure 7.8d, rather than spoon and fork. Hold two forks in the right hand and spread them to the length of the item to be served, insert them under it and lift carefully, adjusting the distance if there is a likelihood of breaking in the middle; transfer to the plate then use a spoon to serve any sauce that is in the dish.

Fig 7.8 *use of serving-spoon and fork*

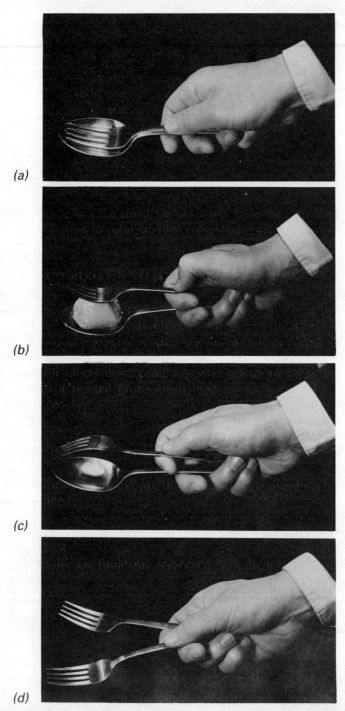

(a)

(b)

(c)

(d)

7.4 POINTS OF ETIQUETTE FOR WAITERS

It is important to remember that a waiter is under constant observation by the customer, indeed he should consider himself as a performer. As a result whilst he is in the dining room he should take every precaution to conduct himself in a manner which does not cause offence to any guest. The following points may be of assistance:

1. Stand upright at all times when you are under customer observation so as to convey an impression of efficiency.
2. Walk energetically taking measured steps, but do not run, as this would suggest a state of confusion.
3. Treat all your guests with the type of deference that you would proffer to an important person.
4. Demonstrate grace of manner by
   * good formal greeting
   * proper voice intonation
   * courtesy and tact in dealing with guests.
5. Be sure to avoid any sign of familiarity with guests.
6. Take care not to listen – nor appear to listen – to guest's conversation.
7. Work efficiently and quietly at all times.
8. Avoid giving the impression that you are hoping to receive a tip.
9. Never display indifference to your guests.
10. Do not carry out conversation with nor show signs of irritability with other members of staff in the dining room.
11. Refrain from touching your hair in the dining room as this is an unhygienic practice.
12. Never lean against walls or sideboards.
13. Deal efficiently with guests' favourable comments or complaints.
14. Remember to say 'thank you' to your guests for giving you their custom.
15. Bid them goodbye when leaving.

7.5 DEALING WITH A DIFFICULT CUSTOMER

A waiter must be able to deal with an unwanted customer who may be either drunk or under the influence of drugs. This kind of aggressive customer may quickly resort to violence and is likely to lash out with his fists or use a broken glass to threaten staff. The solution is to refuse to serve such a customer and to ask him to leave.

It is important not to become involved in a fight and only reasonable force is allowed when endeavouring to throw out a belligerent customer. Should a struggle ensue, the waiter must call for assistance and ensure there is a reliable witness who can either help to eject the drunk or give evidence of what took place.

It is not unknown for the person who has been physically ejected to sue the waiter for malicious wounding. It is advisable to telephone the local police station for the assistance of a constable or, if the situation becomes extremely dangerous, to dial 999. The wine waiter should be aware that it is an offence to sell liquor to a person who is already under the influence of drink.

7.6 THE STILL-ROOM

In a conventional set-up, the still-room acts as a link between the kitchen and the restaurant; it comes under the direction of the head chef but does almost all its business with the waiting-staff.

The still-room makes all the hot and cold beverages and keeps supplies of all the ancillary items needed for breakfast and afternoon-tea meals, as well as the various adjuncts for lunch and dinner. The foodstuffs prepared and supplied include:

porridge – made in bulk and served against an order
boiled eggs – usually cooked in an automatic timing machine for from two to six minutes, according to the customer's request
toast – this is made in a large-scale toaster for serving in toast racks, cut in half or cut in fingers for pâté, etc.
Melba toast for placing on the table at lunch and dinner
very thinly sliced brown bread and butter for serving with fried whitebait, etc.
biscuits for serving with cheese or afternoon tea
butter dishes filled with curls or pats, on a container of ice and garnished with a sprig of parsley
chilled fruit juices, including orange, grapefruit, tomato, pineapple, and tropical – freshly pressed or dispensed from a container, as purchased
cold beverages such as milk, cream and iced coffee
proprietary beverages including Horlicks, Bournvita and Ovaltine
bread rolls, croissants, brioches, sliced French bread, grissini and starch-reduced rolls
proprietary brands of breakfast cereals, either in individual packets or loose in a cereal bowl

poached fruits including prunes and apples, prepared in the pastry section but served from the still-room for breakfast
halves of grapefruit, grapefruit and orange segments as cocktails
preserves, including marmalade, honey, and jam in several varieties
hot beverages, including coffee and hot milk and several varieties of tea.

Coffee is made in bulk, using water at approximately 98°C; it should be held at 83°C, as a higher temperature will cause it to become bitter; the milk is kept hot at 79°C. Tea may be made with leaf tea or teabags, and in teapots rather than in an urn. To make tea correctly the pot must be warmed and the correct amount of tea placed in it; freshly boiled water is poured over to fill the pot which is then left to brew for four minutes before pouring. Herbal teas are made in the same way.

To make Melba toast, cut a sandwich loaf into 4 cm slices, and toast them on both sides, keeping flat; cut three crusts off each slice then cut horizontally through to give two thin slices. Cut off the remaining crust which was left on as a protection and place the slices under a salamander to colour the untoasted sides; they will curl up as they take colour under medium heat. Serve inside a lily-shape table napkin or in a bread basket, usually at the beginning of a meal.

In some establishments the still-room is responsible for the preparation of afternoon-tea sandwiches, for the fruit basket, and for the cheese board and its adjuncts.

All issues have to be authorised by means of a signed check stating the number of portions of everything required, as was shown in Figure 6.1.

7.7 THE PLATE-ROOM

The washing of used cutlery, crockery and glassware is carried out in the dish-washing area under the direction of the head plate-man who is often known as the *argentier* or silverman. The reputation of an establishment relies a lot upon the quality and hygiene of the washing up and the sheen of the silverware, plates and glasses.

Most places use an automatic dish-washing machine which produces the desired result with the minimum of maintenance and supervision; it can deal with every kind of restaurant utensil and delivers them sterile, dry and free from smears. It will still be necessary to polish the silver in a burnishing machine so as to brighten the polished surface, doing this on a rota system so that all items, including coffee- and tea-pots, candelabra and silver flats are done on a regular basis.

Silver plated cutlery stains easily, particularly when it comes into contact with acidic ingredients. These stains must be removed by one of the several methods available. One of the most popular methods is the use of a proprietary metal alloy consisting of a perforated aluminium-like plate used in conjunction with a special activator that through electrolytic action removes tarnish or stain and is ready for rinsing and drying within a very short time.

Some establishments possess fine examples of gold or silver centrepieces with which to adorn table-settings for very special functions; these require very careful cleaning and safe storage in the responsibility of the head plate-man.

How to deal with a spillage

Accidents can happen, no matter how carefully a waiter goes about his job and should an accident happen he must be able to cope with it promptly and in an efficient manner so that the customer has little or no cause to make a complaint. By doing his job in a careful and unhurried way, the waiter can avoid disturbing the even tenor of the atmosphere of the restaurant and can keep the clatter of equipment to a minimum by avoiding dropping things on the floor.

Should food be accidentally spilt over a customer the waiter should use a dampened cloth to wipe it off, meanwhile making his apologies and suggesting that the establishment be happy to have the garment dry-cleaned, or to pay for having it done. Prompt and efficient action can prevent the incident from developing into a crisis and it is in such a situation that the waiter's skill is called upon to function to the full.

Wine spilt on the tablecloth can be dabbed with a wet table-napkin then covered with a clean napkin, if necessary removing the equipment from that part of the table and slipping a used menu under the cloth but above the felt cover. The clean napkin should be rolled from corner to corner so making it easy to unrol over the spillage. Where a bad spillage occurs it might even be necessary to re-lay the table completely or to offer to move the customers to a different table.

QUESTIONS

1. List some of the uses to which a guéridon is put.

2. Outline the role of the still-room and give a full list of its duties.

3. Explain the following forms of service: (i) family; (ii) silver; (iii) plate-cum-silver.

CHAPTER 8

SERVICE PROCEDURES FOR HORS D'OEUVRES

8.1 INTRODUCTION

There are two broad categories of hors-d'oeuvre, the cold hors-d'oeuvre as described in this chapter, and the hot ones which are not so well-known and not very often featured because they need to be set up in the restaurant in the form of a buffet; they consists of small pastry goods, fritters, brochettes and toasted items, mainly of Russian origin and are dealt with in Chapter 9.

There are two main sections of cold hors-d'oeuvre, the mixed ones that are usually displayed on a tray or trolley for customers to select up to a dozen varieties, and the single hors-d'oeuvre which is normally an à la carte item. Amongst the latter are a number of hot items but they are unlike those included in a hot hors-d'oeuvre selection.

The name is difficult to translate into English but implies a course that is outside, or additional to, a meal. It is, always and only, a first course and as such should be light, sharp and fresh-tasting so as to stimulate appetite and start the saliva flowing. By saying that an hors-d'oeuvre should be light means it ought to be a reasonably small portion. The sharpness comes from the use of vinegar which is widely used for dressing most hors-d'oeuvre but is tempered by oil that provides smoothness. Many kinds of pickled and smoked items are served which indicates the use of salt in the preserving process. However, the use of oil, vinegar and salt, together with herbs and spices makes it difficult to suggest a suitable wine that will overcome the sharpness of the chosen hors-d'oeuvre.

8.2 HORS-D'OEUVRE VARIES

These are the cheapest kind of hors-d'oeuvre and can be described as a mixture of many different things, neatly dressed in raviers and displayed on an hors-d'oeuvre trolley or tray for a customer to choose from. Raviers are hors-d'oeuvre dishes and should be used. The statement that this is a cheap course is not to suggest that these hors-d'oeuvre are of inferior quality, but simply that a good hors-d'oeuvre chef can make many delectable dishes from the left-over foods normally available in a busy kitchen. Even the great chef Escoffier said it was possible to make a good hors-d'oeuvre out of discarded cabbage stumps!

The normal items include many that are bought in ready-made, as well as salads and other items thought up by the *hors-d'oeuvrier*, according to how inventive he is. The following list shows the wide variety and that it is possible to ring the changes daily.

Meat:	cornets of salami and ham, beef salad, salad of pig's trotters, ears or cheek, potted meat, brawn, sausage salad
Fish:	anchovies, rollmop herrings, smoked herring fillets, sardines, tunny fish, herring or herring roes à la portugaise, mussels
Vegetables:	artichokes, cauliflower, leek, celery and button onions à la grecque, creamed sweetcorn, olives, radishes, celeriac, French beans, pimentoes, mushrooms, gherkins, pickled red cabbage, stuffed tomatoes
Salads:	coleslaw, beetroot, cucumber, fécampoise, potato, rice, Russian, tomato, shrimp
Eggs:	egg mayonnaise, stuffed hard-boiled
Miscellaneous:	haricot or butter beans, pastas, pickled walnuts

An hors-d'oeuvre trolley usually holds twenty oblong raviers.

The filled dishes are loaded onto the trolley (see Figure 3.9) and the cold fish plates and serving spoons and forks are placed on the shelf. The trolley is wheeled next to the customer who has ordered a mixed hors-d'oeuvre and as he looks at the dishes and makes his choice so the waiter places some on the plate, using separate serving gear for each ravier and turning the wheel to bring the next range of dishes level with the customer. The waiter must pay due regard to the colour scheme as he fills the plate and to make the selected course look attractive. Care must be taken in replacing the serving implements in the raviers as the handles may get caught when rotating the trays of dishes, thus causing them to fall off. As the raviers become empty the person in charge of the trolley should replenish with full ones from the kitchen so as to maintain an adequate supply.

The plate of hors-d'oeuvre is placed in front of the customer who will eat it, using a fish knife and fork regardless of whether the client has chosen more meat than fish or even no fish at all. The cruet of vinegar and olive oil is placed on the table for the customer to help himself. The peppermill and cayenne-pepper-shaker may also be offered. In some establishments a plateful of buttered brown bread is served with a mixed hors-d'oeuvre.

If a wine is requested, Chablis, Moselle or Custoza, served 8–10°C, are the most suitable.

8.3   HORS-D'OEUVRE ROYAL OR HORS-D'OEUVRE DE LUXE

This selection of several kinds of hors-d'oeuvre is the antithesis of the mixed hors-d'oeuvre dealt with in 8.2, being composed of the finest and most expensive of the single ones discussed later in this chapter. It usually consists of a selection of about six varieties from caviar, foie gras, smoked salmon, gulls' eggs, salami, oysters or mussels, smoked breast of goose, poutarge (salted pressed mullet roes), rillette (potted meat), and fresh prawns or dressed crab.

The chosen selection is arranged in separate dishes and put together on a gadroon tray, usually with a decorative centrepiece to enhance the presentation. The normal accompaniments are offered.

It is not just the most expensive items that constitute a royal hors-d'oeuvre – rather those that are rare or have only a short season. Some may be combined, e.g. caviar in a cornet of smoked salmon, a peeled prawn wrapped in a slice of smoked salmon, crabmeat in a cucumber barquette, etc. If raw foie gras is available a shallow-fried slice may be served warm with hot vinegar dressing.

The dishes may be decorated with picked parsley, watercress, radicchio, Belgian endive, chicory, corn salad, mustard and cress, and contrasted with the colours of radishes, cucumber, tomato, gherkin, olives, hard-boiled egg, etc.

8.4 SERVICE OF CAVIAR

This is the most expensive of the single hors-d'oeuvre and as just one dessertspoonful is priced at £20 or more, the presentation and service must match the quality of the commodity. Caviar is the brine-treated roe of sturgeon caught in the rivers running into the Black Sea. There are several grades, the best being the Malossol, Beluga having the largest size of grain. The size of grain varies from 1 mm up to about 4 mm and the colour can be black, grey, green brown or even golden, according to the species of sturgeon. It is sold in tins or earthenware containers and must be stored at 2°C.

For service the whole tin or portion jar is inserted into a silver timbale full of crushed ice, or on an ice socle which is a block of ice carved into the shape of an urn, a swan, an eagle, a fish, etc.

Caviar au Blinis

Blinis are yeast pancakes, 10 cm in diameter, made of buckwheat; they are fairly thick and spongy and served hot from the kitchen, inserted into a folded table-napkin. Serve one onto a plate, cut slits crossways and spoon the chilled caviar into the openings (see Figure 8.1). Serve with a half of lemon and sauceboat of soured cream, or spoon the cream into the centre as shown in Figure 8.1 and place the other blinis on the table; the customer uses a small broad-bladed knife to eat the caviar. It used to be customary to eat caviar with a knife and a spoon carved from ivory.

Caviar nature

Spoon the portion of caviar into the centre of a cold fish plate and place spoonfuls of sieved yolk and white of hard-boiled egg, finely chopped onion and chopped parsley around the side; place a sideplate of warm de-crusted toast folded in a napkin on the side together with a small knife; a fresh dish of butter is placed nearest to the customer.

It is the custom to drink vodka or champagne with caviar.

8.5 SERVICE OF FOIE GRAS AND PÂTÉS

Genuine *foie gras* is the enlarged liver of a fattened goose; it originated in the Alsace region of France but nowadays is produced in countries such as Hungary and Israel. It is available cooked whole

Fig 8.1   *service of caviar*

in tins, earthenware jars and in pastry cases; it is also exported in a chilled raw state. Inferior but good-tasting foie gras are made of duck, chicken and animal livers, often in the form of a pâté whereby it is made as a purée, often containing small pieces of truffle.

Real foie gras as a cold hors-d'oeuvre is presented in the original jar, buried in a timbale of crushed ice, or in a glass bowl and glazed with port-wine jelly, or in a tall baked pastry-case. The cover is a cold meat plate and a small knife and the waiter serves it by dipping a grapefruit or dessertspoon into a silver jug of boiling water and scooping out shell-shape pieces, allowing two to four per portion, arranged as shown in Figure 8.2. The accompaniments are a dish of hot brioches or fingers of warm toast, wrapped in a napkin, and a dish of butter pats. Some establishments offer chopped port-wine jelly and watercress to enhance the colour balance.

Pâté de foie gras can be made from any kind of liver and is canned in tunnel-shape or long, round, tins; this is cut into 5 mm thick slices and may be decorated with a round of truffle and glazed with aspic jelly. The texture is different from that of the real goose liver.

Suitable wines include champagne, Gewürztraminer from Alsace, Beaujolais, and Sauternes.

Fig 8.2 *service of foie gras*

Fresh foie gras is often served hot as an hors-d'oeuvre, cooked slightly underdone in butter and served on a plate with a garnish of radicchio or cos lettuce and hot vinegar swilled around the cooking pan. It is eaten with a small knife and fork, without accompaniments.

8.6 PREPARATION AND SERVICE OF SEAFOOD COCKTAILS

The French name is Cocktail de Fruits de Mer which indicates a mixture of several kinds of shellfish cut into small pieces, placed on top of some shredded lettuce and covered with cocktail sauce. It may be made with shrimps, prawns, lobster, crayfish, crawfish, mussels, crab, and sometimes with cooked flaked white fish and salmon, either singly or in any combination. In many establishments these cocktails are made in the larder but in a first-class establishment they are made in front of the customer by the waiter who will have collected the ingredients from the larder.

To prepare **Prawn Cocktails** for four persons requires 250 g shelled prawns, 4 nice prawns with the heads left on, 0.5 dl each of mayonnaise and double cream, 0.25 dl of tomato ketchup or 0.5 dl very red sieved tomato flesh, quarter of a lettuce, Tabasco sauce, Worcester sauce, milled pepper, 1 lemon, and some paprika pepper.

The method is as shown in Figure 8.3: pour the cream into a soup plate, whisk lightly with two forks until it starts to thicken, then mix in the mayonnaise. Cut the lemon in half, insert the prongs of a fork

Fig 8.3   *preparation of cocktail de fruits de mer*

into one half and press down to squeeze the juice into the sauce; add the tomato flesh or sufficient bottled tomato ketchup to give a pink colour, flavour with a few drops each of Tabasco and Worcester sauces and a turn of the peppermill and the sauce is made. Add the shelled prawns and mix in, and if liked, a little brandy may be added.

Shred the lettuce fairly thinly and share between four cocktail glasses; spoon the prawns and sauce on top and sprinkle with a little paprika pepper. Cut the remaining lemon into four pieces and make a slit so one can be hung over the edge of each glass and finish with one of the whole prawns from which the tail shell has been removed.

Serve on a d'oyley on a side plate with a grapefruit spoon and a dessert fork as shown in Figure 8.4 accompanied by a plateful of thinly sliced triangles of buttered brown bread; the Tabasco and a shaker of cayenne may be offered.

Fig 8.4 *presentation of seafood cocktail*

This kind of cocktail is one of the most popular of all the single hors-d'oeuvre and its success is due to the good quality of the contents and an attractive presentation. To this end special cocktail containers are used; one is made of silver with an inner glass lining, the other is a shallow glass dish that fits into an outer glass; both containers are meant to be filled with crushed ice; or an ordinary Paris goblet may be used.

Suitable wines include Oppenheimer, Sylvaner and Château Grillet – all served at 9–10°C, but the richness of the sauce overwhelms most dry white wines.

There are many other kinds of food cocktails made with combinations of fish or with fruit, which will be found under Fruit Cocktails later in this chapter.

8.7 SERVICE OF SMOKED FISH

There are four kinds of smoked fish in general use as cold hors-d'oeuvre and a few others, such as smoked sturgeon and tunny fish, which are not so well-known.

The best kind of smoked fish is **Scotch smoked salmon**, it has a rich strong flavour, a scented aroma and a deep orange colour; the raw side of salmon is cured with salt then smoked in oak shavings. Some establishments do this in the kitchen but most of them purchase it ready-made; poor quality salmon is pale in colour and breaks easily because it has a dry texture.

An à la carte portion consists of three or four very thin slices weighing a total of approximately 40 g, served on a silver flat with lemon quarters and mustard and cress. The cover is a cold fish plate and a fish knife and fork and the waiter rolls the slices, one at a time on the prongs of a serving fork, unrolling each across the plate; the lemon and cress are added and a plateful of brown bread and butter, a peppermill and cayenne shaker are served.

Smoked salmon is sometimes served in the shape of cornets, filled with shrimps, prawns, crabmeat or caviar.

The best wines to accompany smoked salmon include Fino sherry, Gewürztraminer, Chablis, Pouilly Fumé, Sancerre, and Lugana – served at 8–10°C.

Smoked trout are served from the larder, whole, on a paper d'oyley on a silver flat, garnished with lemon and mustard and cress or parsley and accompanied by a sauceboat of horseradish sauce. The waiter must cut off the head, remove the skin from both sides and open out the trout so as to pull the backbone away; the two fillets are placed on a fish plate with the lemon and cress and served with buttered triangles of brown bread and the sauceboat of sauce on an underplate. A fish knife and fork is used. A Californian Fumé Blanc is very good with smoked trout.

Smoked mackerel are usually bought as fillets, either plainly smoked, covered with crushed peppercorns, or dusted with herbs. A portion is a fillet of approximately 100 g, with a quarter or half of lemon, mustard and cress, horseradish sauce and brown bread and butter. A fish knife and fork is used. Tokay d'Alsace or a Chablis is good with these fish.

Smoked eel is cut into portions approximately 10 cm long from the whole eel and the waiter must remove the skin and backbone so as to serve two pieces of fillet. It is served on a plate with lemon, mustard and cress, horseradish sauce and brown bread and butter (see Figure 8.5). Sometimes a fan of gherkin is used to garnish it. Suitable wines are chilled dry sherry or Bourgogne Aligoté.

Fig 8.5 *(a) smoked trout; serve whole*

(b) smoked mackerel; serve a whole fillet

(c)   smoked eel; serve cut into thin slices

Gravelax (also spelt as Gravad lax or Gravlaks) is a side of salmon marinated with salt, spices, sugar and dill; some brandy may be added. It is served carved into slices, with a sauce made of sour cream, mustard and chopped dill, and brown or rye bread and butter.

8.8   SERVICE OF OYSTERS

These are in season from September until 30 April each year, which is why it is said they can be eaten only when there is an 'r' in the month. Oysters are opened raw by the oyster-man in the larder; he releases them from the shell, replaces them in the deep shell on a layer of crushed ice in a soup plate or oyster dish, allowing six or twelve per portion. They are graded according to size and the price charged per portion of six is decided by the grade served; half a lemon and some parsley are placed in the centre.

The waiter places the plateful of oysters on an underplate in front of the customer; an oyster fork is placed at the right-hand side, a finger-bowl of warm water with a slice of lemon in it at top right, a plateful of brown bread and butter, and a side-plate containing Tabasco, cayenne and peppermill is placed nearby. Some restaurants serve a sauceboat of shallot sauce with oysters – this consists of finely chopped shallots in malt vinegar.

The customer uses the oyster fork to pull the beard from the side of the oyster; he seasons one to taste then picks up the oyster in the shell and pours it into his open mouth, either chewing or swallowing it. It is necessary to offer a clean table napkin after a dish of oysters has been finished. A suitable drink is Black Velvet which is a mixture of champagne and stout, Champagne, Muscadet de Sèvre et Maine, and Chablis, all served at 5–8°C. Figure 8.6 shows a service of oysters.

Fig 8.6 *service of oysters*

8.9 SERVICE OF SNAILS AS A HOT HORS-D'OEUVRE

Snails are normally served six per portion in the metal dish in which they were cooked in the oven; they are placed with the open end upwards to keep the hot butter inside. Place the dish on an underplate with the snail tongs on the left and the snail fork on the right, as shown in Figure 8.7. The customer spears the snail with the fork, chews it, then picks up the shell in the tongs and drinks the butter; brown bread and butter or an extra roll is served. Suitable wines include Châteauneuf-du-Pape, or a red Burgundy.

Fig 8.7 *service of snails*

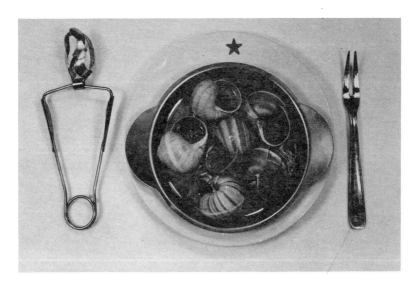

8.10 SERVICE OF SMOKED RAW HAM AND CHARCUTERIE ITEMS

There are several kinds of cured hams which are served raw, including **Parma** from Italy, **Bayonne** from France, **Serrano** from Spain, **Westphalia** from Germany, and **Prague** ham from Czechoslovakia. These are available ready-sliced in vacuum packs but a good-class restaurant will carve slices to order from a whole one on the bone, doing it on the clamp illustrated in Figure 3.10, serving three or four very thin slices per portion. This kind of ham goes very well with fruit and is sometimes served with a slice of melon (as shown in Figure 8.8), with a peeled and cored pear, or a fresh fig. To serve, place a dessert knife and fork in inverted V-shape on a large plate, put two slices of de-rinded melon on top and drape the slices of ham over them. Customers will find a medium to dry white wine suitable for this course, e.g. Orvieto, Soave, Frascati, or a wine from Alsace.

An **Assiette de Charcuterie** is a selection of sliced cured or smoked cold sausages including salami, mortadella, coppa, garlic sausage, liver sausage, haslet and some of the hundreds of other kinds. The word comes from *chair cuite*, which means cooked flesh (meat) but

Fig 8.8 *service of smoked ham and melon*

refers mainly to pork products. Although it is usual to offer a selection, a customer may choose to eat one variety only.

To serve, arrange the thinly cut slices overlapping on a meat plate, garnish with gherkins and parsley and offer grissinis, pumpernickel or rye bread and butter pats; a small knife and fork is used. Recommended wines are the same as for smoked ham.

8.11   SERVICE OF COLD AND HOT VEGETABLES AS AN HORS-D'OEUVRE

The list of vegetables suitable for serving as a cold first course includes asparagus, globe artichokes, corn-on-the-cob, seakale, samphire, and a number of salads which are mixtures of vegetables. In addition there is the selection of raw vegetables known as **Crudités** which consists of lengths of carrot, cucumber, celery, endive, courgette and pimento, with radishes and spring onions, served chilled with several dips, but this is really for customers to nibble while waiting for their order to be taken.

Asparagus – lay a meat fork on the table in front of the customer so that the prongs are pointing to 11 o'clock and the handle at 5 o'clock; place a meat plate on it so that it rests firmly and is tilted slightly towards the left. Serve the portion of asparagus, using a spoon and fork, so that the tips are pointing to 8 o'clock (see Figure 8.9); ladle the vinaigrette or mayonnaise sauce over the tips and place a finger bowl at the top left-hand side of the cover. The remaining sauce should be put on the table and also a small side-plate to receive the tough ends that cannot be eaten. The customer picks up a spear of asparagus in his fingers and chews from the tip end, dipping into the sauce several times before discarding the toughish end portion. A knife and fork is not appropriate although a dainty person may request an asparagus tong with which to hold the asparagus spear.

Fig 8.9   *service of asparagus*

Hot asparagus is served in the same way, using a hot plate and serving a warm sauce as Hollandaise, Mousseline or Melted Butter. An asparagus plate (which has a shallow well at one edge) may be used. A good wine is Tavel Rosé, also Vinho Verde, Orvieto, or a Moselle.

Globe artichoke – serve the whole cold artichoke onto a meat plate and put a side-plate at the top left-hand side as a receptacle for the discarded end leaves that are only partly edible. A knife and fork is necessary for getting to the central part and the sauceboat of vinaigrette is placed as shown in Figure 8.10 for the customer to dip each leaf in as he eats it. A finger bowl is necessary and a replacement table napkin afterwards. A hot globe artichoke is served onto a hot meat plate, accompanied with a sauceboat of warm Hollandaise Sauce or Melted Butter. It is usual to serve a young red wine such as a Beaujolais with cold asparagus and a dry to medium which such as Mâcon, Vouvray or Vermentino with a hot artichoke. **Mushrooms** are served hot as an hors-d'oeuvre either stuffed and grilled or deep fried in batter; they are served on a hot fish plate with a small knife and fork, and hot garlic bread is offered.

Fig 8.10   *service of a globe artichoke*

Corn-on-the-cob is usually served hot, the warm meat plate being laid on top of a large fork so arranged as to tip the plate forward. The waiter inserts a holder at each end of the cob and serves it across the plate; he then ladles the hot melted butter which acts as the sauce, at the bottom of the plate. The customer picks up the cob using both hands to hold it and rotates it as he nibbles away at it. The customer will help himself to more butter from the sauceboat as he needs it; a finger-bowl is essential (see Figure 8.11). Any kind of medium dry white wine is suitable for sweetcorn.

Fig 8.11 *service of corn-on-the-cob*

Mixtures of vegetables include **Ratatouille** which consists of stewed aubergines, courgettes, tomato and onion, served lukewarm with Melba toast; baby artichokes cooked à la grecque; stuffed pimentos; stuffed aubergines; tomatoes filled with rice; tunny fish; crabmeat or vegetable salad; celeriac in creamed mayonnaise; mooli salad, etc. All these may be served as an hors-d'oeuvre. Among the many well-known salads, the best are:

Salade Niçoise – French beans, sliced potato, quarters of tomato, anchovy and black olives

Salade Russe – carrots, turnips, beans, peas, diced salami, lobster and anchovy, all mixed with mayonnaise

Salade Parisienne – russian salad with slices of lobster

Salade Waldorf – celery, apple and walnuts with mayonnaise, in a hollowed-out apple

Salade Windsor – celery, chicken, ox tongue, mushrooms, truffle, and rampion

134

Salade de Légumes – bouquets of spring vegetables with asparagus tips

These salads are arranged in lettuce or radicchio leaves in a ravier or salad bowl and the ones not already dressed with mayonnaise or French dressing can be flavoured and garnished with crisply fried rashers of bacon, fried bread croûtons and hot vinegar.

Any dry to medium white wine is suitable for these salads but most customers realise that vinegar in the dressing detracts from the taste of any wine.

8.12 SERVICE OF FRUITS AS HORS-D'OEUVRE

The fruit most commonly used is grapefruit, followed closely by melon, and by fruit juices, but there are many other fruit hors-d'oeuvre including avocado pears, fresh figs, kiwi fruit, custard apple, mango, passion fruit, persimmon and banana.

Grapefruit Cerisette There are several kinds of grapefruit some sweeter, juicier, or a different colour from those in everyday use. Cut in half through the circumference and use a grapefruit knife to remove the central pith and to loosen each segment. Place a cocktail cherry in the centre of each half and serve in a coupe on a d'oyley on a side-plate. Serve to be eaten with a grapefruit spoon or teaspoon, and the sugar sifter placed on the table for the customer to help himself. See Figure 8.12.

Fig 8.12 *service of grapefruit-half*

Halves of grapefruit may be sprinkled with brown sugar and cooked under a salamander to melt and caramelise the sugar; they are served hot in a coupe.

The only suitable wines are oloroso sherry or sweet Madeira. For other grapefruit hors-d'oeuvre , see section on Fruit Cocktails later in this chapter.

Melon frappé   Many kinds of melon are grown including **honeydew**, which is the most popular, **cantaloup** which has orange-coloured flesh, **charentais** which is a very sweet, small, oval melon suitable for one or two persons only, **Ogen** and **Galia** which have netted skins and a musky flavour and odour, and **water melon** which has pink flesh with black seeds all through, and is not much used in restaurants.

To test for ripeness press the stalk end which should be softish, cut in half, remove the seeds with a spoon then cut into wedges, chill and serve; it is advisable to cut the rind straight at the base to prevent the slice rocking while it is being eaten.

The cover is as shown in Figure 8.13, a dessert spoon and fork placed on a dessert plate crossways with the melon in the middle; a charantais melon is served either whole or half, in a coupe. Caster sugar and a small dish of ground ginger are offered and a teaspoon of each is dusted over the melon, or the sugar sifter may be placed on the table for the customer to use. Some larder chefs like to free the flesh from the melon skin, cut it into slices across and make them into a pattern by pulling every other one slightly out. Sometimes melon is garnished with slices or segments of orange, kiwi fruit, etc.

Fig 8.13   *service of melon slice*

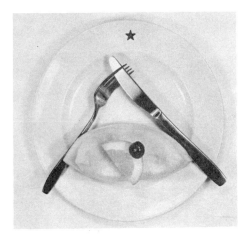

Melon Oporto is a whole melon with the flesh scooped out, replaced and mixed with port, then served chilled in crushed ice; it is served in goblets or coupes. There are many other ways of serving this fruit.

A fairly strong, sweet wine such as port, oloroso sherry or sweet Madeira is suitable for melon. See also section on fruit cocktails later in this chapter.

Figs – fresh figs in season can be peeled and cut into quarters to show the pink colour and black seeds; there are green, white, purple and black varieties of figs and when cut open they resemble a flower. Serve on a dessert plate with a dessert knife and fork. Suitable wines include Muscadet and Traminer. Figs can also be served in partnership with Parma ham.

Fig 8.14   *service of avocado pear*

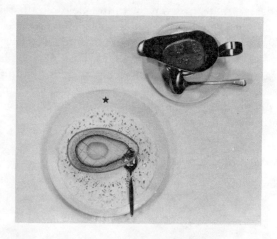

Kiwi fruit – the ripe fruit can be served in an egg-cup, the top being cut off so that the customer can scoop out and eat the soft green flesh with a teaspoon; the skin is too rough to eat. Other items, e.g. scrambled egg, may be served in hollowed-out kiwi fruit and it may be used to garnish other hors-d'oeuvre e.g. on slices of melon.

Avocado pears are used mainly as a cold hors-d'oeuvre, either plain or with French dressing or mayonnaise, yoghurt, cream cheese, shellfish, tuna, taramasalata, or cut into slices, made into a mousse or a dip or a spread. They can also be garnished with lettuce, olives, radishes, tomato, hard-boiled egg, celery, etc., and finished with paprika, parsley or lobster coral. They may also be made into **Guacamole** with cottage or cream cheese, lemon juice, Tabasco, and Worcester sauce and used as a dip for a buffet.

To serve as a single hors-d'oeuvre, cut the avocado pear in half through the length, remove the large stone and place in a silver, glass or china avocado dish on a leaf of lettuce or radicchio as shown in Figure 8.14. Fill with the selected garnish, e.g. shrimps mixed with mustard-flavoured creamed mayonnaise, garnish with slices of pimento-stuffed olive and sprinkle with sieved yolk of hard-boiled egg. Place on a d'oyley on an underplate and serve with a grapefruit spoon and dessert knife. Offer brown bread and butter or Melba toast.

Fig 8.15 *service of tomato juice*

Serve with a medium white wine such as hock, or Graves; if French dressing is used in the dish, a dry sherry is best.

Fruit cocktails – the following are the best-known fruit cocktails which are served as an hors-d'oeuvre:

Avocado – diced avocado and melon balls in lemon juice with a cherry on top; mandarin segments may be added.

Florida – orange and grapefruit segments and a cocktail cherry on top

Exotique – melon balls, nectarine and kiwi slices, with a strawberry on top

Grapefruit – segments of grapefruit with a cocktail cherry on top

Hawaii – peeled grapes, pineapple chunks, mint leaves

Melon – small balls of yellow and green melons, cut with a spoon cutter, flavoured with port or kirsch; a cherry on top

Miami – segments of grapefruit and orange, with small pieces of pineapple

Orange – segments of orange with a cocktail cherry on top

Singapore – pineapple chunks, mandarin segments and sliced banana

Many other combinations, always including citrus fruits, are made; very often the rim of the goblet in which these are served is frosted with plain or coloured sugar. Drinks are not offered with these cocktails as some may be flavoured with kirsch, cointreau or maraschino.

Fruit juice is available in many flavours including orange, grapefruit, pineapple, apple, tomato, vegetable, passion fruit and mixtures of exotic fruit such as apricots, guava, mandarin, papaya, paw paw, peach and banana. In some establishments the orange juice is freshly pressed to order but the canned and tetrapacked kinds have a fairly fresh flavour and odour. Serve in a goblet or fruit-juice glass on a d'oyley on a side-plate; a teaspoon may be needed and the sugar caster or bowl should be offered.

Tomato juice is served in a goblet or fruit juice glass, on a d'oyley on a sideplate with a teaspoon; many customers like to add salt, pepper and Worcester sauce so these must be placed on the table at the time of serving. Figure 8.15 shows the service of tomato juice.

No drink would be offered with fruit or tomato juice.

8.13 MISCELLANEOUS HORS-D'OEUVRE – HOT AND COLD

Canapés à la Russe These are usually offered during the reception before a banquet or dinner party; they are small pieces of toast or savoury biscuits covered with pieces of egg, fish, meat or vegetable, glazed with aspic and arranged on a silver dish to be offered around.

Eggs

Gulls' eggs are bought hard-boiled in the colourful shell and served in a nest of mustard and cress. The customer may shell the egg himself and eat it with a small knife and fork off a fish-plate. Brown bread and butter is offered on one side-plate and a selection of seasonings on another. A finger bowl should be provided.

Quail's eggs are available throughout the year and two or three small ones are served per portion, in the same way as gull's eggs.

Egg mayonnaise is often ready-plated for service and is eaten with a small knife and fork; Hovis or wholemeal bread and butter is offered.

Quiche is an egg and cream flan with cheese, bacon or mushroom filling, a wedge is cut from the whole flan and transferred with serving-spoon and fork onto the hot fish plate in front of the customer. A good dry white white wine such as Alsace is suitable.

Fish

Assiette de Fruits de Mer is a selection of several kinds of shellfish arranged on salad leaves on a large cold plate, sometimes with a garnish of hard-boiled egg, cucumber or tomato. In some restaurants the selection is superbly displayed with whole fish on the opened shells embodied in crushed ice; the customer can take what he wants so he may need an oyster fork, lobster pick, fish knife and fork, finger bowl, extra napkin, sideplate for empty shells, plate of seasonings, sauceboat of mayonnaise and a plateful of brown bread and butter.

This kind of dish served hot is called *à la nage* because the shellfish have been 'swimming' in the cooking liquid, or in other words, are plain-boiled. Champagne may be served.

Fish Mayonnaise is usually ready-plated in an individual dish and need only be placed on a d'oyley on an underplate with a fish knife and fork. A suitable wine is Chablis.

Dressed Crab is sometimes served in portions in a small crabshell so all that needs to be done is place it on a fish plate, surround it with a heart of lettuce, quarter of tomato and hard-boiled egg and offer mayonnaise from a sauceboat. It is eaten with a fish knife and fork. If arranged in a large shell serve a spoonful of the dark and white meat onto a few leaves of lettuce then add the garnish. Brown bread or rolls may be offered and suitable wines to suggest are Alsace or Chablis.

Potted Shrimps are bought in small cartons packed in various weights; they only need to be turned out onto a few leaves of lettuce or radicchio and garnished with a segment of lemon. A fish plate and fork is used, brown bread and butter is served and an appropriate wine would be Chablis.

Taramasalata is a purée of smoked cod roe, oil and soaked bread-crumbs, flavoured with lemon juice. It is served in a small earthen-ware or glass dish from which it can be eaten; or it may have to be served from a larger dish by the waiter. It is either spread onto hot toast or eaten with a small fork and knife.

Whitebait are often featured as a hot hors-d'oeuvre, serving a smaller portion than for a fish course. The pile of small fish is served from the silver dish onto a hot fish-plate, using a serving-spoon and fork, without crushing the food. A lemon segment and bunch of fried parsley are served and the cayenne and peppermill are offered. Whitebait are eaten whole with a fish knife and fork.

Grilled sprats and **sardines** are often served as hot hors-d'oeuvre; they are accompanied with lemon, parsley, maître d'hôtel butter and brown bread and butter. Vinho Verde or Dão are suitable wines.

Mussels are excellent as an hors-d'oeuvre and can be served raw in the half shell in exactly the same way as oysters, or cooked as for Moules Marinière as described in Chapter 9. Suitable wines for cold mussels are champagne, Chablis, and Muscadet de Sèvre et Maine, and for hot mussels, a Muscadet or Gros Plant.

Other possibilities

Meat Terrine or **Pâté Maison** is often featured on all menus because of its popular appeal. The name is interchangeable and the dish is based on the livers of birds or animals made into a coarse or smooth texture with bacon, brandy, cream, eggs, herbs and spices, baked in an earthenware dish; chefs have their own formula for making pâté and some use game instead of liver. Pâté is served in the same way as foie gras, cutting into shell-shape spoonfuls, or slices with a hot knife or it can be served as shown in Figure 8.2 accompanied by hot toast and butter pats. A dry white wine such as Mâcon Blanc is suitable to drink with any kind of pâté.

Mousses are often featured as an hors-d'oeuvre and can be made from avocado, chicken, foie gras, ham, salmon, etc., set with gelatine and lightened with cream. They may be served in individual dishes or larger glass bowls, decorated and glazed with jelly. The small version is placed on a d'oyley on an underplate to be eaten with a teaspoon; the waiter must serve spoonfuls from the larger container, dipping a dessertspoon into a jug of hot water and placing several oval pieces in the centre of a cold fish-plate.

QUESTIONS

1. Distinguish between the service of an hors-d'oeuvre varié and a charcuterie hors-d'oeuvre.

2. Say with which hors-d'oeuvre brown bread is served in preference to toast.

3. State the ways in which melon frappé and melon Oporto can be served.

4. Distinguish between cold and hot hors-d'oeuvre and give a list of six items of each kind.

CHAPTER 9

SERVICE PROCEDURES FOR SOUPS, EGGS, FARINACEOUS AND FISH DISHES

In the classical menu there were as many as fifteen courses and the soup, egg, farinaceous and fish courses were numbers 2, 3, 4, and 5 in the lengthy sequence. Nowadays it is usual to select one course from the group, hors-d'oeuvre, soup, egg and farinaceous, then to continue with a fish or meat course.

9.1 SERVICE OF THICK SOUP

In a menu written on classical lines the soup course follows the hors-d'oeuvre and comes before the fish course. A table d'hôte or set menu will include a thick and a clear soup; an à la carte menu will show as many as a dozen different soups, some cold ones as well as hot, from the main types which are: *consommé*, *bouillon*, *broth* and *potage* (the thin soups); *purée*, *velouté*, *cream*, *brown roux* and *bisque* (the thick soups). There are certain principles which govern the types of soups that are suitable for serving at lunch, as against those which are really only suitable for serving at dinner.

Thick soups are normally served in a soup plate which is placed on a meat plate as the under-plate; for several portions to be served from a large tureen it is usual to ladle it into the soup plates from the tureen placed on the spirit lamp to keep it hot. The soup is served from the left-hand side of the customer, the waiter holding it in his right hand; he should be able to carry three platefuls at a time. Figures 9.1 and 9.2 shows this service, from the guéridon, and on the table.

Single portions of thick soup are sometimes served from the kitchen in an individual tureen as shown in Figure 9.3. The soup plate

Fig 9.1   *service of soup from the guéridon*

Fig 9.2   *service of soup at the table*

Fig 9.3 service of thick soup

on its under-plate is placed in front of the customer and the salver with the bowl of soup positioned just beyond the inside edge, so as to prevent spilling when pouring the soup into the soup plate. Only a single portion should be served from a salver in this way and the bowl of soup must be poured out away from the side where the customer is seated.

Diced fried bread croûtons are served with most kinds of thick soup and should be sprinkled over the served soup, using a teaspoon to take them from the sauceboat in which they are normally served. Toasted rounds of French bread may be offered from a sauceboat; dry water biscuits are served with chowder soups, and diablotins with any other kind of thick soup.

Among the well-known soups in this category are **Conti** (lentils), **Crécy** (carrot), **Dubarry** (cauliflower), **Favorite** (French beans), **Parmentier** (potato), **St-Germain** (peas), **Solferino** (potato and tomato), **Tomate** (tomatoes), and **Washington** (sweetcorn). Bisques are thick soups made of shellfish such as crab, lobster or shrimps.

The kinds of wine suitable for serving with thick soups are Madeira, and fino or manzanilla sherry; a full-bodied dry white is needed for bisques of shellfish; white Côtes du Rhône is good with clam chowder, and Chianti with **Minestrone**.

9.2 SERVICE OF CLEAR SOUPS

Clear soup usually means **consommé** which is a well-flavoured stock that has been clarified with minced shin of beef and egg-white so as to give a crystal-clear appearance. It is usually served in a two-handled consommé cup on a saucer on an under-plate, as shown in Figure 9.4 and is drunk with a dessert spoon rather than the usual soup spoon. There are hundreds of different garnishes used with consommé, most of them being put into the soup just before it is served from the kitchen. Very often cheese straws are served as the accompaniment and these should be offered to the customer, the rest of them being placed on the table. The best known consommés include **Célestine** (julienne of savoury pancake), **Colbert** (a small poached egg), **Madrilène** (tomato, pimento and celery-flavoured with vermicelli and diced tomato), and **Royale** (diced savoury egg custard).

Bird's Nest Soup is a consommé in which the small nests of a species of swallow found in Java and Malaya, are poached.

Clear Turtle Soup is made by flavouring chicken or beef consommé with a mixture of herbs including basil, bay-leaf, coriander, mar-

Fig 9.4 *service of consommé*

joram, peppercorns, rosemary, thyme and sage. It is garnished with turtle-flesh cut into dice, lightly thickened with arrowroot, and a small measure of dry Madeira or sherry is added in front of the customer. Cheese straws and lemon quarters are offered. Figure 9.5 shows the methods of service.

Fig 9.5 *service of clear turtle soup*

Potage Lady Curzon is an example of kitchen presentation of turtle soup; the clear turtle soup is poured into a soup cup, curry-flavoured whipped cream is piped on the surface and is glazed quickly under a salamander immediately prior to service.

Petite Marmite is also a clear soup but one that should be served in a miniature version of the pot in which it is supposed to be cooked. It is a well-flavoured clear stock garnished with small pieces of beef and chicken, carrot, turnip, leek and celery. The pot is placed in front of the customer, the lid removed so as to assail the nostrils with the subtle aroma and toasted croûtons of French bread are offered from a sauceboat, placing them on the side-plate or next to the marmite pot. Grated Parmesan cheese can be offered, sprinkling it from the sauceboat into the soup. Figure 9.6 shows the service.

Fig 9.6 *service of petite marmite soup*

French Onion Soup is also a clear soup and is usually served in an earthenware bowl, covered with round slices of French bread, sprinkled with cheese and gratinated under a grill. It is served on an under-plate and eaten with a dessert spoon.

Suitable wines for clear soups include medium dry sherry and sercial Madeira, served at 12–14°C; dry Montilla is also good with clear soup.

Cold Soups

The most popular cold thick soups are **Vichyssoise** and **Gazpacho** but during hot weather many of the cream and velouté soups such as asparagus, chicken and green pea, may be served chilled. A good quality consommé should set like a wobbly jelly when chilled but sometimes melted gelatine is added to give the required limpidity.

Vichyssoise may be served in a soup bowl or soup plate and have a swirl of lightly whipped cream and a sprinkling of chopped chives added at the point of service.

Gazpacho is sometimes served with ice cubes in it and is always accompanied by a selection of small diced fried bread croûtons, dice of raw cucumber, green pimento and tomato, and finely chopped onion, which the waiter should sprinkle into the soup, in front of the customer, using teaspoons.

Cold Consommé can be finished by flavouring it with a measure of Madeira, port, sherry, claret or other wine. In some cases this is done with hot consommé in the restaurant but is more usually added by the soup cook when making the consommé.

Bortsch Polonaise which is a clear duck soup may be served chilled accompanied by the same garnishes as for hot Bortsch which includes sour cream, raw beetroot juice and very small puff-pastry patties filled with minced duck. The cream and beetroot juice are spooned into the soup in front of the customer, and the patties are handed separately.

9.3 SERVICE OF EGG DISHES

Hot egg dishes need to be cooked to order and served without undue delay, as, if they are left in the hotplate they quickly become overcooked and indigestible.

Oeufs en Cocotte – the eggs are served in the small cocotte in which they were cooked, and the garnish may be on top or underneath the eggs. The cocotte is served on an under-plate, with a teaspoon, as shown in figure 9.7, the peppermill and the uncapped bottle of Worcester sauce may be offered.

Oeufs sur le Plat – the eggs are cooked in a shallow fireproof dish, as shown in Figure 9.8 and the dish is placed on an under-plate. Often a garnish of a rasher of bacon or chipolata sausage is added so a small knife may be needed in addition to a dessert spoon and fork. This dish is sometimes referred to as shirred eggs.

Oeufs pochés – poached eggs may be served plainly on rounds of buttered toast or in tartlet cases filled with a garnish such as chopped

Fig 9.7   *service of oeufs en cocotte*

Fig 9.8   *service of oeufs sur le plat*

mushroom, asparagus, chicken, etc., mixed with a suitable sauce; the eggs are coated with some of the same sauce. They may be served from a silver dish onto a hot fish plate and a small knife and fork are appropriate.

Oeufs Farcis Chimay – these are stuffed hard-boiled eggs coated with Mornay sauce and gratinated with grated cheese. They may be dished in a shallow egg-dish from which they can be eaten, or served from a larger dish onto a hot fish plate by means of a serving spoon and fork. Figure 9.9 shows a single portion of four halves of egg for eating with a dessert fork.

Fig 9.9   *service of oeufs farcis chimay*

Omelette – there are several kinds of omelette (i) the normal oval shape with or without a filling, (ii) a flat omelette like a thick pancake, and (iii) soufflé omelette which is usually served as a sweet omelette. The oval kind is made with two large size eggs for a table d'hôte dish and three eggs for an à la carte order. A larger omelette can be made for serving to two or three people by cutting it into sections. It is the usual practice to cut the end-tips of the omelette off then to lift it by means of two forks on to the plate in front of the customer, as shown in Figure 9.10. Any sauce surrounding the omelette must be scooped up with a spoon and poured around on the plate.

Fig 9.10   *service of an omelette*

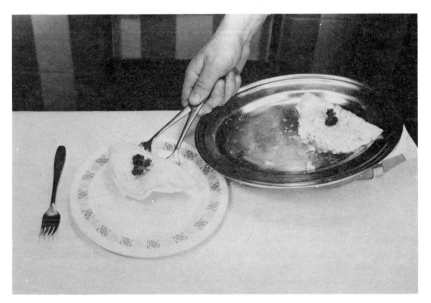

A flat omelette such as **Omelette Espagnole** is lifted from the serving dish onto the customer's plate by means of two serving forks spread out under it. All omelettes are eaten with a joint knife and fork. The word *baveuse* is used to denote that the centre of the omelette is only lightly cooked and not hard.

It is not easy to recommend any wine that matches these egg dishes and an ordinary house white wine is adequate.

9.4 SERVICE OF FARINACEOUS DISHES

The farinaceous course on a menu is often combined with that of the egg dishes, and both are more suitable for lunch than for dinner. Farinaceous dishes include all the hundreds of different kinds of Italian pastas of which spaghetti and macaroni are the best known, also savoury rice dishes and the various kinds of continental dumplings such as gnocchi and späetzle. These items can either be served in small portions as a first course or if desired, as a full portion instead of soup; they are frequently used as a garnish with meat and fish dishes and the rice dishes can be served as a vegetable.

Pastas can be classified as (i) long; (ii) short; and (iii) filled pastas; all may be served with several kinds of garnishes and there is also a wide variety of suitable sauces, e.g. à la Milanaise – mixed with julienne of ham, mushroom and tongue and bound with tomato sauce. Long pastas such as spaghetti and noodles are usually cooked *al dente*, which means very slightly hard at the centre; they are usually tossed in hot butter before the garnish and sauce is added then presented in an earthenware dish for the waiter to transfer into a soup plate. Sometimes they are portioned into individual egg dishes to be placed directly in front of the customer. The implements for eating it are a joint fork on the right and dessert spoon at the left-hand side so the customer can roll up the pasta around the prongs of the fork and hold it in shape inside the bowl of the spoon, conveying it to the mouth from the fork.

To serve from a guéridon, place the dish of pasta on the lamp, mix and serve it with two forks into the centre of a soup plate, or hold the two forks in the right hand and the soup plate on an under-plate on the left hand, as shown in Figure 9.11. Short-length pastas and filled ones such as ravioli are served like this but using a serving-spoon and fork. A **pasticcio di lasagne** is made by baking layers of pasta with various sauces and fillings in the form of a pie; it is served cut into portions.

It is essential to offer grated cheese with all kinds of pastas, serving it from a sauceboat as shown in Figure 9.12, or from a special cheese container which holds more than a normal sauceboat. Parmesan is a very pungent kind of cheese and it can be very finely ground which makes it the most suitable cheese for pastas; Gruyère and Emmenthal are also used, either alone or mixed with Parmesan. A well-known pasta dish is **Linguine ai Cinque Formaggi**, which consists of buttered noodles which the waiter sprinkles with five different kinds of grated cheese such as Parmesan, Gruyère, Emmenthal,

Fig 9.11 *guéridon service of spaghetti*

Cheddar and Edam. When white Piedmont truffles are in season they may be grated raw over a dish of pastasciutta. The truffle should be held in a gloved hand.

Gnocchi means dumplings, though not the kind that are usually served with boiled salt beef. This kind of small dumpling can be made

Fig 9.12 *service of grated cheese*

from either chou paste, semolina, or dry mashed potato, in the form of oval or round flat cakes, gratinated with a sauce and grated cheese. Gratination is done in an egg dish which is served on an under-plate on a d'oyley, as shown in Figure 9.13.

For this course, a pilaff of rice or a risotto with a garnish in it and possibly a sauce to surround it, is served in preference to ordinary plain boiled rice. It is dished in the kitchen in an earthenware dish from which it can be eaten, or for spooning into a hot soup plate; grated Parmesan is offered.

Suitable wines for farinaceous dishes are Valpolicella, Bardolino, Merlot, Barbera, or Chianti, according to whether the pastas are finished in a red meat sauce or in a cream sauce it should be either a red or a white wine.

9.5 SERVICE OF FISH

Fish is available as flat and round varieties; flat fish include plaice, sole, brill and turbot and round fish include cod, haddock, monkfish,

Fig 9.13 *service of gnocchi*

salmon and trout. Small fish can be served whole whereas large ones are cut into fillets or slices, the menu terms for these being:

darne – a slice cut (including the bone) through a round fish;
tronçon – a slice cut (including the bone) through a flat fish that has been cut into half down the backbone;
paupiette – a fillet spread with fish forcemeat and rolled up;
suprême – a slice cut on the slant from a large fillet such as turbot or cod;
délice and *zéphyr* are fanciful names for a fillet of fish, such as sole.

Fish that is plain boiled is normally served with an accompanying sauce whereas shallow-poached fish fillets are coated with sauce which is an integral part of the dish. The most popular way of serving fillets and suprêmes of fish is that of shallow-poaching and coating with white wine sauce which contains the reduced cooking liquid. The sauce adds considerably to the flavour of the fish and the dish is often glazed to a gold brown under a salamander. Many garnishes are added, the most popular being **Bercy** (shallot and parsley); **Palace** (shallot, mushroom and tomato); **Bonne Femme** (shallot, parsley, mushroom); and **Véronique** (grapes).

Serving grilled or poached sole or plaice

Present the fish to the customer then lift it with two forks onto the plate and remove the surrounding fins from head to tail, using the two forks; lift the two uppermost fillets by sliding a fork underneath, pull off the bone attached to the head and place it on a side plate then replace the top fillets on the underneath fillets and serve immediately, adding the lemon and parsley. The maître d'hôtel butter is then served from the sauceboat or dish; placing it on the fish as shown in Figure 9.14. Grilled, poached or shallow-fried trout are usually cooked whole with the head on, and after presenting it, the waiter cuts off the head; if requested to bone the fish, he should remove the central bone by cutting through from the back and opening the fish, pulling the bone from the tail-end up to and including the head. The bones lying along the belly should also be removed by passing a fish knife from the centre towards the edge which will dislodge all the curled ventral bones. Figures 9.15(a) and (b) show how these movements are made. Any garnish such as lemon, parsley or potatoes should be laid at the side of the fish, and in the case of fish shallow-fried à la meunière, the surrounding butter and lemon juice should be spooned over. When serving a whole small fish it must be laid across the middle of the plate, with the head to the left-hand side.

Grilled or poached darnes of salmon and cod, and **tronçons of turbot** – present the dish to the customer then return it to the sideboard or to the guéridon and peel off the skin from around the slice, twisting it onto a fork while holding the fish firmly with a fork stuck into the bone which can then be pulled away (Figure 9.16). The appropriate sauces include hollandaise, mousseline, béarnaise, melted butter, or egg sauce; and anchovy or maître d'hôtel butter for grilled fish. A whole poached salmon is sometimes carved in the restaurant. The skin will have been removed in the kitchen and the portion is cut as shown in Figure 9.17 without bones, with a slice of lemon, sprig of parsley, plain boiled potatoes and hollandaise sauce or hot melted butter, which the waiter should serve from the sauceboat using a dessert spoon. The fish may be moistened with some of the cooking liquid and it is usual to serve a ravier of thinly sliced cucumber with hot poached salmon, in which case vinegar should be offered. Cold poached salmon is cut in the same way as hot whole fish, placing the section on a leaf of lettuce, and adding the garnish of one quarter of a hard-boiled egg, tomato sections, sliced cucumber and sauce mayonnaise.

Truite au bleu – this is an à la carte dish made with a live trout which is taken from the tank, stunned, gutted and placed into a dish of vinegar which will cause it to turn blue all over. It is then boiled in an individual trout kettle in court-bouillon and served in this container, which has an inner drainer with which to lift out the trout. Melted butter or hollandaise sauce may be served with it.

Deep-fried fish in breadcrumbs or batter is served with a quarter of lemon, fried sprig of parsley and tartare sauce, or in the case of fish à la Orly, with hot tomato sauce. Deep-fried whitebait are served onto a hot fish-plate in a bunch, with a quarter of lemon and fried parsley, but no sauce. The peppermill and cayenne cellar are placed on the table and a plateful of buttered quarter-slices of brown bread.

Suitable wines with poached fish are Chablis, Graves, Mosel, and Vouvray. Fresh salmon deserves Meursault, Corton Charlemagne or a German Spätlese.

9.6 SERVICE OF SHELLFISH

There are two kinds of shellfish – crustaceans which are lobsters, crabs, crawfish, crayfish, scampi, shrimps and prawns, and molluscs which are oysters, mussels, scallops, whelks and winkles.

Lobster

Cold lobster – the edible part of a lobster is only two-fifths of the total weight, the rest being the shell, it therefore makes the portion look larger if it is served in the half shell, which is usually cut in the larder but may have to be done by the waiter in front of the customer. Figure 9.18(a) shows how the tail is cut down the middle from the end of the head and Figure 9.18(b), how it is then turned the other way and cut through the head to give two equal halves. It is usual to break off and crack the large claws before cutting the lobster. It is necessary to discard the sac from inside the head and to detach the flesh in the tail part before placing the half-lobster on a large plate and garnishing it with the quarters of hard-boiled egg, tomato and lettuce that are an important part of the service. Mayonnaise is served onto the plate from a sauceboat, using a dessert spoon. It is necessary to supply an extra table napkin, a finger-bowl and a plate for the shells; the customer may ask for the lobster crackers and pick so that he can break open and delve inside the shell for every scrap of flesh.

Fig 9.14   *(a)   as received from the kitchen*

(b)   removing the fin bones

(c)   lifting off the top half

(d) removing the centre bone

(e) replaced ready to serve

*(f) an alternative method of removing the back
     bone*

Fig 9.15   *filleting a trout*

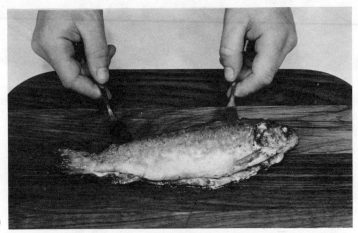

(a)

(b)

An alternative method of service is as shown in Figure 9.19 where the flesh from the body and claw are placed on lettuce leaves, with the quarters of tomato and hard boiled egg arranged around.

Hot plain boiled lobster is served in the same way as cold lobster but without any garnish, except for a sauceboat of melted butter or Sauce Beurre Blanc, which is reduced white wine and white wine vinegar with butter whisked into it.

Fig 9.16 *removing the skin from a fish steak*

Fig 9.17 *portioning a whole poached salmon*

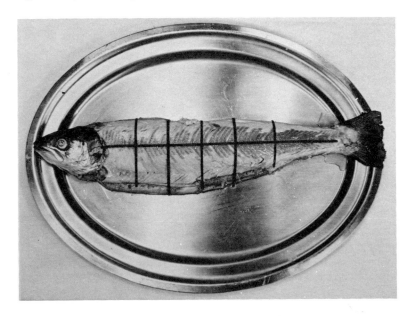

Fig 9.18 *cutting a cooked lobster*

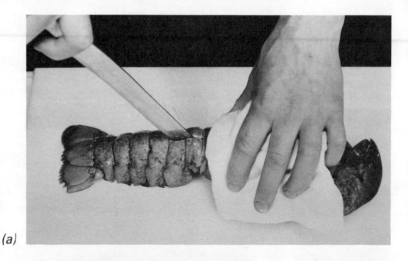

(a)

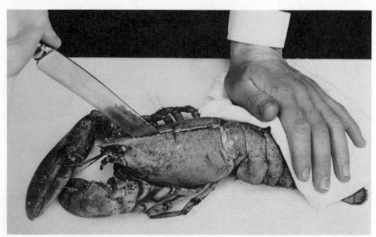

(b)

Lobster Américaine This well-known dish is made by cutting a live lobster into sections and cooking it with butter, garlic, tomato and shallot in brandy, white wine and fish stock. The pieces of lobster are served in a silver timbale, coated with sauce and decorated with the tip of the head and tails; a timbale of pilaff rice is served with it and the waiter should arrange it in a circle on the plate and spoon the pieces of lobster and sauce into the centre.

Lobster Newburg This is slices of cooked lobster reheated in butter with marsala or Madeira wine and covered with cream which is

Fig 9.19 *service of cold lobster*

thickened as a sauce with egg yolks and to which brandy may be added. It is usually served in a silver timbale accompanied with a dish of rice pilaff.

There are dozens of ways of serving hot lobster, many of them being done in the half shell which the waiter must lift onto the plate in front of the customer, using two large forks.

Crayfish

Crayfish are fresh-water crustaceans which, like lobsters, turn from dark blue to red when cooked. They are often served à la Nage, allowing six or more per portion, according to their size. Service is in a timbale containing some of the cooking liquid and some of the crayfish may be arranged over-hanging the edge.

Crayfish (écrevisses) are found in rivers and are very small, weighing only up to 100g each. The chef has to decorticate each one before cooking. This means removing the intestinal tract from the middle phalanx of the tail with a knife or by twisting the central underflap and pulling it out whole. If this is not removed in its entirety the crayfish will have a bitter taste. It is usual for the chef to truss crayfish with the claws.

Confusion exists between the names *crawfish* and *crayfish* – the former is sometimes called a sea crayfish, a langouste, or a spiny lobster. It looks like a large lobster but is pale pink and white in colour and is usually featured as a cold buffet presentation dish, with the flesh cut into round slices and coated with jellied mayonnaise.

Scampi

Scampi are known as Dublin Bay Prawns or langoustines and are similar in size to crayfish but pale orange-white in colour. The shelled tails are coated in breadcrumb, deep-fried and served in a pile with lemon, fried parsley and tartare sauce. They can be shallow-fried à la meunière or à la provençale, when they are presented in an earthenware dish for the waiter to serve onto the hot fish-plate; occasionally they are served cold in the shells for the customer to remove.

Crab

Crab is usually served cold as an hors-d'oeuvre or as a fish course. Dressed crab is presented in the cleaned shell, the flaked white flesh kept apart from the softer dark meat and garnished with sieved yolk and white of hard-boiled egg and chopped parsley, or spoonfuls of both kinds of meat can be arranged on lettuce leaves and garnished with quarters of hard-boiled egg and peeled tomatoes. Mayonnaise is served at the side of the plate.

Crab is also served as a hot dish, often in scallop shells, coated with a sauce and gratinated. The waiter must transfer the scallop shell from the serving dish onto the plate, using a service spoon and fork.

Scallops

Scallops are removed from their shells, poached, sliced and replaced in the deep shell which has been piped around with potato; the fish is coated with sauce and glazed to a gold brown colour. By placing the shell on a plate lined with a d'oyley there is less chance of the shell tipping over or sliding around. As shown in Figure 9.20 the customer is given a fish knife and fork, but usually only the fork is used, in the right hand, the other being required to hold the shell steady. There may however, be some large pieces of scallop in it that need to be cut

Fig 9.20 *service of scallops*

up to be eaten. Scallops may also be shallow-fried and served with rashers of bacon as a breakfast dish or for a luncheon entrée.

Mussels

Mussels are often served in the half shell, coated with sauce made from the cooking liquid thickened with beurre manié or cream. Large ones may be served in a soup plate, as shown in Figure 9.21 placed on an under-plate. The customer may prefer to pick up the half shells and eat the mussels directly which means that an additional table napkin, a finger bowl, and a plate for the empty shells must be provided. A plateful of thinly sliced brown bread and butter, or hot garlic-flavoured French bread should be offered.

Oysters

Oysters are usually served cold as an hors-d'oeuvre but may be poached and served in scallop shells as in Huîtres Florentine when they are placed on a bed of buttered leaf spinach and coated with mornay sauce and gratinated with grated cheese. The waiter transfers

Fig 9.21 *service of mussels*

the shell to the customer's plate by means of the serving-spoon and fork and the customer eats with a fish fork and dessert spoon. The customer needs his left hand free to prevent the shell toppling over.

Brochettes of fish and shellfish are prepared by impaling pieces of white fish, scampi, mussels, oysters, etc. on a skewer, with mushrooms, bacon, pimento and bay leaves. It is grilled and served on a bed of rice pilaff and the waiter transfers the brochette to the plate then withdraws the skewer by pulling it with the prongs of a fork, meanwhile holding the contents in place with a spoon or second fork. A sauce such as sauce diable or béarnaise may be served, pouring over or spooning it at the side.

Vol-au-vents of fish and shellfish are puff-pastry cases filled with hot pieces of the chosen fish, mixed with fish sauce, mushrooms, truffle, etc. An individual vol-au-vent is served by holding it between a serving-spoon and fork, turned inwards so as to grip it fairly firmly. A large vol-au-vent is cut into portions and extra filling from a silver timbale is added onto the plate. A fish knife and fork are used.

Bouillabaisse is a stew of pieces of fish and shellfish some of which can be left in the shell. There is plenty of cooking liquid and it is usual first to ladle this into the soup plate over slices of French bread and when the customer has eaten this, to serve a mixture of the various kinds of fish and more liquid, into the same or a clean soup plate. The customer requires a soup spoon and fish knife and fork; more French bread may be offered.

There are several other kinds of fish stew including *Bourride*, *Blanquette*, *Chaudrée*, *Cotriade*, *Matelote*, *Meurette*, *Potée* and *Waterzoi*; these are distinguished by the kinds of fish and the flavourings used.

Wines that are suitable to serve with shellfish include champagne, Alsace Riesling, Chablis, Muscadet, Moselle, Verdicchio, Condrieu, Vouvray and Chiaretto del Garda. Those with a rich sauce require a richer wine such as Tokay d'Alsace or Monbazillac.

9.7 HOT HORS-D'OEUVRE

Although they are called hors-d'oeuvre, the items that constitute a hot hors-d'oeuvre selection are so much more substantial than those normally associated with this course that they are not served as a first course, but later in the meal, either in the place of the farinaceous dish, or as a light entrée or main course. For this reason they are included here.

Each item of a hot hors-d'oeuvre selection is fairly light and delicate on its own but as a wide variety is offered, and all are so appetising, the end result can be a meal in itself, especially since pastry figures largely in the selection. Amongst the following list there are many of Russian origin as served in the homes and hotels of Czarist Russia. The best known include:

Allumettes – puff-pastry fingers filled with fish or chicken forcemeat
Attereaux – very small skewers of items of fish, meat and vegetables, dipped into a sauce, egg and crumbed and deep-fried
Barquettes – oval pastry cases filled with various mixtures of fish or meat
Beignets – deep-fried fritters of pieces of fish, meat, etc., or of chou pastry

Bouchées – small vol-au-vents with various fillings in a sauce

Cromesquis – croquette mixtures wrapped in caul or a pancake, dipped in batter and deep-fried

Cutlets – small shallow-fried cutlet-shapes of fish or meat mixtures

Croquettes – dice of fish, meat, etc., bound with sauce then moulded into cork-shapes and deep-fried

Croûtes – hollowed-out pieces of fried bread filled with mixtures such as brains, livers, bone marrow, etc.

Fondants – croquette mixtures moulded into pear-shapes, egg and crumbed and deep-fried

Huîtres Villeroy – poached oysters dipped into Villeroy sauce, crumbed and deep-fried

Nalesnikis – cottage cheese and egg mixture wrapped in pancakes, dipped into batter and deep-fried

Pâtés – small puff-pastry patties filled with fish or meat mixture

Piroguis – crescent-shapes of cheese, fish, meat or vegetable mixtures; shallow- or deep-fried, or baked

Quichelettes – tartlet cases filled with savoury egg and cream custard containing grated cheese, lardons of bacon, ham, mushrooms, etc.

Ramequins – cheese-flavoured chou buns, or cheese-flavoured egg-custard tartlets

Rissoles – puff-pastry turnovers of mixtures of fish, poultry, game, meat, etc., deep fried

Soufflés – small soufflés of vegetables, ham, oysters, cheese, etc.

Subrics – batter flavoured with foie gras, brains, cheese, spinach, etc.; shallow-fried in spoonfuls

Tartlets – filled with cheese, egg, fish, meat or vegetable mixtures bound with sauce

Timbales – dariole moulds of forcemeat filled with salpicons of fish, meat, game, etc., poached, demoulded and served with a sauce

Varenikis – raviolis with cheese, fish or meat filling

Vatrouskis – brioche pastry patties filled with cream cheese mixture

Visniskis – brioche pastry patties filled with fish mixtures

If the hot hors-d'oeuvre are displayed in the restaurant the customer may go to the buffet and help himself; if served from the kitchen the waiter will be given a trayful from which the customer may choose those he fancies, which will be transferred to a hot plate in front of him.

QUESTIONS

1. Describe the service procedures for (a) Petite Marmite, (b) Consommé, (c) Clear Turtle Soup.

2. Suggest wines that are suitable for drinking with soup.

3. Describe the service of eggs in cocotte.

4. Say why it is considered correct to cut off the ends of an omelette.

5. State the differences between the service of long as against short pastas.

SERVICE OF POULTRY, GAME AND MEAT DISHES

10.1 INTRODUCTION

This chapter deals with the service of all the main meat courses and it includes many of the most popular table d'hôte dishes as well as those that come under the heading of à la carte. Table d'hôte foods are those that have been prepared in advance for a particular meal and can be served immediately, whereas à la carte dishes are cooked to order. Some à la carte dishes are prepared or finished at the table in front of the customer, often with the use of the spirit lamp, so it is important for the waiter to assemble all the ingredients and equipment required to serve the dish correctly and quickly. In some cases carving is done by the waiter as in cutting a grilled chateaubriand into two or three portions, dividing a whole roast chicken or duck, or a best end of lamb. Or it may be the complete cooking of a piece of meat or fish and its accompanying sauce; this is known as lamp work or guéridon service as described in Chapter 12.

10.2 ENTREES AND RELEVES

The commonplace word for the main course of an ordinary meal is entrée, a term that was used to denote the first course of a full meal at the time when a repast consisted of only two courses – the *entrée* and the *remove* or *relevé* – both of which consisted of several dishes. Nowadays the two words are used only on a banquet menu or where there are two meat courses, the entrée being a fairly light item of meat without any garnish and the relevé being a more substantial piece of meat with a garnish and accompanied with vegetables.

Typical luncheon entrée dishes include the offals, braised steaks, vols-au-vent, shallow-fried breadcrumbed cutlets and small escalopes, stews and hot-pots, and the rechauffé dishes; typical entrées for dinner include tournedos, suprêmes, escalopes, sweetbreads and the various small cuts.

Relevés include pot-roasted and braised joints of beef, veal and lamb, whole game birds, whole poultry, and joints of venison; these would be cooked and served with an appropriate garnish.

The forgoing paragraphs show that there are a number of distinctions between dishes that are suitable for serving at lunch and those that are more suitable for dinner; they also demonstrate that the relevé is not usually served at lunch-time. In the logical sequence of a menu, white meat such as veal and poultry should be served before a red meat such as beef or game, because of the strong distinction between the flavour and texture of each.

10.3   CARVING AND SERVICE OF POULTRY

There are occasions when it is appropriate to carve a whole item of poultry in the restaurant; this is because it looks larger and better than the same cut portions served flat in a dish. A customer can derive much pleasure at the sight of the whole bird and its garniture, whether pot-roasted, plainly roasted or boiled.

(a)   Chicken

To carve a four-portion chicken into fair and even-size portions, first present it to the customer then lift it by means of a table fork and drain any cooking liquid from inside; place it on its side on a plate, then with a sharp table knife cut the leg away from the carcase, holding it with the fork as shown in Figure 10.1(a); remove it completely by pulling with the fork as shown in Figure 10.1(b). Cut the leg into two pieces through the centre bone as shown in Figure 10.1(c) place it on another plate and remove and cut the other leg. Next stand the bird upright and cut halfway along the breast down through the wing joint; pull it away and cut the piece of breast on the other side of the bird. Now cut along each side of the breastbone and cut off the two remaining sections; this is shown in Figure 10.1(d)(e) and (f). The pieces are then portioned as the drumstick and outer breast piece, and the thigh and inner breast piece.

The usual garnish for roast chicken consists of gravy and bread sauce, served in sauceboats; game chips and watercress on the dish with the bird, and sometimes grilled bacon rolls and chipolatas.

Fig 10.1 *carving a roast chicken*

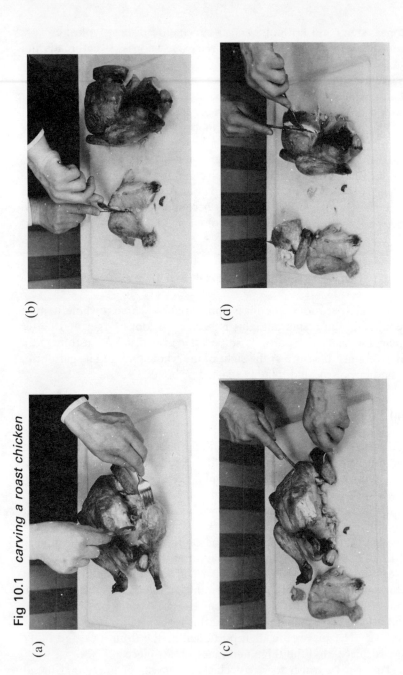

(a)

(b)

(c)

(d)

Chicken en cocotte or *en casserole* is pot-roasted and served with a thick sauce and a garnish; it is removed from the pot and carved as for roast chicken. A grilled chicken is carved by severing the two legs from the body and dividing them in two pieces through the joint; the breast is cut into four pieces and the portions are served as the drumstick and outer breast piece, and thigh and inner breast piece. Accompaniments are grilled tomato, mushroom, streaky bacon rasher, straw potatoes and watercress. For a grilled devilled chicken the bird will have been spread with mustard and dipped in bread-crumbs before grilling; hot sauce diable is served.

A spatchcocked chicken or *poussin* is cut open to represent a crouching frog; it is grilled and can be decorated with eyes made from slices of hard boiled egg, beetroot or truffle.
A *poussin* is a baby chicken, the smallest being served whole for the customer to tackle, the slightly larger ones being cut in half to give two portions. They are served in the same way as chicken, sometimes being filled with a breadcrumb-based stuffing. A popular way of serving roast poussin is Poussin à la Polonaise in which the cooked bird is covered with fried breadcrumbs, sieved hard-boiled egg, and chopped parsley.

Suitable wines are white, rosé and red such as Montrachet, Saint Peray, Montefalco d'Assisi, Rosé d'Anjou, a Hock, or a Moselle; these are served at 8–10°C. It is in order to suggest a good red wine with roast chicken.

(b) Duck

To carve a pot-roasted or roast duck in view of the customer, follow the same procedure as for roast chicken except that as the breast is flat and not very well fleshed it is usually only possible to cut two portions, one on each side of the breast.

The garnish for roast duck consists of gravy, apple sauce, and sage and onion stuffing, served in sauceboats, and game chips and watercress on the dish with the duck. A pot-roasted duck is usually served as *Caneton à l'Orange* or *Caneton aux Cerises* in which the cooking liquid is made into a sour-sweet sauce, poured over the portions of duck and its garnish of orange segments or stoned cherries.

Duck is classed as dark meat so a rich red wine such as Côtes du Rhône, Pomerol or St Emilion is to be recommended; a rich white such as an Alsace wine is equally good.

Wild duck is a game bird and will be found in that section. A goose or gosling is carved in the same way as turkey but the breast meat is much shallower.

(c) Guinea-fowl

This bird is nearly as big as an average ordinary chicken but thinner and the flesh is slightly darker and fairly dry; for this reason a guinea-fowl is often pot-roasted and served with a thick sauce and appropriate garnish. Whichever way it has been cooked, the bird is always carved in the same way as a chicken. Roast guinea-fowl is served with roast gravy, bread sauce, game chips and watercress. It is usual to serve a red wine with guinea-fowl – a Château Margaux, St Estèphe, Bardolino, or Pauillac.

(d) Turkey

A whole roast turkey is almost an essential item of Christmas fare as often served from a carving trolley; a portion consists of thin slices of breast and leg meat, a grilled chipolata sausage, chestnut stuffing, roast gravy and bread sauce. Cranberry sauce is popular and sometimes a slice of boiled ham is served with roast turkey. Suitable vegetables are Brussels sprouts, braised celery, broccoli, and roast or fondante potatoes. It requires great skill on the part of the person who does the carving to obtain the maximum number of portions from the bird whilst serving neatly carved slices that represent a good portion. Most establishments do the carving in the kitchen.

Recommended wines include Pinot Blanc or Hock, in fact any dry or medium white; it is also permissible to suggest an old claret or burgundy with roast turkey.

(e) Stews of poultry

Several different kinds of stew are made from chicken, the most popular being the sautés in which cut raw chicken is shallow-fried in butter then finished cooking in a minimum of brown or white sauce and served with a garnish. *Fricassée* is the best-known white stew of chicken, the usual garnish being button mushrooms and onions. Heart-shaped fried-bread croûtons are frequently added as part of the garnish.

When serving several customers from one dish the waiter must ensure that each is served fairly by pairing the winglet piece of the breast with the drumstick and the thigh with the strip of white from the inner breast. It would be wrong to serve all leg-meat to one person while another receives two pieces of breast. Just sufficient sauce to mask the pieces of chicken is spooned over, together with the right amount of garnish.

Curried chicken is a stew of pieces of chicken, some of which may contain bone, it is served in the same way as all curries by forming a circle of plain boiled rice in a soup plate and arranging the pieces of chicken coated with the sauce, inside it. Accompaniments of a grilled Bombay duck and a poppadum are served onto the side-plate, then the tray of small side dishes known as sambals such as mango chutney, sliced banana, chopped apple and desiccated coconut, etc., is offered, a teaspoonful of each being scattered over the chicken or at the side of the plate.

Capilotade is a brown stew made with pieces of ready-cooked chicken together with mushrooms and onions and is served onto the plate by means of serving-spoon and fork. *Chicken à la King* consists of slices of cooked breast of chicken reheated in butter together with sliced mushroom and strips of green and red pimento; it is flavoured with sherry and bound with chicken sauce, egg yolk and cream, and served in a dish with triangles of toast or with a separate dish of pilaff of rice. Some establishments serve the chicken mixture on a round of toast and flash it under a salamander to glaze.

(f) Miscellaneous dishes

A suprême of chicken is the whole breast cut from one side of a chicken with only the wing-bone left attached. It can be cooked plainly in butter or shallow-fried after being covered with bread-crumbs; there are many classical garnishes for this popular item. *Suprême de Volaille sous Cloche* is the breast cooked with mushrooms in cream, in a special dish that is covered with a bell-shaped glass which gets steamed up during the cooking. The whole thing is placed in front of the customer, on a plate, and the cover removed so that the aroma assails the nostrils thus stimulating the taste buds.

A breast of chicken cooked by stuffing with a hard piece of savoury butter and deep frying, is called *Suprême de Volaille à la Kiev*; it is served plainly with a frill on the end of the bone.

Shallow-fried suprêmes usually have the wing-bone covered with a paper cutlet frill which should be left on when serving it, the idea being that the customer may pick it up to chew any meat left around the bone.

A vol-au-vent is often served as a luncheon dish, either as an 8 cm diameter individual vol-au-vent or a larger one for two to three people. The filling consists of diced cooked chicken, button mushrooms and sometimes diced sweetbread, mixed with chicken sauce. An individual vol-au-vent is served as it is, lifting it between an inverted serving-spoon and fork, and the larger one has to be cut into portions with a sharp knife and transferred to the plates, adding the chicken mixture plus some of the extra that is usually supplied. It is not necessary to serve the sprigs of parsley.

The only item of poultry offal in wide use is the liver which is usually served in the form of a brochette or as a pilaff in a mound of braised rice.

10.4   CARVING AND SERVICE OF GAME BIRDS

Game birds are only available at certain times of the year, as shown in Appendix 2. The flesh is dark and tends to be dry but with careful cooking can be very tasty and succulent and have a wonderful aroma. All young roast game birds are served on a croûton of fried bread spread with a paste made from its liver, cooked with bacon, onion and herbs; game chips, watercress, a sauceboat of roast gravy and one of fried breadcrumbs are the traditional accompaniments. Older birds which are inclined to be tough are usually cooked by braising.

(a)   Grouse

This is the most expensive kind of game bird and is the one with the shortest season. It is usually served whole for one portion but a slightly larger one may be cut in half for two portions. It is the practice to cook it underdone, either plainly roasted or the breasts only, lightly sautéd. The legs tend to be tough and can be kept for use in a *Salmis* which is a game stew which takes its name from the main item, e.g. Salmis de Grouse. Some chefs dress a roast grouse with sprigs of purple or white heather but this should not of course, be transferred to the plate.

(b)   Partridge

This small, one-portion bird is served whole, plainly roasted, or the two breasts are removed, lightly sautéd and garnished with, e.g. grapes, olives, apple, etc., and a sauce made from the bones.

(c) Pheasant

This is the most popular of all the game birds and can be cut into four portions though some are only big enough for two. In a book published as long ago as 1612, the author of *The Haven of Health* said 'fesaint exceedeth alle foulees in sweetnesse and wholesomenesse – it is meat for princes and great estates' and this high esteem has persisted unto the present age.

Pheasant can be cooked in several ways but is most popular when plainly roasted, served on a large fried croûton of bread spread with a paste made from the liver, with game chips, watercress, fried breadcrumbs, roast gravy, bread sauce and often the piece of fat bacon which is usually tied across the breast to prevent it drying out. Pheasant can be carved in the same way as for chicken but a fairly big one can be sliced in the same way as a turkey.

When pot-roasted, a pheasant may be stuffed with foie gras, rice, truffle, or a forcemeat, which should be served with the pieces of bird and covered with the sauce.

A *suprême* of pheasant is a breast cut from one side of a plump bird, without skin or bone; it is cooked in butter and may be served with chestnuts, chestnut purée or other nuts, an exotic fruit, celery, asparagus, etc.

Only the finest red wine should be recommended for drinking with pheasant, partridge or grouse and a very expensive château-bottled claret or a superb Burgundy such as Chambertin or Aloxe-Corton is absolutely appropriate; it should be served at 17°C.

(d) Wild duck

A wild duck is prepared differently from an Aylesbury duck and is often given à la carte treatment in a duck press in front of the customer. *Canard Sauvage à la Presse* is the epitome of guéridon work and the full recipe will be found in section 12.4; it is the dish that made the Parisian restaurant, Le Tour d'Argent, world famous. There every duck bears a numbered label which is given to the customer as proof of his patronage.

Wild duck is also served plainly roasted with the same accompaniments as for all game birds and can be carved into joints, but is more usually cut into very thin slices called aiguillettes.

(e) Other game birds

The *quail* is now bred in captivity which means that it is not subject to the seasons as are other game birds. It can be served roasted but is more usually pot-roasted and served with garnishes such as cherries, grapes, quinces, chestnut purée, rice, foie gras, or pineapple.

The quail is a small bird and is served whole either on the bone or boned and stuffed; it is sometimes finished to cook inside a pastry case, thus it is always served whole.

The other birds are also small, the smallest being the snipe which is often finished by the waiter in front of the customer. The recipes for this and for woodcock are given in Section 12.3. The other birds that are sometimes featured on menus are the *teal* which is a small wild duck and the *pigeon* which does not have a season and is quite plentiful and is therefore not a true game bird.

A young pigeon is sufficient for one portion, the flesh is dark but fairly bland and it can be cooked by roasting, grilling, shallow-frying or pot-roasting, with a garnish such as crayfish, cèpes, mushrooms, chestnuts, peas, or cabbage.

A *salmis* is a quick stew made of cooked pieces of game bird with mushrooms and truffle; the meat is reheated in brandy then covered with a rich sauce made from the trimmings and bones of the carcase, white or red wine and brown sauce.

10.5 SERVICE OF GAME ANIMALS

Furred game includes *venison* which is the flesh of the various species of deer, and *hare*. Rabbit is not game but is usually included under this heading.

Venison

A large joint of roebuck which is the kind of deer in general use, would be the saddle or leg, the latter also being known as a haunch. It is usual to hang the joint to mature then to marinade it in red wine with aromatic flavourings so as to make it tender and give additional flavour. It is usually roasted and served with sauce made with the marinade and a garnish such as spiced pears, apples or braised chestnuts. The carving is done in the same way as a leg or saddle of lamb as described in section 10.7

Steaks and cutlets of venison are also served but because of the lack of fat in the animal it is the practice to shallow-fry quickly rather than to grill, and to serve with a rich sauce and garnish such as cherries, chestnuts, cucumber, orange and mushrooms.

Hare

Hare is often served in the form of a rich brown stew known as a *civet*; in fact that is the name given to all stews made with pieces of furred game. Jugged hare is the equivalent of *Civet de Lièvre* and is served accompanied with a sauceboat of redcurrant jelly.

The French name for a saddle of hare is *Râble de Lièvre* and consists of the back and middle part of the animal in one piece, larded, marinated and roasted. It is served with a rich sauce made from the marinade, and a garnish such as cherries, chestnuts, orange segments, etc. If it is large enough for two portions the waiter will carve it into very thin slices parallel with the backbone. Redcurrant jelly or a sauce of grated horseradish mixed with redcurrant jelly is served separately.

Furred game requires a full-bodied red wine such as a vintage claret, a Côtes du Rhône, or Bull's Blood from Hungary, served at 17°C.

Game birds are often served cold with a composed salad and both feathered and furred game are often made into a hot or cold game pie or a game pâté.

10.6 SERVICE OF BEEF DISHES

Large joints of beef including the wing rib, sirloin, fillet and baron (a 'Baron of Beef' consists of the two sirloins in one piece on the bone), are often carved in the restaurant by the trancheur, using a heated carving-trolley which he takes to the table to serve each customer with his requirements. Figure 10.2 shows the way to carve a roast contrefilet (boned sirloin) of beef. These joints can be either roasted, boiled, braised or pot-roasted, served with the requisite gravy or sauce, a suitable garnish and the normal accompaniments.

If the meat is carved by the chef in the kitchen it is dressed on a silver or earthenware dish and the waiter should transfer the portion onto the plate using a serving-spoon and fork, arranging the slices of meat overlapping at the top right-hand side of the plate. The silver dish will have been brought from the kitchen with a lid on top which should be removed and placed upside down on the sideboard and the dish taken to the table by means of a folded waiter's cloth. The dish must be balanced evenly over the left forearm and hand as shown in

Fig 10.2 *carving a boned sirloin (contrefilet)*

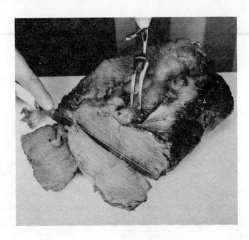

Figure 10.3. The dish should be held flat over the edge of the plate and the meat and its garnish is transferred neatly onto the plate as shown in Figure 10.3(b), then the vegetables are brought from the hot-plate and served in the same way, and finally the hot gravy or sauce and any other accompaniment such as horseradish sauce, is ladled around rather than over the meat. The service must be carried out assiduously to avoid any chance of the food getting cold. Roast beef in the English style is served with a portion of Yorkshire pudding, roast gravy, watercress, and a sauceboat of cold horseradish sauce or grated horseradish. Boiled salt beef is served with trimmed carrots, turnips, leek, onion and celery and some of the cooking liquid; a boiled suet dumpling is a traditionally British garnish. Boiled beef in the French style is also served with a boiled vegetable garnish plus a cold vinaigrette-based sauce, coarse salt and a dish of small gherkins. Braised and pot-roasted joints of beef are served with some of the name garnish and the thick sauce.

A whole fillet of beef cooked *à la Wellington*, inside a coating of duxelles and a covering of pastry, is served cut into approximately slices 1 cm wide.

The small cuts of beef are also suitable for shallow-frying, particularly the entrecôte steaks and there are several classical sauces and garnishes that are very appropriate for these items. Some can be cooked in the room and details of these flambé dishes are included in section 12.3.

Fig 10.3 *the service of sliced meat*

(a)

(b)

Grilled meats

When taking the order for a grilled item of beef it is essential to ask the customer how he wishes it to be done, to note this on the check and ensure it is understood by the grill-cook. Some customers like their meat grilled very rare (*saignant* or *au bleu*), others like it cooked medium rare (*à point*), while others request it to be well done (*bien cuit*).

The cuts of beef suitable for grilling and sautéing are:

1. sirloin steak (entrecôte) which can be had as ordinary, double thickness (entrecôte double) or flattened very thinly (entrecôte minute);
2. pieces cut from the fillet of beef are (a) chateaubriand, for two or more portions, cut from the thick part, (b) fillet steak, a 200 g (7 oz) slice cut from the thickest part, (c) tournedos, a round piece from the middle part, (d) fillet mignon, a flattened piece from the thin end of the fillet;
3. a rump-steak, cut $1\frac{1}{2}$ to 2 cm thick, or à point steak, a fairly thick slice from the corner part of the rump – both these are usually served with a grilled slice of the suet fat;
4. T-bone steak and porterhouse steaks – these are cut from an unboned sirloin, the latter including a part of the fillet.

The garnish for grilled beef consists of straw potatoes, watercress and beurre maître d'hôtel, that is, parsley and lemon butter; the accompaniments are a variety of mustards including English, several varieties of French, and German, served by the waiter with a small bone spoon onto the side of the plate. Sometimes a grilled steak may be accompanied with a warm sauce such as Sauce Béarnaise.

Roast and grilled beef require a fine quality red wine such as Nuits St Georges, Pommard, Côte de Beaune or Romanée-Conti from Burgundy, or Brunello di Montalcino from Italy, all served at room temperature of 17°C.

The stews of beef include *Carbonnade de Boeuf Flamande* which is made with beer; *Currie de Boeuf* served with plain boiled rice, popadums, Bombay ducks and sambals; *Goulash de Boeuf* which is usually served garnished with small chou paste dumplings called gnocchi; *Ragoût de Boeuf* which is a rich brown stew cooked slowly with a vegetable garnish; *Sauté de Boeuf Strogonoff* which is a quickly-made stew of strips of the tail end of fillet flavoured with lemon juice and cream, and *Estouffade* which is a red wine stew, garnished with button mushrooms and onions.

The offals of beef include kidney, oxtail and tripe which can also be made in the form of a stew. Stews are particularly suitable for service as lunch entrées and they may be eaten with a spoon and fork from a deep plate, but are more usually apportioned into shallow individual cocottes from which they can be directly consumed, the accompanying vegetable and potato being served onto a side-plate at the right-hand side.

Steak and kidney pie, and steak, kidney and mushroom pudding are usually presented whole in the dish they were cooked in, the pie with a frill around it, the pudding surrounded with a table napkin. A portion is cut out and spooned onto the plate.

10.7 SERVICE OF LAMB AND VEAL DISHES

The roasting joints of lamb and veal are the best end, shoulder, saddle and leg; it is possible to cut a baron from a carcase of lamb, keeping the two legs attached to the whole saddle as a single joint. The carving of a best end of lamb or veal is shown in Figure 10.4, each cutlet being cut separately then replaced on the serving dish with the garnish; the normal portion is two cutlets, each one being topped with a cutlet frill.

A *crown of lamb* is a pair of best ends turned inwards around a mould so as to take the form of a hollow crown. A whole cauliflower is placed inside when cooked; cutlet frills, stoned olives or cherries

Fig 10.4 *carving a best end*

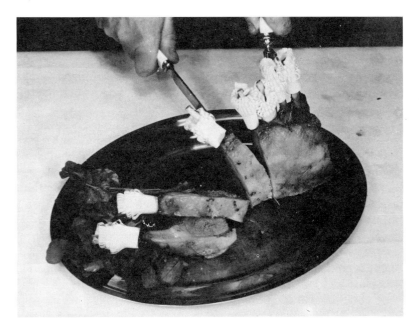

are placed on each bone and a glazed vegetable garnish around the edge of the dish. It is cut into cutlets and served with some of the garnish. A *Guard of Honour* is a pair of best ends set upright on the serving-dish with the bones interlocked.

To carve a *saddle of lamb* or *veal* on the bone by the French method, cut slices each side of the backbone and parallel to it going down as far as the horizontal bones as shown in Figure 10.5; the chump end is then sliced in the opposite direction. The two fillets found underneath should be removed whole then cut into small round slices on the slant. The carving for a saddle in the english style is shown in Figure 10.5(b), where the meat is cut against the grain. A boned and rolled saddle is cut in the opposite direction as shown in Figure 10.6.

To carve a leg of lamb or mutton, start at the knuckle then as the slices become larger, cut smaller ones from each side, as shown in Figure 10.7. It is usual to bone, roll and tie a shoulder before cooking as otherwise the bone structure prevents ease of carving.

The accompaniments for roast lamb are roast gravy, mint sauce and redcurrant jelly. The accompaniments for roast veal are thickened gravy, slices of thyme and parsley stuffing and, sometimes, a slice of boiled ham.

Suitable wines for roast lamb are Beaujolais, a Médoc or Bardolino; for veal, either red or white wine may be served, including any of the popular brands of Liebfraumilch.

The grills of lamb and mutton which include mainly cutlets and chops are served garnished with straw potatoes and watercress, and maître d'hôtel butter may also be served, allowing one slice per cutlet. Other suitable garnishes include pommes soufflées, grilled mushrooms and tomatoes and one of the other flavoured butters. It is incorrect to serve mint sauce with grilled lamb.

A mixed grill consists of a lamb cutlet and kidney, a rasher of bacon, a sausage, mushroom and tomato, garnished with straw potatoes, watercress and parsley butter; these items should be arranged neatly on the plate and the various mustards offered.

Shallow-fried items of lamb and veal include breaded cutlets, escalopes and plain noisettes, rosettes and grenadins, the latter being a fairly thick round escalope; a médaillon de veau would be about 5 cm in diameter and $1\frac{1}{4}$ cm thick, allowing two per portion. *Escalopines* are small escalopes cut three or four per portion; the Italian name is *piccata* and recipes for these as a flambé dish are included in section 12.3.

A cutlet of veal can be served shallow-fried or grilled but possibly the most high-class way of serving one is as *Côte de Veau en Papillote*

Fig 10.5a   *method of carving a whole saddle French style along the meat grain*

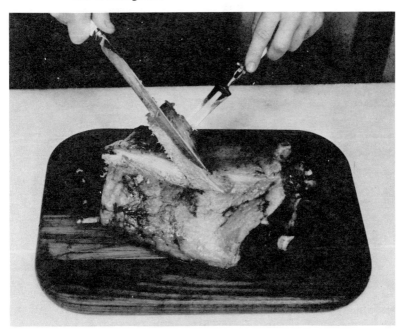

Fig 10.5b   *alternative method of carving a saddle English style against the meat grain*

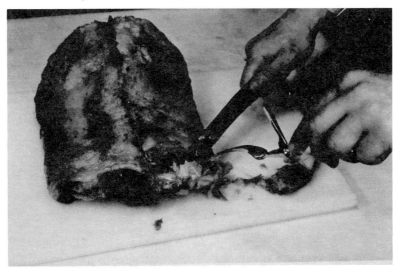

Fig 10.6 *carving a boned and rolled saddle*

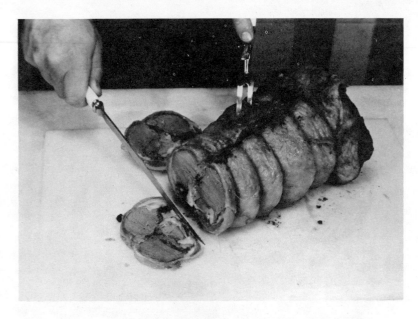

in which it is cooked in the oven inside a paper case which swells and colours with the heat. It should be presented to the customer and then pierced with a sharp knife and opened to allow the aroma to assail the customer's olfactory senses; the waiter then serves it onto the plate together with the duxelles sauce which is inside the case. The other popular item cooked in this way is a red mullet but it is possible to prepare many other one-portion foods *en papillotte*.

The stews made from lamb and veal are (a) white – blanquette; fricassée; Irish stew; (b) brown – curry; haricot which despite its name does not include any beans; cassoulet which does contain haricot beans; daube; sauté; navarin; pilaff which is a stew served with braised rice; and hotpot. Osso buco is a dish of stewed pieces of knuckle of veal.

Among the offals of lamb and veal are heart, liver, kidney, trotters, sweetbreads and calf's head. *Calf's head* can be served in several ways, the most popular being plain boiled with a piece of the brain and tongue and sauce vinaigrette, or as *Tête de Veau en Tortue* which is made in the form of a stew well-flavoured with herbs and spices. *Haggis* is made from lamb offals and is usually served according to certain rules of protocol on Burn's Night (25 January).

Offals and made-up dishes such as shepherd's pie, moussaka, cromesquis, crêpinettes, croquettes and rissoles are served only as

Fig 10.7   *carving a leg of lamb*

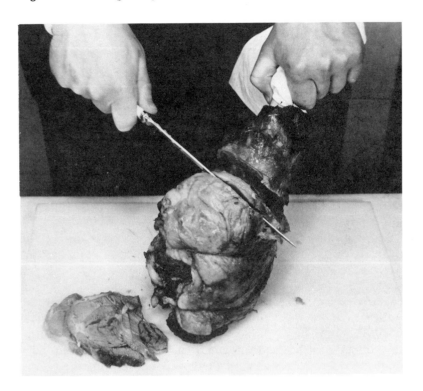

luncheon entrées, as are kebabs of lamb and brochettes of veal sweet-bread. A *pojarski* of veal is prepared from finely chopped veal, soaked breadcrumbs and cream, moulded cutlet-shape and shallow-fried; this is strictly a luncheon dish although small ones are some-times featured at fork-buffet meals.

10.8   SERVICE OF PORK AND HAM DISHES

The large joints are the loin and the leg which when cured becomes a ham or gammon; a whole sucking-pig is also featured occasionally. Roast pork is served with roast gravy, and a sauceboat each of apple sauce and sage and onion stuffing. A ham is boiled but may then be finished by braising or by being enveloped in pastry and baked; Madeira sauce and apples, peaches, pineapple, soubise, sauerkraut, pasta, and many classical garnishes are suitable.

The grilled cuts are pork chops and the trotters, the latter usually being boned and covered with breadcrumbs. The garnish for a grilled pork chop consists of straw potatoes, watercress and a brown sauce such as sauce diable, sauce Robert or sauce charcutière – apple sauce is not served. A grilled gammon-rasher is also served with watercress and straw potatoes but is also popular with a grilled ring of pineaple or half a peach, in which case one of the above sauces or Madeira sauce is served.

10.9   SERVICE OF NOUVELLE CUISINE DISHES

This is a method of service in which the cooked food is arranged on the plate by the chef who does it very artistically so as to set off the main ingredient to best advantage, together with its garnish and sauce. The sauce is sometimes marbled by contrasting two different-coloured sauces. The plate is usually an expensive one that will further enhance the aesthetic look and is covered with a silver dome-shape cloche or dish-cover. The waiter takes the plateful of food from the kitchen and puts it in front of the customer, then with a dramatic flourish he whips off the cover thus drawing the guests' attention to the picturesque presentation.

The effect of this form of service is to de-skill the role of the waiter and to relegate him to the status of a menial table-clearer but this is in accordance with the concept of nouvelle cuisine which is to eliminate all unnecessary and complicated procedures on both sides of the hotplate and to create a smoother, less muddlesome atmosphere so that the facilities of an establishment can be concentrated onto the service of a few dishes of the highest possible quality. It is considered unwise to try to serve too many customers at once and there is an upper limit to the number of covers that can be dealt with in a given period of time.

Many of the old classical traditions have been abolished and chefs have been encouraged to create new and exciting food combinations using exotic materials, yet the cooking methods must be simple and decided by the commodity itself and how the chef considers it is best handled. A similar simplistic approach is expected of the service staff.

The form of service derives from that of the middle-class stately Victorian household where the butler took each filled plate from the master at the head of the table and placed it in front of each member of the family in their order of precedence. He took pride in his job, was probably dressed for the part with knee-breaches, white gloves and the rest of an elaborate braided uniform; he did his work conscientiously and professionally, just as it has to be done today.

10.10 GUIDE TO SELECTION OF VEGETABLES AND POTATOES

Vegetables and potatoes are established as an integral part of the meal, the reason being that they perform a dual function in man's diet:

1. they provide a nutritional balance by contributing much roughage and vitamins to the diet;
2. they make a gastronomic contribution to the meal experience by adding variety and contrast to the food offerings.

Therefore the food service worker must be in the position to provide the correct advice to customers who may seek his advice when making a choice, particularly for à la carte menus. Note that in classical menus root vegetables are not served for dinner.

Principles of potatoes and vegetable combinations with main courses, in conventional menus

In general, the guiding principles in selecting vegetable and potato combinations are that they should provide contrast, variety, harmony and suitability to the senses involved in food appreciation, as described in Chapter 2.

In consequence, when advising customers on their choice, colour, texture, flavour and temperature must be considered. Another important consideration must be function — a cream potato is ideal for serving with a dish containing a tasty sauce, whilst it would be wrong if served with a grilled dish, unless specifically requested by the customer. The following may be taken as examples of good combinations, by providing a balance which has a purpose and meets a need:

Poached salmon, hot – new boiled potatoes, fresh garden peas, and cucumber salad
Comments – clearly the plain boiled potatoes are required to be taken in conjunction with this dish which is flavoursome and delicate. Equally the peas form an excellent colour contrast and add seasonality to the dish. The cucumber salad – ideally with curly lettuce – will add crispness to an otherwise soft combination.

Roast lamb – buttered French beans, glazed carrots and roast potatoes
Comments – The green French beans and orange carrots will provide an excellent colour contrast and freshness to the meal. Roast potatoes are flavoursome and they are not required to absorb any sauce.

Grilled fillet steak – asparagus spears with some Hollandaise sauce, and chipped potatoes
Comments – A delicate vegetable which adds elegance to the steak, and appropriately fried potatoes which give a crisp texture.

Duckling with orange sauce – broccoli in butter and potato croquettes
Comments – In this dish the broccoli adds colour and freshness, whilst the croquette potatoes can be used effectively to absorb the sauce and give a crunchy texture.

Mixed grill – sautéed mushrooms, stuffed tomatoes and French-fried potatoes
Comments – The distinctive flavour of mushrooms and tomatoes add

to the mixture of flavours in the dish. The fried potatoes are ideal with this dish, which is frequently taken in order to achieve a high-calorie meal.

10.11 SERVING OF SALADS

Salads are used in several ways in a meal and can be classified as

(a) the made-up kind usually served as part of an hors-d'oeuvre selection, as shown in Chapter 8;
(b) a single hors-d'oeuvre served on its own as a first course, e.g., fish salad or chicken mayonnaise;
(c) a main-course such as ham salad or chicken salad, dressed with mayonnaise;
(d) a vegetarian dish;
(e) a warm salad consisting of the usual salad vegetables sprinkled with hot fried-bread croûtons or pieces of bacon and a hot vinegar dressing;
(f) the side salads served as an accompaniment to grilled or roast meats – the ones dealt with below

Salads are also classified as being either simple or composed, *simple* implying just a quarter of lettuce or a plain mixture of salad greens with tomato, cucumber, etc., whereas *composed* salads combine more complex ingredients in a dressing with only a few salad leaves to garnish them.

There are hundreds of different formulas for making salads the most popular ones being listed below. They are prepared by the larder cook, in a salad bowl or crescent-shape salad dish, dressed and served with either a sauceboat of vinaigrette salad dressing which is often described as *French dressing*, cream mixed with lemon juice and seasonings, or mayonnaise. Brillat-Savarin, author of *The Physiology of Taste*, tells the story of a Frenchman who made a fortune out of dressing salads in the homes of the rich in London, taking his case of ingredients from house to house, dressing the salads with various flavours of vinegar and oil, soya sauce, ketchup, meat essence, caviar, truffle and anchovies, before going on by carriage to the next place. Head waiters often like to dress a salad for a special customer, possibly starting by rubbing the salad bowl with crushed garlic, adding salt, pepper, French or English mustard, vinegar, oil, and chopped fresh herbs, etc., then the crisp leaves of salad, turning it over and over to create a harmonious result. Other ingredients used

Table 10.1 *a selection of salads with appropriate dressings*

Name	Ingredients	Dressing
Aîda	julienne of raw artichoke bottoms, hard-boiled egg white, green pimento and chicory; sliced tomatoes around the dish	mustard-flavoured vinaigrette
Alice	a hollowed-out apple filled with small balls of apple, redcurrants and walnuts	acidulated cream
Beaucaire	julienne of apple, celeriac, celery, chicken, ham, and mushroom, mixed together, with rings of beetroot and potato around	mayonnaise
Bean sprout	bean sprouts, celery, green pimento, water chestnuts, almonds and pineapple, cut up and mixed	vinaigrette
Caesar	cos lettuce with diced anchovy, Parmesan and fried croûtons of bread on top	raw egg yolk, lemon and oil
Coleslaw	shredded white cabbage, carrot and onion; pineapple, dried fruit, nuts, apple, etc. may be added	mayonnaise
Delmonico	mixed diced apple and celeriac	mayonnaise
Demidoff	crescents of carrot, celeriac, turnip and truffle, mixed with chopped onion	vinaigrette
Eve	diced apple, banana, pineapple and fresh walnuts, served in a hollowed-out apple	acidulated cream
Française	hearts of lettuce, sprinkled with chopped chervil, tarragon and parsley	vinaigrette

Italienne	diced carrot, turnip and salami, peas, diamonds of French beans and chopped anchovy	mayonnaise
Japonaise	orange segments, dice of tomato and pieces of pineapple	acidulated cream
Lorette	julienne of beetroot and celery on lamb's lettuce	vinaigrette
Manon	segments of grapefruit on lettuce leaves	sweetened vinaigrette
Margaret	dice of cucumber, potato, tomato and prawns, tossed together and placed on lettuce	mayonnaise
Mascotte	separate bunches of asparagus, crayfish, quarters of gull's eggs and cockscombs	mustard cream
Mignon	dice of cooked artichoke bottom and shrimps with slices of truffle on top	creamy mayonnaise
Mikado	poached oysters, diced red and green pimento and boiled rice, all tossed together	mustard vinaigrette
Mimosa	seeded grapes, orange segments, sliced banana sprinkled with sieved yolk of hard-boiled egg, on leaves of lettuce	acidulated cream
Niçoise	diced French beans, quarters of tomato, sliced potato; decorate with anchovy, capers and black olives	mayonnaise
Panachée	quarters of lettuce, sliced hard-boiled egg, beetroot and tomato, and any other salad vegetables	vinaigrette
Rachel	julienne of artichoke bottom, celery, potato and truffle, mixed gently together	mayonnaise

Name	Ingredients	Dressing
de Saison	any salads in season, with tomato, egg, cucumber, etc.	vinaigrette
Véronique	julienne of beetroot, celery and crisp lettuce; fried lardons of bacon and sliced hard-boiled egg, arranged neatly in a dish	vinaigrette
Waldorf	diced apple, celery and walnuts filled into a hollowed-out apple	acidulated cream
Windsor	julienne of celery, chicken, ox-tongue, raw mushrooms and truffle, mixed together and garnished with rampion	vinaigrette

in making a salad dressing are yoghurt, Rocquefort cheese, sugar, paprika, chives, gherkin, Worcester sauce, Tabasco, cider and brandy. *Thousand Island Dressing* consists of chopped red and green pimento, chives and hard-boiled egg added to vinaigrette. *Russian Dressing* consists of chopped onion, lemon juice, Worcester sauce and chilli vinegar mixed into yoghurt, *Green Goddess Dressing* is made of anchovy essence, chopped capers, gherkins, chives, garlic, onion and parsley, added to thin mayonnaise. Table 10.1 shows a selection of salads with appropriate dressings.

Too much dressing will spoil a salad and over-mixing it will bruise the crisp leaves and cause them to go soggy, which will detract from the customer's enjoyment. They should look dainty and be colourful when placed in a crescent salad dish at the top left-hand corner of the meat plate; if considered necessary lay a small fork across it.

QUESTIONS

1. List the main accompaniments for (a) the various items of poultry, and (b) roast game birds.
2. Give a list of six dishes that use game animals and state their composition and accompaniments.

3. Why is English mustard served and how should it be made? Compare French and English mustards.

SERVICE OF DESSERTS, FRUITS, SAVOURIES, CHEESE AND COFFEE

11.1 GENERAL RULES OF SERVICE

In the sequence of courses of a meal, the sweet course comes after the main dish but before the coffee which concludes a meal. It is only at a very long, formal meal that all these four courses of dessert, fruit, savoury and cheese would be served at one and the same repast. Usually a customer chooses only one or at most, two of them, and the coffee. It should be noted that coffee does not count as a course in its own right, not even when served with petits fours or after-dinner mints.

Some customers, especially those from France, prefer to have cheese before the sweet because to them it seems gastronomically incorrect to finish a savoury-tasting main course, then to have a sweet dish, then another savoury dish; they use the argument that a meal should end with a light sweet. It should also be borne in mind that most French cheeses are very mild. The French menu term for the sweet course can be either Les Desserts or Les Entremets. The English word 'dessert' comes from the French word '*desservir*' which means to clear the table, which is what has to be done before starting to serve the sweet. The term 'entremet' comes from the time when a full meal consisted of two main courses each composed of many disparate dishes; the second, which included the roast, also contained some sweet dishes and these acted as a breathing space between the heavy viandes, therefore the term 'between dishes' which is '*entre mets*' in French, was used to describe them.

11.2 SERVICE OF HOT SWEETS

If a table of two people choose one hot and one cold sweet the waiter must serve the cold sweet first and then the hot one, so as to avoid it getting cold while the cold sweet is served. Hot sweets must be served on hot dessert plates; cold sweets should be served on chilled plates or dishes. The following are examples of methods of serving sweets.

Apfelstrüdel, which is a Continental sweet made by wrapping chopped spiced apple in wafer-thin pastry, is cut into slices 4–5 cm wide, placed on a hot sweet plate and set in front of the customer; the hot custard sauce is ladled around rather than over, or, if whipped cream is served this is spooned on top and down the sides.

Apple Charlotte can be made in either individual or six-portion moulds. After being turned out, the large one has to be cut with a table knife, between the slices of bread, before serving the portion by means of a serving-spoon and fork, adding more apple from the centre to provide a reasonable portion. Custard or apricot sauce is served from a sauceboat with a small silver ladle or serving-spoon, ladling it around the charlotte.

A *baked apple* can be cooked plainly, or inside a pastry casing so it is necessary to grip it between the inverted serving spoon and fork but without such pressure as would squash it, then to lift it onto the plate. Custard sauce is served from a sauceboat.

Baked egg custard is often cooked in an individual pie-dish from which the customer can eat it by means of a dessertspoon and fork. If baked in a large pie-dish it is necessary to take several spoonfuls to make a portion, serving it carefully because of its fragile nature. There are several versions of this kind of pudding, including *Bordure Beau Rivage*, *Cabinet Pudding*, *Diplomat Pudding*, *Crème Brulée*, *Bread and Butter Pudding*, and *Crème Caramel*, all of which require delicate handling in serving, so as to look appetising.

Fruit Fritters are made with apple, banana, pineapple, etc. normally allowing two or three pieces per portion; they are usually glazed with icing sugar to make them look more appetising. The usual sauce served is apricot which should be ladled onto the plate and not over the fritters.

Lemon Meringue Pie is cut into wedge-shape pieces and transferred onto the plate by means of serving-spoon and fork. A triangular-shape pie-server is very suitable for serving portions of flans and gateaux but its use is normally confined to the domestic scene.

Milk Puddings can be made of rice, sago, semolina and tapioca, usually in single portion pie-dishes from which it can be eaten by the customer, or it may be spooned onto a plate by the waiter. *Rice pudding* in the French style is baked with the addition of yolks of egg and butter which makes it richer and less runny.

A *sweet omelette* is filled with any kind of jam, mincemeat, apple purée, etc., or it may be a plain sweet one, flavoured or flamed with rum or other spirit or a liqueur. It is the rule that the two ends be cut off before transferring it to the hot plate by means of two forks held underneath the omelette, thus serving only the very soft part.

Pancakes are served folded in four or rolled up, usually with a filling inside, allowing three or four per portion. The lemon slice and any sauce should be placed on the pancakes and the sugar sifter offered. A dessertspoon and fork are used.

Fruit pies are presented surrounded with a pie-frill and a wedge-shaped piece of pastry is cut and laid on top of the pie whilst the fruit filling is served onto the plate, then the piece of pastry is laid over it. *Custard Sauce* (which is called *Sauce Anglaise*) is spooned over the fruit but not over the pastry, otherwise liquid cream is offered. *Apple Pie à la Mode* has a ball of vanilla ice cream instead of custard or cream.

Hot sweet *Soufflés* are made in many flavours such as chocolate, coffee, praline, vanilla, or a liqueur such as Grand Marnier. Timing is important as any delay in serving will cause it to collapse so making it look unappetising. A dish of stewed fruit is sometimes served but no sauce.

Soufflé Puddings differ from soufflés in that they are cooked in dariole moulds, turned out and served coated with a sauce such as Sauce Sabayon.

Zabaglione is a classical Italian sweet made like an egg flip, flavoured with a sweet wine and served in a tulip-shaped glass. It is eaten with a teaspoon and accompanied by sponge finger biscuits, known as *biscuits à la cuiller*, which should be offered to the guests and then the remainder placed on the table. The glass of warm zabaglione is placed on a small d'oyley on a side plate.

11.3 SERVICE OF COLD SWEETS

Cold sweets should be served onto chilled plates and not onto plates that have come lukewarm from the dish-washing machine; the sweet should be served onto the centre of the plate.

A *Bavarois* is set in a charlotte mould, turned out and decorated with whipped cream. To serve, cut a portion with a knife and transfer it to the cold plate, adding some of the cream and if set in jelly, some of that too.

Blancmange is served as for bavarois, either cutting a portion with a knife, or scooping several spoonfuls to make a reasonable-sized serving.

Charlotte Russe is vanilla bavarois mixture, set in a mould lined with sponge finger biscuits, and the servce is as for ordinary bavarois.

A *Chartreuse* is made by lining a charlotte mould with jelly, then with slices of fruit such as banana, and filling it with vanilla or other flavoured bavarois.

A *Compote* is stewed or poached fresh or dried fruit in a very sweet syrup; it is usually served with liquid double cream and sponge finger biscuits. Fresh fruits used include halves of apple, whole apricots, blackcurrants, cherries, figs, gooseberries, pears, plums and rhubarb; dried fruits include figs, prunes, apple rings, and dried mixed fruits; they must be cooked slowly so as to retain their shape.

Crèmes au Caramel are cooked in dariol moulds and when cold, demoulded onto a dish. To serve, grasp gently with serving-spoon and fork turned inwards, so that they act as a pair of pincers, and transfer to the plate; serve some of the caramel juice over the crème caramel.

Créoles are made of moulded rice set with gelatine, with a garnish of fruit and a covering of apricot glaze; to serve, take a large spoonful of the rice with a portion of the fruit on top and cover with some of the glaze. If decorated with cream, serve some of that too.

Fruit Fools can be made with any kind of purée of fruit mixed with whipped cream; it is portioned into coupes and when set, decorated with whipped cream. It is served on a d'oyley on an under-plate, with a teaspoon to eat it, and sponge finger biscuits are offered on a side-plate.

Fruit salad can be served from the bowl onto a chilled sweet plate or into a small glass bowl or coupe. Liquid cream is offered and if accepted, poured over the fruit. The sugar sifter should be placed on the table. The cutlery is the usual dessert-spoon and fork, as for all sweets. Fresh fruit salad can be enhanced by the addition of a small measure of kirsch or maraschino but wine is not really suitable for drinking with it. A ball of ice cream is sometimes served on the salad.

Jelly is usually set in a glass bowl, or turned out of a mould, often with segments of fruit in it, and it is advisable to dip a serving-spoon into a jug of hot water so as to facilitate service. Liquid cream may be offered and poured around.

Junket is best set in individual pots suitable for eating from, as it is almost impossible to spoon it from a large bowl onto a plate. The rennet which sets the milk barely coagulates it and it is necessary to eat it using a teaspoon, with finger biscuits as an accompaniment.

A *Mousse* can be served in a glass or a coupe, the container being lined for example, with melted chocolate couverture; or it may be set in a mould and turned out onto a dish for service, decorated with a swirl of whipped cream. A teaspoon is the most suitable implement for eating it.

Profiteroles are small baked chou-paste buns, filled with whipped or pastry cream, arranged in a bowl and covered with either hot or cold chocolate sauce. A portion of approximately four is served onto a dessert plate and covered with the chocolate sauce from the bowl or from a separate sauceboat.

Cold rice sweets are named *Condés* and *Impératrices*, the latter being made by mixing equal parts of Condé rice and vanilla bavarois. These are set in individual moulds or coupes, or in a larger mould for portioning, the condés usually being garnished with poached fruit and decorated with whipped cream.

Cold soufflés are made to look like a risen sweet soufflé straight from the oven but are in fact, made of cooked egg mixture lightened with whipped cream and set with gelatine. Flavours include vanilla, strawberry, praline and most of the sweet liqueurs. To serve, dip a spoon into hot water and scoop spoonfuls onto a dessert plate.

Yoghurt can be served as a sweet either in the container in which it was purchased, or turned out into a dish or coupe; finger biscuits should be offered.

11.4 SERVICE OF FRESH FRUIT

Some establishments keep special fruit knives and forks and have special plates for the service of fresh fruit, whereas others use an ordinary sweet plate and a dessert fork and small knife. When serving a bowl or basket of fruit it is usual to place it on the table in front of the customer for him to make his choice. A finger-bowl half full of cold water with a rose petal rather than a lemon slice, is placed on the left-hand side, and the plate and cutlery is positioned in the normal place. If the guest selects cherries or grapes, an additional bowl of cold water should be supplied for the guest to rinse them in, as the finger-bowl is only used for removing any strong flavour from the fingers.

A basket of fresh fruit should contain a variety of good quality fruit and possibly a bunch of green or black hothouse grapes for which a pair of grape scissors must be provided; in addition there may be an assortment of nuts for which a pair of nutcrackers and a salt cellar is required. Waiters must be capable of preparing certain of these fruits in front of the customer, as detailed in the following.

Pineapple

Cut off the leaf end and shave off sufficient of the skin so as to be able to cut the required number of slices; gouge out the centre core then cut round slices approximately 5 mm thick (see Figure 11.1). Ask the customer if he requires a few drops of kirsch over it and place the sugar sifter on the table. It is eaten with a fruit knife and fork, off a fruit or dessert plate.

Orange

If a waiter is asked to prepare an orange he should cut off the top then almost cut through the bottom, impale the top piece on a fork then push the prongs through the bottom and into the flesh. Use a sharp knife to pare all skin and pith from around the orange, letting this fall onto a plate on the guéridon, then cut segments from in between the membrane, or place the fruit on a fruit plate and cut into round slices. Arrange the pieces neatly and serve accompanied with caster sugar (see Figure 11.2).

Fig 11.1   *preparing and serving fresh pineapple*

Apple and Pear

Cut a slice from the bottom, push a fork through this and into the centre of the fruit; hold it up and peel from top to bottom or by rotating it, letting the skin fall onto a plate. It can be cut into quarters so as to remove the core, still using the fork to hold it steady, then arrange neatly on a fruit plate.

Peach

Sometimes a customer may request the waiter to skin a peach. This is done by impaling it on a fork, dipping first into a jug of very hot water for about ten seconds, then immediately into cold water. Cut a

Fig 11.2 *preparation of an orange for dessert*

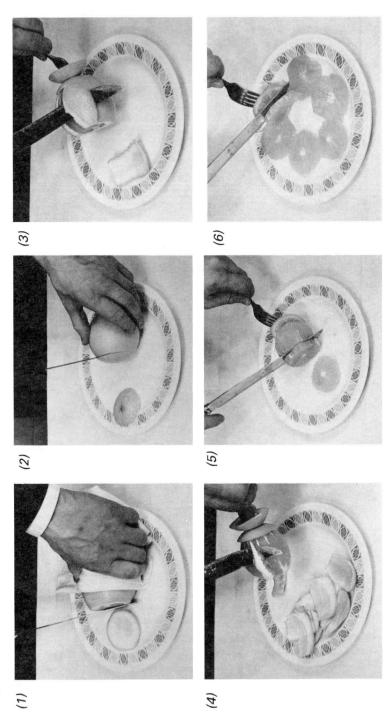

shallow incision around the circumference then use a folded napkin to press the skin off, or peel it away with the tip of a knife. Cut the peach in half, discard the stone and cut the flesh into segments. Arrange neatly on a plate and serve with a fruit knife and fork, caster sugar, and if desired, a sauceboat of liquid double cream.

Strawberries Romanoff

This may be done in the pastry department, or may be prepared in front of the customer by first presenting the dish of strawberries and then hulling them by holding the stem firmly and pushing off the strawberry as shown in Figure 11.3, using a folded napkin. Flavour some lightly whipped cream with a little Curaçao or Grand Marnier liqueur, add the strawberries and crush them lightly with a fork to give a rose-pink colour. Spoon onto a chilled dessert plate, garnish with a few of the smaller strawberries and serve with sponge finger biscuits.

Some people like to drink a glass of vintage port with an apple or a sweet muscat wine with the other fruit. Sweet sherry or Madeira, or a tawny port goes well with nuts.

11.5 SERVICE OF CAKES AND PASTRIES

The wide variety of cakes and pastries add much to the eye appeal of a sweet trolley and most of these are suitable for serving as a sweet course, as well as for afternoon tea, and as part of a post-banquet buffet.

French pastries means a collection of individual cakes such as éclairs, chou buns, millefeuilles, fondant fancies, macaroons, tartlets and barquettes with fresh fruit or other fillings such as frangipane, cream meringues, cream horns, florentines, etc. A variety of these is displayed on a silver dish on a d'oyley and shown to the customer to take his pick, or the waiter will serve them by means of a serving-spoon and fork onto a small plate. Cake tongs are not normally used.

Gâteaux are large round, square or oblong cakes, which have been cut open, and sandwiched together with cream or butter cream. Names of well-known gâteaux include Mocha (coffee); Chocolate; Printinière (various coloured and flavoured buttercreams); Black Forest (morello cherries and chocolate); Pithivier (puff pastry filled with frangipane); Millefeuilles (puff pastry sandwiched with baker's custard and jam with marbled fondant topping); St Honoré (cream-

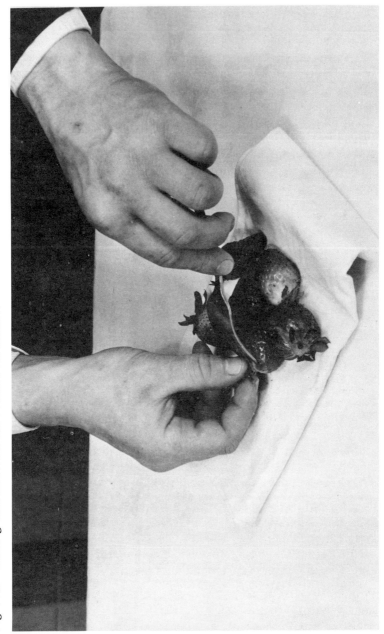

Fig 11.3 *hulling strawberries for Fraises Romanoff*

filled puff-pastry base with a border of chou buns); and various kinds of cheesecake. *Torten* are large-size gâteaux, flavoured with a liqueur, sandwiched with butter cream and decorated in a very elegant manner. Names of these include Sachertorte; Linzertorte; Dobos; Praline and Kirsch torten.

To serve a portion of gâteau or torten cut an even-sized wedge-shaped slice, preferably using a knife dipped into hot water which will help to give a clean cut and avoid making crumbs. Transfer to a cold sweet plate, keeping it upright so that the decoration is still at the top, using the serving-spoon and fork in each hand, or if permissible, a cake slice. Place in front of the customer with the pointed end towards him and offer liquid cream from a jug. For this sweet a dessert-spoon is placed at the right-hand side and a dessert-fork to the left but if cream is not served a cake fork or dessert-fork is placed at the right-hand side.

Suitable wines for serving with hot and cold sweets include Sauternes or Barsac, Piccolit from the Veneto region of Italy, or Asti Spumante; sweet Champagne, Muscat de Beaumes de Venise, Malmsey Madeira, or a German Beerenaüslese, and of course demi-sec Champagne, are also very suitable.

11.6 SERVICE OF ICE CREAM SWEETS

Ice cream and the flavoured water ices can be served in many forms including *Bombes*, *Coupes*, *Parfaits*, and *Iced Soufflés*.

Sorbet is a delicate water ice made with fruit and a wine or liqueur flavouring, plus the addition of Italian meringue. Sorbet is often served as a sweet but its correct role is as a course served midway through an elaborate meal such as a banquet, when it is customary to include a sorbet between the two main dishes. Other water ices are Granité, Marquise and Spoom but these are not often served.

An *Ice Mousse* is made by mixing whipped cream into Crème Anglaise then whisking it until very frothy before moulding and freezing. *Ice Puddings* (Poudings Glacés) are made with the same mixture as Ice Mousse but frozen in a soufflé dish to come above the rim so as to give the impression that it has risen.

A *Bombe* takes its name from the shape of the mould and is a combination of several colours and flavours of very creamy ice cream set in various ways, usually an ordinary ice cream as the outer lining. The bombe is turned out and decorated with whipped cream. It should be cut into wedge-shaped portions, using a knife dipped into hot water. This slice and some of the decoration and garnish is placed on a chilled dessert-plate to be eaten by means of a dessert-spoon and fork. Sponge finger biscuits are usually offered. There are hundreds of different names of garnishes given to bombes, according to the combination of colours and flavours as added to the bombe mixture, as well as the way they are arranged in the mould e.g. *Bombe Frou-Frou* is rum-flavoured bombe with crystallised fruit inside vanilla ice cream with added diced crystallised fruits and chopped nuts, set in a dome-shape mould. It is served in the same way as a bombe.

A *Coupe* takes its name from the silver or glass stemmed dish in which the ice cream is served. There are hundreds of names for this kind of sweet, according to the flavour of ice creams and garnishes used. An example is *Coupe Clo-Clo* which is made by putting two balls of strawberry ice cream containing chopped candied chestnut into the chilled coupe, a whole marron glacé on each ball, finishing with a piped border of raspberry-flavoured whipped cream. A *Coupe Jacques* is made by placing a scoopful each of vanilla and lemon ice into the bowl, adding kirsch-flavoured diced fruit salad and a whirl of whipped cream. The coupe is served on a d'oyley on an underplate with the ice-cream spade on the right of the plate; fan-shape wafers, rolled biscuits or sponge fingers are offered, the remainder being placed on the table.

Biscuit Glacé is made by filling an oblong mould with rich ice-cream mixture to which Italian meringue has been added, flavoured and coloured with liqueurs, etc., and set in variegated layers. It is served cut into slices, with wafer biscuits.

Sweet champagne or a sweet liqueur can be drunk with ice cream, but as a rule no wine is served with any of the above.

11.7 SERVICE OF SAVOURIES

These small, dainty and flavoursome preparations are a British invention and are served as a course, only in English-speaking countries, including the USA. Most savouries are made by putting various ingredients on squares or rounds of toast or fried bread, the fillings being mushrooms, sardines, cheese, ham, smoked haddock, bone marrow, etc. They can be called Canapés, Croques or Croûtes.

The following are the best-known savouries:

Anges à Cheval – three oysters, each rolled in a rasher of bacon, grilled and placed on an oblong piece of buttered toast

Buck Rarebit – a hot poached egg on top of a Welsh rarebit

Canapé Diane – three pieces of chicken liver each rolled in a rasher of bacon, grilled and served on toast

Canapé Ivanhoe – creamed smoked haddock purée piled on a round of toast, with a grilled mushroom on top

Champignons sous Cloche – small white mushrooms cooked in cream and lemon juice, under a bell-glass cover

Champignons sur Toast – grilled field mushrooms on toast

Croque Madame – a fried sandwich of ham, cheese and a fried egg

Croque Monsieur – a fried sandwich with ham and Gruyère cheese, inside the bread

Diables à Cheval – prunes and chutney wrapped in streaky rashers, grilled and served on toast

Marrow Bone – this is a 15–18 cm length of leg bone of beef, boiled and served as a hot savoury so that the customer can enjoy the nutritional contents. To serve, it is placed upright with a napkin folded around it and is eaten by means of a silver marrow-bone scoop. Melba toast, salt and pepper should be offered

Scotch Woodcock – scrambled egg on toast, decorated with a trellis work of anchovy fillets and capers

Welsh Rarebit – cheese mixture flavoured with beer and mustard, spread on toast and gratinated.

Some savoury soufflés are served as the Savoury course.

All savouries must be served very hot on a hot side-plate with a dessert-knife and fork to eat it with; the salt and pepper, peppermill, cayenne pepper, bottle of Worcester sauce and pot of mustard, may be placed on the table for customer's use.

A good Burgundy or Barbera are suitable wines for all kinds of savouries.

11.8 SERVICE OF HOT SANDWICHES

There are several well-known hot toasted sandwiches suitable for serving as supper dishes, or as a substitute for a full meal for a person who has not much time to eat a full meal.

A *Bookmaker's Sandwich* is made by pressing a grilled minute steak between two long slices of bread or toast, with made mustard and grated horseradish. It is pressed so the juice from the meat impregnates the bread.

A *Club Sandwich* is served hot by layering three slices of toast with lettuce, mayonnaise, sliced chicken, tomato and grilled bacon. To keep it from collapsing it may be necessary to pierce each quarter with a toothpick but it is important to serve this kind of double- and triple-decker sandwich as hot as possible and in good shape when transferring it to a hot medium-sized plate; a small knife and fork are used.

There are many other of these substantial hot sandwiches in the repertoire, but in general they are served as supper meals that go well with a mixed salad and with a drink such as coffee, beer, or a glass of wine.

11.9 SERVICE OF CHEESE

This course is served after, or in lieu of a sweet and it is usual to keep a good selection of cheeses on a board or trolley in the restaurant, so that it is always to hand. The range of cheese available may vary according to the kind of clientele; it may, for example, consist of only English or only French cheeses, but in general the array is made up of the best-known cheeses from several countries, so as to cover the various types which can be categorised as follows:

Hard – Cheddar, Cheshire, Dunlop, Double Gloucester, Emmenthal, Gruyère, Sbrinz, Provolone

Blue Vein – Stilton, Gorgonzola, Danablu, Rocquefort, Lymeswold, Mycella

Soft – Caithness, Herve, Carré de l'Est, Brie, Camembert, Bel Paese

Semi-hard – Gouda, Port Salut, Caerphilly, Pont l'Evêque, Harlsberg, Getost, Fynbo, Leicester, Wensleydale, Edam, St Paulin, Limburger

Fresh Cream – Gervais, Petit Suisse, Quark, Ricotta, Mascarpone

Flavoured Fresh Cream – Boursin, Roulé

Goats' Milk – Bressane, Chevreton

Ewes' Milk – Pecorino

What the customer basically wants to know is if a certain cheese is mild, medium or strong, as shown below:

Mild – fresh cream cheeses, flavoured cream cheeses, cottage cheese, processed cheese, Saint Paulin, Bel Paese, Lancashire

Medium – Brie, Camembert, goats' cheese, Emmenthal, Cantal, Comté, Cheddar, Cheshire, Caerphilly, Gloucester

Strong – all the blue cheeses, Munster, Pont l'Evêque, matured goats' cheeses, mature farmhouse Cheddar

English farmhouse cheeses compare favourably with factory-made cheese as they are allowed to mature for nine months to one year; some are left to mature for as long as two to three years, giving an exquisite nutty and slightly sharp flavour. They are made as *Cheshire* – both white and red, *Cheddar*, and *Lancashire*. As with all cheeses, they need to be brought to room temperature by removal from the refrigerator or store, at least an hour before serving.

One waiter may be given responsibility for the cheese tray or trolley. He has to keep it clean and replenished during service, and to do the actual service, and must be able to offer advice and information on the available range. He must be capable of naming and describing each cheese, as it is not common practice to stick labels into them. Customers are not allowed to serve themselves as this could lead to waste or extravagance. Cheese must be cut into portions according to the original shape and any foil must be removed before the cheese is placed on the customer's plate. Two or more knives should be used on the board so as to avoid mixing the flavours.

The accepted accompaniments should be kept on the trolley or close to the tray. They may include any of the following: celery, radishes, spring onions, watercress, grapes, apple, walnuts, white or brown bread rolls, slices of French bread, grissini, ryvita, water biscuits, crackers, pumpernickel, mixed cheese biscuits, wholemeal biscuits, and of course, butter curls. The celery should be crisply iced and preferably English as this has more flavour than imported celery. The radishes and spring onions must be kept on ice and fresh butter curls or pats are required, not those that have been on the table throughout the meal.

Suitable drinks

It is possible to suggest an individual wine with each kind of cheese – for example, port is traditionally served with Stilton. However, the simple rule is that a sweet wine is unsuitable for any kind of cheese and that red is more suitable than white wine. But both beer and cider are also suitable drinks and, as is well known, the original ploughman's lunch was Cheddar cheese, home-baked bread and beer. Examples of appropriate wines are:

Brie and Camembert – fruity red wine such as St Emilion

Cheddar and Cheshire – Burgundy or Côtes du Rhône

Emmenthal and Gruyère – a young white wine or a Beaujolais
Gorgonzola – Barbera
Rocquefort – French regional wine or Châteauneuf-du-Pape.

To serve cheese, cut the required size of portions without being too
mean or too generous, and use the prongs of the cheese-knife to place
the pieces on a side-plate; a customer may choose one or several
different kinds and may like a lot or only a little, but in general a
portion should be approximately 80 g, cut in neat pieces of reasonable size rather than thin slivers (see Figure 11.4). A side knife is used

Fig 11.4 *service of cheese*

and the salt and pepper pots should be replaced on the table, and if a cream cheese such as petit suisse is chosen, a bowl of caster sugar is necessary.

The box or basket of cheese biscuits is offered, then placed on the table for the customer to take some more. The waiter may ask if the customer prefers bread. A fresh dish of butter curls or pats is placed on the table as well as the vase of celery. Sometimes tomatoes are placed on the tray as decoration around the several cheeses, but it is not intended that these should be served.

When a party of several people are at the table and one or more of them does not partake of a sweet, savoury or cheese course, a plate should still be put in front of that customer even though it may stay empty. This indicates to the Station Head Waiter that the customer is not being neglected.

11.10   SERVICE OF COFFEE

This beverage rounds off a meal, both lunch and dinner, and its quality can make or mar the entire meal. Equally important is the way in which it is served, which should incorporate all the rules and protocols of service. A good cup of coffee properly served gilds the lily of the fine cooking and service that has gone before, a poor one ruins a good meal.

There are many different types and blends of coffee, and several ways of making it, each having its adherents. Management decides which kind of coffee will suit its customers and what kind of machine will be used to make it in the stillroom. Some restaurants have a coffee-making machine on each sideboard in the restaurant so that the waiter can make it close to where customers are, but generally coffee is made in bulk by the stillroom staff, who dispense it in pots of various capacities, according to the number of servings required.

Some customers prefer coffee made from lightly roasted beans because they give a mild and smooth flavour. Coffee made from medium roasted beans has a deep and strong rich flavour but without bitterness. Dark roasted is usually described as Continental coffee and gives a stronger but no harsher flavour. The best coffee beans are the Arabica from Central and South america; the Robusta beans from Africa are of poorer quality but can be mixed with Arabica to produce a satisfactory blend. The beans may be purchased ready roasted for grinding in the stillroom, or as vacuum packs of ground coffee under a brand name.

Among the finest coffees are:

Mocha – from Ethiopia; is often requested by connoisseurs who appreciate its 'winey' flavour

Mysore – from India; reputed to be the smoothest of all, yet full of flavour

Costa Rica – in demand by discerning coffee-drinkers who like its slight acidity and delicate flavour

Java – an exceptionally rich coffee with a heavy flavour.

Coffee-making machines

The large-scale '*Café Set*' is usually called a coffee still because it is housed in the stillroom; it may be heated by electricity or gas. A central boiler feeds hot water into containers set at each side, where it runs onto the correct amount of ground coffee, usually 225 grams per 4.5 litres of water, or $\frac{1}{2}$lb per 1 gallon. It is maintained at serving temperature all day long but is best if served within the hour as it tends to darken and develop a bitter flavour. Milk is heated in the other container and a jug of each can be dispensed very quickly. Coffee left over from a previous meal should not be reheated for service to customers and it should never be boiled as this destroys its flavour and aroma.

Cona coffee is made in a machine of the same name which consists of two bowls, the one underneath being full of cold water which is heated from the hotplate on which it is standing as shown in figure 11.5. When the water comes to a boil it rises into the upper bowl, in which a measured amount of ground coffee has been placed; when it cools the infused coffee is drawn back into the lower bowl by the vacuum created by the change in atmospheric pressure, where it is kept hot for service until required.

An *electric filter machine* is clean and easy to use by filling the reservoir with cold water and placing the right amount of ground coffee inside a filter cone in the coffee container. When the machine is switched on the water will come to a boil, rise up and filter through the coffee into the pot. On a smaller scale, *Café Filtré* is made by placing some finely ground coffee in a container on top of a pot or cup, and filling it with boiling water which then filters through the coffee into the pot or cup.

A *cafetière* is a glass beaker set in a handled cradle as shown in Figure 11.6; it has a lid with an attached plunger. A measure of ground

Fig 11.5 *(a)   Cona coffee machine*

(b)   electrical coffee filter

Fig 11.6 *a cafetière*

coffee is put into the container which is then filled with freshly boiled water; the lid is placed on, left to infuse for up to five minutes then the plunger is pushed slowly to the bottom so trapping the grounds. The coffee is then ready for pouring.

A *percolator* is a jug which is filled with cold water, with a perforated container set at the top into which a measure of ground coffee is placed. As the water starts to boil it rises up a central tube into the coffee and drains back into the pot, doing this all the time until removed from the heat or switched off. The jug may be made of polished aluminium or stainless steel in an elegant coffee-pot shape.

Espresso coffee is made by forcing steam produced under pressure through a perforated container full of dark-roasted and finely-ground coffee. It comes out as a small cupful of black, full-flavoured coffee that holds all its aromatic essences.

A *cappuccino* is made by adding two parts of hot milk to one part espresso coffee, mixing it on the steam jet of the machine.

Decaffeinated coffee is available as instant, ready ground or beans, under various brand names and is often requested by customers in place of ordinary coffee, as being less stimulating and less likely to keep them awake at night.

Coffee is served at breakfast by placing a jugful each of coffee and hot milk on the table in front of the customer with the handles directed to the right. The cup, saucer and spoon will be in position on the right hand side of the cover.

To serve coffee for lunch and dinner, collect the jugs of coffee and hot milk from the stillroom, together with a basin of sugar and the required number of hot coffee cups known as demitasses, which hold about 1.5 dl, and place them on a folded tray cloth on the salver. Place the cup on the saucer then go to the right of the customer and ask if he wants his coffee with milk and if he takes sugar. If the reply is in the affirmative, serve a spoonful of sugar in the cup then position the tray so that the spout of the coffee pot is just above the cup then tilt it as shown in Figure 11.7, to fill the cup three parts full then turn the tray slightly and tilt the milk jug to fill the cup almost to the brim. If taken without milk, fill the cup to the top. Serve the other customers at the table then place the sugar-basin, the coffee and milk in the centre of the table, each on an underplate, the handles towards the host, for him to offer more coffee to his party.

The kind of sugar used is selected according to the kind of clientele, the choice being from demerara, caster, spiced sugar,

Fig 11.7 *pouring coffee*

brown sugar-crystals, knobs, or rainbow coffee-sugar crystals. Some establishments keep sugar substitutes for customers who are on a slimming diet. Some restaurants serve cream instead of milk.

Special coffees

Turkish coffee is made by boiling very finely ground dark-roasted coffee in a small copper pan with or without sugar, three times, then it is flavoured with a vanilla pod or rose-water, poured into a small cup without being strained and served accompanied with a glass of cold water.

To make an *Irish Coffee*, heat a specially made irish-coffee glass or large Paris goblet over a lamp, pour in strong black coffee and stir in two teaspoons of sugar; add a measure of Irish whiskey then pour a good layer of double cream over the back of a teaspoon so that it floats on the coffee. Serve, without stirring it, on a d'oyley on a small plate.

The necessary equipment includes the glass, spirit lamp for heating, small jugful of cream, sugar basin, pot of very hot coffee, bottle of Irish whiskey, 6-out measure, teaspoon, serving plate, and d'oyley.

Some of the other spirits and liqueurs used to make this kind of coffee, are shown below, together with the name appropriate to the finished coffee:

Armagnac – Napoleon
Bénédictine – Monks'
Calvados – Normandy
Cognac – Royale
Cointreau – Parisienne
Drambuie – Highland
Tia Maria – Calypso

Vodka – Russian
Aquavit – Scandinavian
Kahlùa – Mexican
Kirsch – German
Kümmel – Dutch
Whisky – Scottish
Rum – Don Juan or Caribbean

It is a good marketing ploy to suggest to a customer what spirits and liqueurs are appropriate for drinking separately with ordinary coffee, for example, Cognac, Armagnac, Tia Maria, Sambuca, Chartreuse, Bénédictine, and many others.

11.11 SMORGÄSBROD

This type of meal usually takes the form of open sandwiches, made on slices of buttered brown or white bread, rye bread, or toast. The fillings are usually generous, arranged artistically, with a garnish to make each sandwich look like a substantial meal. All kinds of fish and meat may be used, examples being smoked salmon, eel or sturgeon, roast beef, turkey, ham, ox tongue and corned beef. Scrambled egg and various kinds of cheese may also be used and suitable garnishes include tomato, cucumber, lettuce, gherkin, anchovy, olives, mustard and cress, mayonnaise, slice of lemon, mixed pickle, and potato crisps. Sometimes some hot dishes are included.

Service of this Scandinavian-type meal is usually self-help from a buffet table from where the customer may take whatever he likes, or the sandwich may be made to order and served on a silver dish on a d'oyley, from which the customer can help himself. It is usual to drink lager with this form of meal.

QUESTIONS

1. Describe the methods and draw an outline of how a slice of gâteau should be served.

2. Define the various types of cheese and state how cheese is served.

3. What are the accompaniments of savouries?

LAMP WORK

12.1 INTRODUCTION TO FLAMBÉ WORK

Flambé work is the cooking or finishing of dishes, by adding a spirit and setting it alight, doing this in front of the customer and usually serving it whilst it is still alight. The item of food and its garnish or sauce are prepared in the kitchen, placed on a guéridon, or mobile table or trolley, which has been equipped with the necessary cooking utensils and serving equipment, and the cooking or finishing is done where the customer can watch closely. In the USA this kind of service is called chafing-dish cookery after the frying pan in which the item is cooked. Here it is known as flambé work or guéridon service, a guéridon being a small mobile table. Some waiters call it lamp work.

The list of dishes that can be cooked in the restaurant is limited and as may be seen by the recipes that follow, only small or fairly thin things can be done properly. This means that the whole process should be completed in less than five minutes as otherwise the proceedings may begin to pall and customers at other tables might assume that the recipient is receiving too much attention. Only a skilled and experienced member of the waiting staff should be permitted to do this work for there are inherent dangers in igniting alcohol in a crowded room and many accidents have resulted because inexperienced staff failed to exercise proper control over the flame from the lamp, and it set fire to the curtains or blew up in the waiter's face. A skilled waiter can pour brandy from the bottle directly onto a flaming dish but a novice may find the flame spreads to the bottle so he should use a measure or sauceboat.

The high price charged for a flambé dish includes the cost of the measure of spirit and the extra skill involved in carrying out the operation; the cost assists in keeping demand within reason since a lower price might make flambé work become too popular and the member of staff responsible for this work would be rushed off his feet while the cooks in the kitchen remained idle. Dishes prepared in the restaurant must not be so highly spiced or seasoned as to cause strong cooking smells in the room nor must the work be carried out with so much aplomb as to cause a lot of noise. The preparation of flambé dishes should be carried out by a waiter who has a flair for showmanship in that he creates a moment of dramatic tension at the setting alight of the dish, which impresses everyone in the room.

There are two kinds of table cooking-lamp – one works on a container of methylated spirit and a wick which if properly trimmed should not give any smell; the other has a replaceable container of butane gas and will give more heat than a spirit lamp. The lamp is made of stainless steel or of silver plate and has a wide flat top on which to place the pan. Lamps must be properly serviced every day and if possible checked to be sure that they contain sufficient fuel to last through the service.

The pans used for cooking must look clean and hygienic, one with a copper bottom will convey the heat better than a stainless steel one; according to the number of portions being cooked, either a 22 cm or 30 cm diameter pan may be used. All the ingredients, cooking equipment and serving dishes must be arranged neatly on the trolley or cart, before starting to do the cooking. It is necessary to use 70° (40%) proof spirits because these catch alight quite quickly when warmed and even a sparse sprinkling is sufficient to cause a good blaze. The following recipes are for two persons.

12.2 FLAMED FISH DISHES

Crabmeat Newburg

30g butter, 200g flaked white crabmeat, 0.5dl dry sherry, 0.25dl brandy, 1dl cream, 2 yolks of egg, 180g cooked pilaff of rice.

Heat the butter turning it around the pan until hot but not brown. Add the crab, stir to heat through. Add the brandy, set alight, then add the sherry and cook to reduce. Pour in the cream, warm through. Add the yolk and stir to mix in and thicken, but do not boil. Arrange the rice in a circle on the plate and spoon the crab inside. (The cream and egg may be mixed together before adding.)

Scampi Provençale

0.5dl oil, 15g flour, 1 clove garlic, 25g finely chopped onion, 100g diced tomato flesh, 0.25dl brandy, 180g scampi, 1dl provençale sauce, 150g pilaff of rice, parsley.

Sprinkle the scampi lightly with flour, put into the pan of hot oil. Cook to colour, add the crushed garlic, onion and tomato and cook slightly. Flame with the brandy, add the sauce, reheat and serve in a circle of rice. Sprinkle the scampi with chopped parsley. Other suitable fish are lobster, prawns, scallops and strips of fillet of dover sole, which may be cooked by either of the foregoing methods.

12.3 FLAMED MEAT DISHES

Beef Strogonoff

0.5dl oil, 20g butter, 20g finely chopped shallot, 5g paprika, 0.25dl brandy, 200g strips of fillet of beef each 5cm×1cm, 1dl cream, lemon juice, 180g cooked pilaff of rice.

Heat the oil and butter until hot, season the beef with salt, pepper and paprika and fry quickly to colour. Pour in the brandy and allow to flame; remove the meat and keep warm. Add the shallot and cook for 1 minute, add the cream, season and reduce until thick. Flavour with a little lemon juice, place the beef in this sauce to reheat but do not allow to boil. Place the hot rice in a circle on a plate, spoon the beef in the centre and sprinkle with chopped parsley.

Grenadin of Veal Etna

40g butter, 4×1cm thick slices cushion of veal, 0.25dl brandy, 50g Mozzarella cheese, 8 asparagus tips, Worcester sauce

Heat the butter and shallow fry the pieces of meat on both sides for approximately 4 minutes. Flame with brandy, sprinkle with a few drops of Worcester sauce and place a thin slice of cheese and four asparagus tips on each piece of meat. Cover with the lid to melt the cheese then serve coated with juices from the pan.

Escalope de Veau Montpensier

Shallow fry two thin, seasoned, slices of veal in hot butter, flame with brandy then add a little demi-glace and cream to form a sauce; transfer to a plate and add the Montpensier garnish of a small bunch of buttered asparagus tips and a slice of truffle as prepared in the kitchen. An escalope of pork can be done in the same way.

A small selection of vegetables is usually arranged on a side-plate and set at the left-hand side of the customer.

Escalopines de Veau à la Crème et Champignons

Shallow fry the small, thin, seasoned slices of veal until light brown, remove to a plate and add some sliced button mushrooms to the pan, season and stir for a minute. Add a little sherry, allow to reduce, then add sufficient cream to make a sauce; pour over the escalopines and serve immediately.

Piccata alla Madera

Shallow fry 8 small slices of veal in hot butter, remove to a plate and pour in a little dry Madeira wine; allow to reduce slightly then add a little jus lié to make sufficient sauce to pour over the piccatas.

Liver Delmonico

40g butter, 20g flour, 4 slices calf's or lamb's liver (1cm thick), 0.25dl brandy, 25g finely chopped onion, 60g sliced mushroom, 0.5dl white wine, 1.5dl brown sauce.

Season the liver with salt and pepper, dust with flour and cook quickly in the butter to colour on both sides; add the onion and mushroom and cook for two minutes. Flame with brandy, add the wine and reduce slightly. Add the sauce, reheat and serve.

Minute Steak Jockey Club

40g butter, 2×120g sirloin steaks beaten until thin, 30g finely chopped shallot, 0.25dl brandy, freshly ground black pepper, 2 slices bread (crust removed), chopped parsley.

Heat the butter, add the shallot and cook for half a minute.

Increase the heat, fry the steaks quickly on both sides for a total of one minute; flame with brandy, place each steak on a slice of bread and sprinkle with chopped parsley and the coarsely ground black pepper.

Monkey Gland Steak

30g butter, 2×110g thin slices of fillet steak, 25g chopped onion, 0.25dl brandy, French mustard, Worcester sauce, chopped parsley

Heat the butter, add the chopped onion and the steaks and cook on both sides. Flame with the brandy then smear the steaks with the mustard. Sprinkle with a few drops of Worcester sauce and serve sprinkled with chopped parsley.

This dish was popular during the 1930s when Voronoff, a celebrated Russian physiologist, recommended grafting monkey glands into human beings as a means of prolonging human life.

Piccata alla Marsala

40g butter, 8–10 small thin rounds of cushion of veal (25g each), 0.25dl brandy, 0.5dl Marsala, 1dl jus lié

Heat the butter and cook the seasoned pieces of veal until coloured on both sides. Flame with brandy, add the Marsala, reduce slightly and finish with the jus lié. Small rounds of pork fillet can be cooked in this way, and are called Piccata or Scallopine di Maiale alla Marsala.

Rognons Flambés

25g butter, 8 lamb kidneys, skinned and cut in half, or 200g veal kidney cut in half or in thick slices 5cm, 0.25dl brandy, 0.5dl port, 0.5dl jus lié, 0.5dl cream, French mustard, lemon juice

(The kidneys should be sautéd but slightly underdone in the kitchen, placed in the silver pan and brought hot to the guéridon.)

Flame with brandy and remove the kidneys to a hot plate. Add the port and allow to reduce; add the jus lié and cream, then season this sauce, flavour with mustard and thicken with the butter; finish with a squeeze of lemon juice. Reheat the kidneys in the sauce but do not allow to boil.

Rognon de Veau Robert

1 veal kidney, 0.5dl brandy, 30g butter, squeeze of lemon juice, 1tsp made English Mustard, 0.5dl dry sherry

(The kidney is cooked whole in a casserole with butter for 15 minutes then brought from the kitchen.)
Place the kidney in the silver pan, flame with the brandy then remove and slice it. Add lemon juice, mustard and sherry to the pan, thicken with small pieces of butter and replace the kidney to reheat but not to boil.

Steak Diane

30g butter, 2×90g pieces of flattened tail-end of fillet of beef, 30g finely chopped onion, 60g sliced button mushroom, 0.25dl brandy, 1dl cream, few drops of Worcester sauce, pinch of chopped tarragon, chervil and parsley

Heat the butter and cook the seasoned steaks quickly on both sides, remove and keep hot. Sauté the onion and mushroom for one minute, replace the steaks and flame with brandy. Add a few drops of Worcester sauce and the cream, reheat and finish with a pinch of the fines herbes. Serve immediately.

Steak au Poivre

2×150g sirloin steaks, 0.25dl brandy, 0.5dl port, 0.5dl jus lié, 0.5dl cream, coarsely ground peppercorns, 25g butter

(The steaks should be coated with crushed peppercorns from the mill and sautéd in the kitchen, transferred to the silver pan and brought hot to the guéridon.)
Pour the brandy over the steaks and flame. Remove the steaks to a plate, cover and keep hot. Add the port to the pan and allow to reduce by half. Add the jus lié and cream, and allow to reduce whilst stirring. Reduce the heat and mix in the butter to thicken the sauce. Place the steaks in the sauce to reheat then serve on two meat plates, coated with the sauce.
Madeira or white wine may be used instead of port and the waiter should enquire if the customer wishes for some of the peppercorns to be scraped off before serving.

Bécasses Flambées

2 woodock, 50g butter, 80g foie gras, 0.5dl brandy, 1dl red wine, 1dl game stock, lemon, nutmeg, salt, pepper

(The woodcock are roasted in the kitchen, each dressed on a croûton of fried bread and brought to the guéridon on a silver dish.)

Pour the wine into the silver pan, add a little grated lemon-rind and seasoning and allow to reduce slowly on the lamp. Cut the woodcock in half, remove the backbone, head and neck. Scoop out the liver and intestines and mash with the butter and foie gras using a fork; spread some on each croûton and send to the kitchen to have them grilled. Place the halves of woodcock into the pan with the wine, flame with brandy and place on plates, together with the heads which have been held in the flame of the lamp for 10 seconds. Add the stock to the pan, thicken with the remaining intestine mixture, season with a pinch of grated nutmeg and lemon juice but do not allow the sauce to boil. Place the pieces of woodcock on the croûtons, add the heads and strain the sauce over them.

12.4 CANARD À LA PRESSE

1 wild duck, 50g sieved raw duck liver, 1dl red wine, 0.5dl brandy

(The duck is roasted in the kitchen, keeping it underdone, and is brought to the guéridon whole.)

Remove the legs and return them to the kitchen for further cooking under the salamander. Carve the breasts into thin slices, overlapping onto a dish; cover and keep hot. Place the carcase into the press to extract the juices for making the sauce. Pour the duck juice and wine into the silver pan, bring to a boil and allow to reduce, then lower the heat and stir in the sieved liver to thicken the sauce and allow to boil for two to three minutes. Place the dish of sliced duck on the lamp, flame with brandy, transfer to plates and coat with the sauce, adding the duck's legs. Serve with pommes soufflées and a salad.

12.5 FLAMED SWEET DISHES

Bananes Flambées

25g butter, 3 peeled bananas cut in half lengthways, 0.5dl rum, caster sugar

Melt the butter and sprinkle well with sugar from the sifter. Place the bananas round side down in the pan, allow to colour slightly then turn over and colour the other side, basting occasionally; add more butter if necessary. Remove the pan from the lamp, pour the rum in at the side, replace on the lamp and allow to catch alight whilst shaking in more sugar. Serve three halves per portion, coated with the caramelised sauce.

Cerises Flambées

180g stoned, cooked cherries, 0.5dl port, 0.5dl kirsch, caster sugar

Pour the port into the silver pan and reduce until syrupy. Add the cherries with some of the thickened cooking juice and sprinkle with sugar whilst reheating. Remove from the lamp, pour the kirsch at the side of the pan, replace on the lamp, allow to catch alight and serve immediately.

Cerises Jubilée

Cook and flame the cherries as for Cerises Flambées and spoon them over balls of vanilla ice cream into coupes

Crêpes Flambées

6 pancakes, 0.25dl brandy, 0.25dl Grand Marnier, 1dl orange juice, juice of half a lemon, caster sugar

Sprinkle the pan liberally with sugar, add the juice of half a lemon and cook on the lamp without stirring until it begins to caramelise. Add the orange juice, reduce the heat then add and fold the pancakes, one at a time, so they are coated with the juice, pushing each to the end of the pan. Remove the pan from the lamp, add the Grand Marnier, replace and flame. Remove the pan from the lamp, add the brandy, place on the lamp and allow to catch alight, sprinkling well with sugar. Serve three pancakes per person, coated with the sauce.

Crêpes Suzette

80g butter, 80g sugar, 16 sugar knobs, 1 orange, 1 lemon, 0.5dl Grand Marnier or Curaçao, 0.5dl brandy, caster sugar

Prepare the Suzette butter by mixing the softened butter and sugar; rub 12 sugar knobs on the orange and 4 on the lemon to flavour them with the oils, then crush them together with the juices of both fruits and mix this well into the butter mixture, adding a little liqueur and brandy. Melt some of this mixture in the pan and coat and fold each pancake in it, adding more of the flavoured butter for each one. Remove the pan from the lamp, pour in the remaining liqueur, replace on the lamp, allow to catch alight and serve three pancakes each, overlapping on a hot plate, and covered with the sauce.

Omelette au Rhum

Pour 0.25dl warm rum over the made omelette, place the dish on the lamp and tilt to allow it to flame, dredging with caster sugar. Serve onto a hot plate.
Other liqueurs and spirits may be used to flame a sweet omelette.

Omelette de Noël

Make a sweet omelette and stuff it with warm mincemeat; pour some warm rum around it on the dish and set alight on the lamp.

Pêches Flambées

4 halves of peaches, 1 lemon, 0.5dl Cointreau, caster sugar, 0.25dl stock syrup or peach juice

Sprinkle the pan well with sugar, add the juice of half a lemon and place on the lamp to caramelise, without stirring. Place the peaches round side down in the syrup and prick them to allow the syrup to penetrate, adding more of the syrup or peach juice. Turn the peaches over and continue to cook. Remove from the lamp, pour the liqueur down one side, replace over the flame and allow it to ignite, dredging well with sugar.

12.6 FLAMED COFFEES

Café Brulot

2dl black coffee, 0.5dl brandy, 4 sugar knobs, 2 cloves, piece of cinnamon, orange, lemon, a few roasted coffee beans

Heat the beans by tossing in a sauteuse on the lamp. Add the brandy, spices and sugar knobs, previously rubbed on the skins of the orange and lemon. Allow to flame, then quickly add the coffee and reheat. Pour into demitasses, leaving the beans, cloves and cinnamon in the pan.

Café Diable

2dl black coffee, 4 sugar knobs, 2 cloves, piece of cinnamon, 0.5dl brandy, 1 orange, few roasted coffee beans

Heat the beans by tossing in a sauteuse on the lamp. Add the brandy, spices and sugar knobs, previously rubbed on the orange skin. Allow to flame, then add the coffee and juice of half the orange. Reheat and pour into demitasses, leaving the beans and spices behind.

12.7 MISCELLANEOUS FLAMBÉ DISHES

Christmas Pudding

Pour some warm brandy over the very hot pudding, and set alight with a taper just as it is taken into the dimmed dining room.

Bombe Vesuvius

Cover a base of sponge cake with layers of vanilla and straw-berry ice cream and some pieces of candied chestnuts. Place a hollow oval dried meringue shell on top and pipe all around with meringue. Colour quickly in a hot oven then fill the meringue with stoned cherries mixed with thickened juice. Pour warm brandy over the cherries and set it alight as the dish is taken into the darkened dining room.

Omelette Surprise Néron

Cover a base of sponge cake with ice cream and place a hollow oval dried meringue shell on top. Pipe all around with meringue, colour quickly in a hot oven then fill the meringue with warm rum and set it alight.

Flamed Consommé

Heat a little dry sherry in a soup ladle over the lamp then tilt slightly to allow it to catch alight. Pour gently into a portion of consommé and serve whilst still flaming.

12.8 USE OF SPIRITS AND LIQUEURS IN COOKING

Although brandy is the spirit most widely used for flambé dishes, some other spirits also have their uses with certain foods, provided that their flavour is in keeping with the main item and its garnish. The spirit must complement the dish because, although the alcohol may be burnt away, the underlying richness of flavour of the drink is left to give character and a rounded taste to the food. The spirit used should be of good quality since the customer may ask to see the label on the bottle, but it need not be the most expensive nor of highly refined quality. For example a three-star brandy is better than an older liqueur one, for cooking purposes. There is no point in adding a lot of spirit as it will overpower the food, nor should several kinds of spirit be used in one dish as they will clash. Only one kind of liqueur should be used in any dish or there will be too mismatched a mixture of tastes and flavours and in the end only one may predominate, so wasting the others.

In most cases it is advisable to remove the meat, fish, etc. from the chafing dish whilst flaming the pan, and to make any sauce before replacing the food. If food is allowed to boil in the resultant sauce it is likely to become stringy. When making Crêpes Suzette, the made pancakes must be turned and folded in the sauce over only a low flame, because they will become chewy if allowed to boil in it. Generally, the spirit should only be allowed to burn for a short time thereby preserving most of its aroma and taste.

Armagnac is a high-class brandy that is usually darker and less refined than cognac and may be used instead of it. Calvados is good with pork and some game dishes. There are several kinds of rum, including white Bacardi and Daiquiri, but for flambé work ordinary dark rum is used, mainly for an omelette or Christmas pudding.

Gin and Vodka do not leave any kind of flavour or aroma in dishes and are not therefore used to flame dishes.

Kirsch and Maraschino are distilled from cherries and their stones, and so are useful mainly in sweet dishes although they are not sweet in themselves. The orange-flavoured liqueurs such as Cointreau, Curaçao, Grand Marnier, Mandarine Napoleon, and Van der Hum, are suitable for duck and pork, and in many sweet dishes.

Whiskies which come from Scotland, Ireland, Canada and USA can be used to flame foods in place of brandy, but they leave a more pronounced taste and aroma. Liqueur whiskies such as Drambuie, Glayva and Glen Mist can be used for flaming fruits.

12.9   UNFLAMED DISHES

A *Chateaubriand* is a piece cut from the head end of the fillet of beef for two or more people, allowing approximately 250g of raw weight per person. It is flattened to about 6cm thickness so that it can be grilled as a steak to the degree of doneness as requested by the customer, though naturally the outside will be fairly well done while the inside is still fairly raw. At one time a chateaubriand was tied inside two outer beef steaks to be cooked, the outer steaks being discarded after they had served the purpose of protecting the actual chateaubriand. A chateaubriand is presented whole then cut into slices 15mm thick. The garnish is watercress, pommes soufflées, or pommes pont neuf, and parsley butter. Sauce Béarnaise is sometimes served as are a variety of mustards and the salt and pepper mills.

Steak Tartare is a raw finely chopped fillet of beef, moulded to the shape of a hamburger, with a raw yolk of egg on top, and surrounded with a selection of finely chopped onion, parsley, and gherkin and whole capers. To serve it, place the yolk in a small dish and mix into it half a tablespoonful each of vinegar and olive oil, a little French mustard, a few drops each of Tabasco and Worcester sauces, milled pepper and salt and, if requested, very little crushed garlic. Now mix in the raw beef and its garnish and mould again into a flat round cake, place on a plate and serve accompanied with sliced rye bread.

QUESTIONS

1. Indicate the reasons why, and say what, special precautions are necessary, prior to the introduction of table or guéridon cookery in a restaurant.

2. What are the principal characteristics of all the meat dishes which are cooked at the table?

3. In ideal conditions when should flambé dishes be served?

4. State which principles should be considered when deciding which particular kind or brand of spirit to use for flaming any given dish in the restaurant.

CHAPTER 13

SERVICE OF BREAKFAST, AFTERNOON TEA, AND SUPPER

13.1 INTRODUCTION

Breakfast, afternoon tea and supper are subsidiary meals as compared with luncheon and dinner, which are the two main meals. Yet these subsidiary meals have the potential of becoming substantial and of replacing either of the main ones.

Although considered as light meals, they fulfil a nutritional need in between the two main repasts and they also make the day more interesting from a gastronomic viewpoint. In a normal waking day it is possible to spend some three and a half hours at the table, with half an hour for breakfast, quarter of an hour for elevenses, three-quarters of an hour for lunch, half an hour for tea, an hour for dinner, and half an hour later on for supper. These six meals break the day into fairly even sessions.

Serving these meals correctly is as important as serving a three- or four-course main meal – in fact, these subsidiary meals can be more profitable than full ones because staff and food costs are less, and in many restaurants, part-time waiters are employed to serve them.

13.2 ENGLISH BREAKFAST

Some people feel fine when they wake up in the morning, while others feel jaded or irascible; both require a good meal to allay hunger and raise the blood-sugar level that has been lowered through being without food for some ten hours during the night.

The irascible ones need not only a good meal to help them recover, but also good service given in a patient and understanding manner, so as to help to prevent the customer losing his temper with the person on breakfast duty, over what may be only a minor detail.

The traditions of the English breakfast originated in medieval days when only two large meals were consumed daily – one between 8 and 9 o'clock in the morning, the other at about 4 o'clock in the afternoon, and this pattern lasted until the beginning of the nineteenth century.

The early meal consisted of cold and hot meats with bread. Ale was served as tea and coffee were not introduced into this country until towards the end of the seventeenth century. Porridge had long been a staple of the Scottish diet and the oatmeal it is made from is very beneficial for good health as it helps to lower the blood cholesterol to a safe level. In England frumenty was eaten for breakfast instead of porridge, and was made by steeping wheat in hot water to make it easy to hull, then drying and boiling it in milk, with sugar and spices. A pint of frumenty with bread and cheese was a typical breakfast for the inmates of workhouses during the eighteenth century and they then had to work exceedingly hard to earn their keep.

The English breakfast as served today is much smaller than it was in most upper-class households up to the beginning of the Second World War, when cold game birds and large cold joints were displayed on the sideboard to add an additional course to the half a dozen hot dishes that were obligatory. A traditional breakfast menu is stereotyped and does not vary very much from one establishment to another; it is only perhaps the quality of the ingredients that differ, according to the price charged in different restaurants. A full English breakfast usually consists of two courses, with bread items and a beverage and the menu is composed from dishes as shown in Table 13.1.

A waiter should know how to prepare a grapefruit half as this is one of the most popular breakfast dishes. Roll the grapefruit so as to release the juice within, cut in half horizontally then use a curved grapefruit knife to cut out the central core and any pips, then cut around each segment to release them from all skin and pith, but leaving segments in the half-skin. Place into a coupe, decorate with a maraschino cherry and serve on a d'oyley on an underplate accompanied by a sugar sifter. Special teaspoons are made to facilitate eating.

A soft-boiled egg, cooked for three to four minutes in the still-room is served in an egg-cup on a side-plate, with an egg-spoon which is of a size between a teaspoon and a coffee-spoon. The top of the shell can be removed by means of an egg-topper which is used like a pair of pincers to remove the shell only. Salt and pepper must be on the table at breakfast time. All other hot cooked dishes are obtained from the kitchen.

Table 13.1 *check-list of breakfast dishes*

First course

Fresh or canned fruit juices – orange, pineapple, tomato, tropical
  (a mixture of banana, apricot, mango, peach, pineapple, etc.),
  vegetable juices, passion fruit juice – served chilled
Stewed fruits (compotes) – apple, pear, prunes, figs – served cold,
  with cream if desired
Fresh fruits – apple, banana, fresh figs in season, grapefruit in
  halves or segments, kiwi fruit, melon, fresh pineapple, sharon
  fruit, tangerines
Hot cereals – oatmeal porridge, rolled oat porridge, cream of
  wheat, Readibrek, Quaker Oats – served with caster sugar,
  cream, honey, syrup, etc.
Proprietary brands of breakfast cereals – All Bran, Branflakes,
  Cornflakes, Grapenuts, Force, Frosties, muesli in several
  versions, Post Toasties, Rice Crispies, Shredded Wheat,
  Weetabix, etc., with cold milk, hot milk or cream
Yoghurt – plain, set, fruit, French, Greek

Second course

Fish – Yarmouth bloaters, grilled kippers, poached finnon
  haddock, kedgeree, fish-cakes, fried cod, scallops and bacon,
  grilled herrings, Arbroath smokies (cured small haddocks)
Eggs – boiled, fried, turned-over, poached, scrambled, shirred;
  omelettes – plain, cheese, ham, Spanish, tomato
Meats – back bacon, streaky bacon, gammon rasher – Danish or
  Wiltshire; sausages and chipolatas – beef, pork, chicken
Cold meat – cold York ham, pressed beef, brawn, ox-tongue
Hot dishes – fried black pudding, fried sliced Bath Chap, grilled
  lamb's kidneys, fried calf's liver
Vegetables – sauté potatoes, French-fried potatoes, potato cakes,
  grilled mushrooms, grilled tomatoes, baked beans

Additional items

Bread – fried bread, French toast, Bermaline, Daren, Hovis, white, wholemeal, French

Rolls, etc. – baps, brioches, crispbread, croissants, Energen rolls, muffins, oatcakes, potato scones, bread rolls, toast – served hot; waffles, Scotch pancakes or buckwheat cakes served hot with maple syrup

Preserves – apricot, blackcurrant, raspberry or strawberry jam, honey of various flavours, marmalade

Butter – curls or pats

Beverages – coffee, decaffeinated coffee, hot chocolate, Instant Postum, Horlicks, milk

tea – *China*: Earl Grey blended with a little Indian and bergamot oil, Gunpowder, Keemun, Lapsang Souchong, Yunnan *Indian*: Assam, Darjeeling; also Ceylon and Kenya

---

13.3 CONTINENTAL BREAKFAST

In this country when a customer orders a Continental breakfast he will be given the French version but in fact each continental country has its own traditional kind of breakfast.

The generally accepted menu is:

coffee with milk
brioche, croissant or bread roll
toast, portion of preserves
butter portion

Optional extras may include chilled fruit juice, cereal, yoghurt, or perhaps a boiled egg, but is not then a true continental breakfast but something in between that and an English breakfast.

Many people in France do not have petit déjeuner as a breakfast, instead they order a Café Complet which is really the equivalent of a continental breakfast and is partaken at any time of the day. By law, tourist hotels in France must serve breakfast, preferably in the bedroom, otherwise in an annexe to the restaurant.

13.4 BREAKFAST SERVICE IN THE RESTAURANT

It is usual to lay tables for breakfast the previous evening, putting a full cover so as to be prepared for every possible request from the menu. The 'cover', which is the word used to describe the complement of cutlery and crockery required for a meal, for breakfast, consists of:

Knives – joint, fish, side
forks – joint, fish, dessert
spoons – tea, dessert, preserve
crockery – breakfast-size cup (3dl), saucer, side-plate, slop basin, under-plates for coffee pot and milk jug
other – cruet, sugar sifter, tea strainer, ashtray, table number, table napkin, flowers in vase, sugar bowl

When the customer arrives at table the waiter must bring the dish of butter-pats, jug of milk or cream, dish of preserve, basket of warm bread rolls or croissants, and rack of hot toast. The hot beverage as chosen by the customer is brought direct from the still-room as soon as the cereal or other first course is finished. Figure 13.1 shows the normal breakfast cover or lay up; any spare cutlery is removed as soon as the order is taken.

The routine of breakfast service varies from one restaurant to another; in some places the customer must go to a buffet table to select his first course and take it to the table allocated by the head

Fig 13.1 *lay-up for English breakfast*

waiter. The waiter presents the menu, takes the order for the main course and beverage and serves them. To obtain these things he has to write out a check each for kitchen and still-room on which is written the customer's room number, if on bed-and-breakfast or board-and-lodging terms, or the price payable if the customer is a non-resident.

When the main course has been eaten the waiter must remove the used dishes and cutlery and move the side-plate to the centre, and if requested, fetch another rack of toast or more hot beverage.

The service of Continental breakfast in the restaurant is straight-forward and the cover laid on the table consists of tea-cup, saucer and teaspoon, small plate and side-knife, under-plates for the hot beverage, a table napkin and bowl of sugar. As soon as the customer is seated the waiter must bring a dish of butter-pats, the warm roll and croissant, dish of preserve and the beverage as ordered. He places these within easy reach of the customer, the handles of the pots directed inwards.

Continental breakfasts vary from country to country but all include a hot or cold beverage and a choice of bread with butter and preserve. The following variations should be noted:

Germany – various sausages, salami and cooked type of cheese
Holland – sliced Edam or Gouda cheese, luncheon meat or ham
Italy – soft-boiled eggs, fruit, cheese, pastries.

Breakfast dishes are also featured on the menus of night-clubs and gaming houses, which stay open until the early hours of the morning.

13.5 TIFFIN AND BRUNCH

Tiffin is an Anglo-Indian word to denote a light meal taken towards the end of the morning. It was originally a dish of curried meat, vegetables or eggs, served with boiled or braised rice, plus the usual sambals of sliced banana, chutney, toasted coconut, chopped apple, peanuts, pickled walnuts and sliced pimento, as well as poppadums and Bombay ducks. It is not often served like this now and is more likely to be the kind of meal described as brunch.

Brunch is a portmanteau word coined from breakfast and lunch; it is a snack meal eaten towards the latter part of the morning and consists of items from the main course of an English breakfast and light lunch dishes.

The dishes served include several items served on toast – baked beans with grilled rashers of streaky bacon, tomatoes on toast, fried, poached or scrambled eggs on toast, toasted cheese, sausages on toast, etc. Other suitable dishes are Frankfurters in a soft finger-shape roll, hamburger in a toasted roll, cheeseburger (that is, a hamburger steak finished with a slice of processed cheese melted on top) and brunchburger (a hamburg steak with a fried egg on top). Flapjacks and waffles can be served with grilled bacon, sausage or tomato, or with maple syrup, diced fruit, cream, etc. Tea, coffee or hot chocolate can be served for brunch.

Elevenses are light refreshments served briefly between breakfast and lunch. At their most basic they are just a cup of tea or coffee and a biscuit, but it is possible to attract customers to partake of a cake with their coffee at this time of day, in fact Danish pastries, cream cakes, doughnuts, slices of torten and filled rolls are ideal. In late Victorian times it was fashionable to take a glass of Madeira wine and a slice of Madeira cake as a mid-morning reviver, or as an appetiser in advance of the midday meal.

13.6 FLOOR SERVICE FOR BREAKFAST

Room service is sometimes known as *floor service* and is the service of food in a residential establishment to people staying in a suite of rooms or a bedroom.

A luxury hotel will employ a number of staff whose duties are solely to serve meals in private apartments. Meals served may be the same as in the public restaurant though the prices charged may be slightly higher. Some hotels have a separate menu printed for floor service but the food is prepared by the chefs in the main kitchen. A smaller or less luxurious hotel may not find it profitable to employ a waiter specifically for floor service and will use a part-timer to serve breakfasts and a waiter from the restaurant for any orders at other times.

Room service of breakfasts

Many hotels encourage guests to eat breakfast in the bedroom, offering a service from about 7.00 a.m. until 10.30 a.m. or even later. Breakfast service in the restaurant has to end early so as to have the room ready for lunch by 12.15 p.m. A guest can order breakfast (i) by using the internal telephone and speaking to the floor head waiter; (ii) by giving the order to the hall porter or receptionist; or (iii) by using the order form as shown in Figure 13.2. Should a guest forget to

Fig 13.2 *breakfast order form for room service*

Hôtel Ambassador

ℋA

Floor Service Breakfast

please hang on outside ( ) door knob before 5.00 am

Room N° __ N° of Persons __ Serve at __ am

Please tick items required or indicate number of portions if more than one

Coffee ☐   Tea ☐   Milk ☐
Hot Chocolate ☐   Tomato Juice ☐
Orange Juice ☐   Grapefruit ☐

Boiled Egg ☐ | 3 | 3½ | 4 | 4½ | minutes
Poached Egg ☐   Scrambled Egg ☐

Porridge ☐   Cornflakes ☐

Roll ☐   Croissant ☐   Brioche ☐
Toast ☐   Butter ☐   Marmalade ☐

have a good day

place his order in advance he may be kept waiting if he places it at the last minute.

It is usual to have a pantry on each or every alternate floor of an hotel, in which waiters assemble the orders. The head floor waiter distributes the orders received to the appropriate pantries which are stocked with all the necessary equipment. Trays are assembled in advance, laid in line according to requested time of serving and with the room number and copy order on each. Orders for cooked food are passed to the breakfast cook in the kitchen who will cook and plate the items to be sent up by service lift at approximately the requested time.

The tray is prepared by covering it with a small cloth, adding a side-plate with a folded serviette, a small knife, a saucer and teaspoon on it ready to add a hot cup at the moment of service. Figure 13.3 shows the completed breakfast tray with the pot of coffee, jug of hot milk, (or pot of tea and jug of cold milk), basin of sugar with a teaspoon in it, dish of butter-pats, plate with small pots of preserves, plate or basket with the warm rolls or croissants, or rack with several slices of freshly made toast, and the hot cups. Some hotels offer a free daily newspaper and deliver it with the breakfast, otherwise a porter will push it under the bedroom door.

The hot beverages may be made on a machine installed in the pantry on each floor or if that is not justified, the beverages will be sent from the still-room. However, it is best to make tea just before serving the breakfast, drawing the boiling water from a kettle or the

Fig 13.3   *breakfast tray for two persons*

tap of a hot-water boiler in the pantry. Toast should also be made as required in a toaster in the pantry. This means issuing a limited range of items to each pantry and controlling the usage; the stock should include tea-bags, sugar, butter-pats, and individual pots of preserve, and there should be a daily issue of bread, rolls, croissants and milk.

Service of hot beverages from the still-room must be carried out quickly. A written order for the required number of pots is sent by hand or by a pneumatic tube system, if installed; otherwise the orders may be phoned directly to the still-room. The means of delivery may be by a dumb-waiter or in a goods or service lift by a liftman.

At the appointed time the waiter carries the breakfast tray to the room, balancing it on the open palm of his left hand and left shoulder, leaving the right hand free to knock on the door before entering. He should listen for the customer to tell him to come in and use his pass key to open the door, say 'good morning' or pass a comment on the weather, and with both hands, place the tray on the bedside table, on the luggage stand, or on the bed. When several guests on one corridor all request breakfast at about the same time, all the trays may be placed on a trolley and wheeled along.

When the customer has eaten breakfast he may ring room service to have the tray removed; if not, the waiter should return to collect it after about half an hour. In some hotels, Continental breakfasts are served by the chambermaids, in the same way as early morning tea.

13.7 AFTERNOON TEA

Afternoon tea is a repast that follows a time-hallowed tradition and conforms to a menu that is practically the same in every establishment and includes a selection of items as shown in Figure 13.4. As can be seen there are a number of sections or courses but it is in order to serve these all at once by putting a dish of each on the low table to allow customers to help themselves. They will probably follow their childhood pattern and eat the bread and butter before the cake.

The pastrycook bakes small-size cakes and pastries and the larder chef cuts dainty sandwiches for afternoon tea; the cakes can be consumed in a few mouthfuls, using a cake fork, which has one flat prong with a sharpish edge to cut the cake into pieces and two more prongs to pierce and convey it to the mouth.

Afternoon tea is normally served in a foyer or lounge so as to provide an informal environment; there may be a pianist or small group of musicians playing appropriate melodious pieces.

Fig 13.4 *afternoon tea menu*

AFTERNOON TEA MENU

White Bread and Butter
Brown Bread and Butter
Jam • Honey • Lemon Curd
Asparagus Spears rolled in Brown Bread
Sandwiches of chicken spread,
cucumber, egg and cress, tomato,
foie gras puree and salmon paste
Sliced and Buttered Fruit Loaf
Biscuits – brandy snaps, chocolate,
digestive, ginger nuts, oatcakes,
shortbread and Shrewsbury
Hot toasted Teacakes, Sally Lunns and Muffins
Chelsea buns, Lardy cake
Gingerbread, Swiss Roll
Macaroons, Madeleines
Fruit Cake, Queen Cakes
Scones filled with Raspberry Jam and Cream
French Pastries – chocolate éclairs, fondant
fancies, strawberry barquettes, rum babas,
cream horns and millefeuilles
Tea with milk or lemon
* * * *
Cornish Cream Tea
served daily from 4–5 pm

Home made Scones with
our own Strawberry Jam
and Clotted Cream

China or Indian Tea

Afternoon tea is usually sold at a set price per person and there is no need for the waiter to take the order but simply to write out a check for so many teas at so much each, then bring the required amount of items, place them on the table and leave the customer to get on with it. The plates full of the various sandwiches, cakes and biscuits are left on the tea table for customers to help themselves, and the waiter is not expected to pour out the tea.

The equipment consists of teacup and saucer, side-plate, teaspoon, small knife, cake-fork, bowl of sugar knobs and sugar tongs, dish each of butter and preserve, pot of tea, pot of hot water, jug of cold milk, tea strainer, slop basin, small serviette, possibly a dish of sliced lemon, plus the number of items from the menu, in reasonable portions.

The waiter should ask the customer which variety of tea he requires and should obtain the pot from the still-room, where it will have been freshly made in a warmed teapot, with boiling water. If it is the policy to use portion-control tea-bags there is no need for a strainer but it still takes five minutes for tea to brew to perfection, whether using loose tea or tea-bags.

Apart from the well-known brands and the caterers' blends, there are a number of special teas which are appreciated by discerning customers and a waiter should get to know the quality of such teas as:

Earl Grey – a tea of luxury quality that is lightly flavoured with bergamot, and used mainly for afternoon tea;
Assam – this tea comes from the finest tea-gardens of North India, and is blended to give a very full, rich, slightly malty flavour that is excellent for drinking at breakfast time;
Darjeeling – this is reckoned to be the finest of all the many kinds of tea and is noted for its bouquet of muscatel grapes that endears it to connoisseurs of a good cup of tea.

It should be remembered that tea is the British national beverage and many British people are heavy tea drinkers and can tell a good cup of tea when they drink it. Customers have their own preference and the waiter should ensure their order is fulfilled correctly as some kinds of tea taste wrong if served with milk and some herbal teas such as camomile and jasmine do not require either milk or lemon and are taken merely to relieve a headache.

Thé-dansant is a popular form of entertainment that combines the ritual of afternoon tea with ballroom dancing. An inclusive charge is made, or customers pay an entrance fee and order and pay for the tea meal separately. A group will play appropriate music to create a sedate and leisurely atmosphere.

A Garden Party is usually held during the afternoon so that afternoon tea is the appropriate meal to be served. Full details can be found in Chapter 14.

13.8 HIGH TEA

This meal is more substantial than ordinary afternoon tea, being made so by the addition of a hot or cold fish, meat, egg or cheese dish, and a sweet. It could also be described as a combined tea and supper meal because for some people, particularly young children and the elderly, it is the last meal of the day.

Many hotels organise the service of high tea for all the children in residence so as to enable parents to enjoy their evening meal alone, or it may be served on a tray in the bedroom from 6.00 p.m. to 7.00 p.m. The menu may include some children's specialities such as Spaceships on Toast with Moon Juice, Spider Cake and Cobweb Pudding, or Singing Angels and Sparkling Shimmer Drink. This system is also a feature of cruise-liner catering, with a number of waiters known for their patience with children being detailed for this extra duty.

Since high tea is a formal meal, the table must be laid as for table d'hôte lunch, complete with cruet and mustard plus teacup, saucer and teaspoon, in order to accommodate the type of menu shown in Figure 13.5 which is suitable for children of 5 years and upwards as well as the elderly.

The planning of this meal is critical since it may be the last of the day and there will be a gap of twelve hours or more until the next day's breakfast. Foods that are indigestible, such as shellfish, should not be served in case they disturb the sleep of the recipients.

The normal pattern of service when there is a sweet is for the customer to eat the sandwiches and cakes first, then the waiter serves the main dish, either hot or cold, and the drink. After clearing the empty plates he serves the sweet but if a sweet is not included, the main dish should be served first. The sandwiches and cakes can be placed on the table for guests to help themselves.

13.9 SUPPER AND EVENING MEALS

Supper and late-evening meals are more of a household meal than a restaurant one and are only served commercially in places such as a

Fig 13.5 *menu for high tea*

MENU FOR HIGH TEA

Assorted Sandwiches
Sliced Fruit Cake
Swiss Roll
Fruit Loaf

* * *

Eggs – Poached or Scrambled on Toast
or
Buck Rarebit
or
Poached Finnon Haddock
or
Cold Ham and Pickles

* * *

Chocolate Mousse
or
Apple Fritter and Custard

* * *

Tea, Ovaltine, Bovril, Barley Water
Roll and Butter

gaming house or night club that stay open to members from late evening to early morning.

The menu is usually à la Carte, with a limited number of dishes that can be made fairly quickly with a small amount of preparation. In these places the meal, though of importance and quite highly priced, is not the prime reason for the customer's presence – the customer has come for the gambling, the dancing, the floor show, the company, or the drink, rather than for a gastronomic occasion. Indeed in some locations there may be only sandwiches or a limited selection of cold meats. Figure 13.6 shows some of the dishes that are appropriate for consumption late at night, the emphasis being more on English savouries such as mushrooms or sardines on toast than on rich sweets.

As the night progresses so may customers' thoughts turn to breakfast so the same menu must accommodate a few traditional breakfast dishes, or an English breakfast may be featured at an inclusive cost, for example, grilled bacon and sausage, mushrooms, tomato and fried egg.

The service should be highly professional because the clientele is usually knowledgeable and cosmopolitan and expects its every whim to be catered for. Customers may leave the table and dance between courses, thus the waiter must be aware of the progress through the meal to each customer on his station.

Flambé work was a prominent feature of food service in night-clubs in the years between the two World Wars and certainly the effect of flaming food is more marked in the subdued lighting of a room of this kind. It is not now so widely practised because of restricted space and more stringent fire precautions.

Restaurants located in the theatreland of major cities can offer pre-theatre dinners and after-theatre suppers, and also during the lengthy intervals between the Acts of some operas, when there is time to leave the opera house for at least a two-course meal. The menu for an after-theatre supper is usually the normal à la Carte with its wide choice of dishes for cooking to order, as at that late hour the table d'hôte menu would most likely be finished.

13.10 FLOOR SERVICE

In a residential establishment such as an hotel or block of service apartments, waiters are employed to serve food in rooms from approximately 7.00 a.m. to 11.00 p.m. daily. The demand is likely to be spasmodic but may call for food in the form of an elaborate meal

Fig 13.6   *night-club supper menu*

À LA CARTE

Avocado Pear with Prawns £4.50
Iranian Caviar £40   Ogen Melon £4
Smoked Scotch Salmon £6.50

* * *

French Onion Soup £2.50   Consommé £3

* * *

Grilled Kippers £3.50   Lobster Newburg £12
Scampi Provençale £7   Haddock Monte Carlo £6

* * *

Beef Strogonoff £12   Spaghetti Bolognaise £6
Suprême of Chicken à la Kiev £12
Gammon Steak and Fried Egg £8
Grilled Sirloin Steak (300g) £12
Vienna Schnitzel £11   Cold Buffet £10

* *

Cream Caramel £5.20   Raspberry Melba £6
Cherry Cheesecake £4.50   Lemon Pancakes £5

* * *

Club Sandwich £5   Welsh Rarebit £4.50
Croque Madame or Monsieur £4.50
Cheeseboard £4

* * *

or merely a sandwich and a bottle of beer, both have to be met without delay, even though the number of waiters is kept low.

An hotel can have a separate section for room service with a head floor waiter, a number of waiters and several commis waiters and there may even be a floor wine waiter. The head waiter will have an office where guests can telephone to request him to bring a menu and wine list and take the order for a meal.

According to the volume of business there will be a floor waiter's pantry on each floor, or one for each two or three floors of the hotel. Each pantry will be equipped with an internal telephone to link it with the bedrooms, the head waiter's office, the kitchen, and the still-room. The equipment required includes cupboards for crockery and cutlery, sink for washing up (or a small dishwasher), hotplate, oven, bain-marie, toaster and refrigerator; there will also be a hot-water fount, possibly associated with a coffee-making machine or if not, a Cona-type machine plus an egg-boiling machine and a butter-pat machine – in short, a miniature still-room and kitchen.

The utensils required include trays for serving meals, crockery, cutlery, glassware, linen and silverware. Each pantry must have its own inventory listing every item of equipment, which should not be allowed to stray and should be totally self-contained.

13.11 ROOM SERVICE

There is a difference between Floor Service and Room Service – the latter is a more economical system in terms of staff, space and equipment, gives a faster service and exerts more effective control.

There are no waiter's pantries for Room Service, only an office situated close to the kitchen and still-room. This gives centralised control, especially if there is space to lay out the trays and trolleys, and the site is adjacent to the service lift.

Orders are received by a cashier over the telephone and given to one of a number of waiting-staff who are free to serve any room on any floor. There is a set menu in each room and customers are restricted to ordering only the dishes listed. A head waiter is in overall charge.

When the cashier receives an order she processes it on the billing-machine and gives a copy to a waiter to fulfil. The check will have the room number, details of the food requested, the price, the waiter's number, the date, and the sequence number of the check. The waiter takes the check to the kitchen, still-room or dispense bar to order the goods, arranges them on a tray or trolley, then has to pass the cashier who checks the items against her copy order.

The waiter takes the tray to the room, via the lift, and asks the customer to sign the order as proof of having received the food and drink as ordered. On returning to the servery he gives the check to the cashier who passes it for payment and the waiter is then available for further duties.

The advantages of this system is that all staff are kept equally busy and are all available at peak periods; the service can be carried out quickly especially if there is a high-speed lift, so there should not be any complaints about hot food being served lukewarm. It is possible to use the Ganymede system as outlined in Appendix 1, to keep hot food piping hot, using the heated pellets during transit.

QUESTIONS

1. Give an outline of the work involved for a three-course meal with wine served in a guest's room on the top storey of a luxury hotel.

2. Describe the service procedure for afternoon tea.

3. How does the organisation of a breakfast served in the room differ from breakfast served in the main dining room?

4. List ten dishes suitable for a supper menu.

FUNCTION CATERING

14.1 DEFINITION OF A FUNCTION

In catering terms a 'function' means a meal served as a special occasion in a room set aside for these purposes and usually for a large number of people. Any party of customers larger than can normally be seated at one table in a restaurant may be given a private room, where available, and a meal served to a larger number than that may be termed a banquet.

A *banquet* is a special meal supplied to a group of persons who belong to a particular association and who wish to meet and eat together because of their like interests, usually annually. This makes it a special occasion and the menu and service should therefore be of a higher standard than for the normal daily routine. A banquet can be held at lunch- or dinner-time and the pattern of operation may vary from one kind to another but it is a formal occasion and traditional protocol should be followed.

An establishment that has accommodation available and the necessary back-up catering facilities will find there is a demand for this kind of large-scale food service, especially at weekends. Additional revenue can be had from relatively little outlay since the food is cooked by the normal kitchen staff as part of their everyday duties and the necessary waiting-staff are engaged on a casual basis and paid only for the actual hours of work in serving the meal.

14.2 SPACE UTILISATION

This is the way in which maximum use is made of available floor-space to ensure that each square metre of space produces a monetary return. It also ensures that each customer at a banquet is seated comfortably and that there is sufficient circulatory space for waiters to carry out their job efficiently.

The *banqueting room* has to conform to the safety regulations and be approved by the local fire officer to accommodate a maximum number of persons. The *banquet manager* draws up seating plans that allow free access to all the exits.

The formal method of seating at a banquet is to have a top table that will accommodate the officials and honoured guests, and sprigs from it to seat the remaining number of people, leaving sufficient space between each sprig for waiters to move in to serve. This style of seating makes the maximum use of available space and can quickly be set up for the meal and moved if the room has to be cleared in readiness for a dance floor.

The individual method of banquet-seating is less formal because groups of friends can be seated at tables of various sizes, or the organiser can allocate each seat as he thinks fit for his members. The following figures demonstrate how different seating arrangements affect the number of available seats. Figure 14.1(a) shows a banqueting room measuring 15 metres × 12 metres furnished with tables of the normal width of 90 cm; the table length per person is 50 cm and the organiser has requested a top table for 15 persons. The full complement is therefore 149. Figure 14.1(b) shows the same room arranged on the individual system with tables for 10 persons each; this gives a seating capacity of 120. By having tables or two different sizes, as shown in Figure 14.1(c) some seating eight, the others eleven persons, there is a capacity of 103.

Using the room for a reception when only a few chairs are required, the number of persons can be as high as 200 without overcrowding, as shown in Figure 14.2. To accommodate a formal meeting or lecture the same size of room can seat an audience of 162, as shown in Figure 14.3. All these examples are meant to assume that there is a separate reception area and cloakrooms, and for some of the functions, a bar in an anteroom.

14.3   CHECK-LIST

When carrying out banqueting business, each function is an individual operation and can take a different form. It is only the service that follows a routine pattern with all the other arrangements being carried out to meet the requirements of the organiser. A Banquet Booking Form as shown in Fig 14.4 covers the formal agreement between banqueting manager and client but the check-list shown in

Fig 14.1 *banquet seating arrangements*

(a)

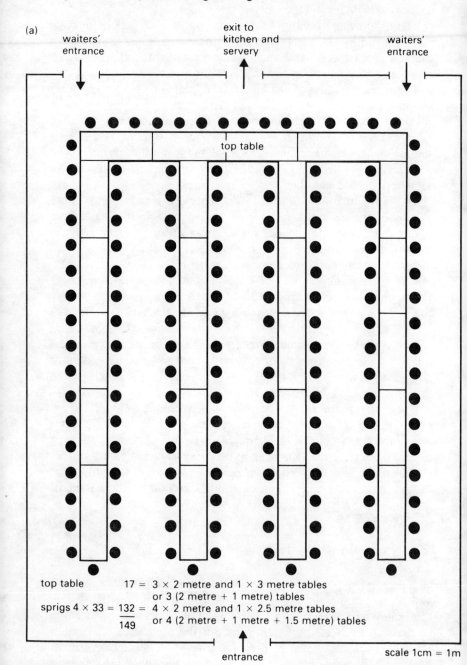

waiters' entrance

exit to kitchen and servery

waiters' entrance

top table

top table	17 = 3 × 2 metre and 1 × 3 metre tables or 3 (2 metre + 1 metre) tables
sprigs 4 × 33 = 132 = 149	4 × 2 metre and 1 × 2.5 metre tables or 4 (2 metre + 1 metre + 1.5 metre) tables

entrance

scale 1cm = 1m

Note: A banqueting room measuring 12 m× 15 m seats 149 guests on the communal seating plan; this allows sufficient space for entrance and exits for customers and waiters

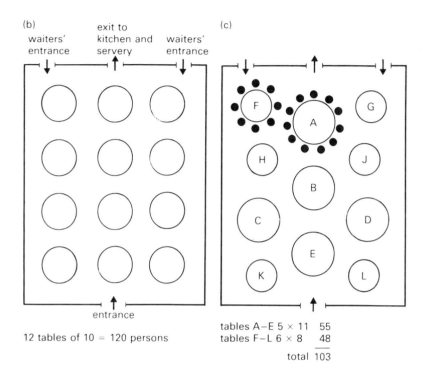

(b)

waiters' entrance   exit to kitchen and servery   waiters' entrance

↓ ↑ ↓

entrance

12 tables of 10 = 120 persons

(c)

↓ ↑ ↓

F   A   G

H   J

B

C   D

E

K   L

↑

tables A–E 5 × 11   55
tables F–L 6 × 8   48
              total 103

This is the same room as shown in Fig 14.1(a) but laid up for a less formal banquet on the Individual Seating plan

Table 14.1 gives a detailed synopsis that informs each key member of staff of his duties connected with a particular banquet.

14.4 STAFFING QUOTAS

The requisite number of waiting staff for serving at a banquet is related to the final number of persons attending and as only a small nucleus of permanent staff is retained, the remainder is recruited from the local pool of extra waiters. These casual workers are paid

Fig 14.2 *room arranged for a reception*

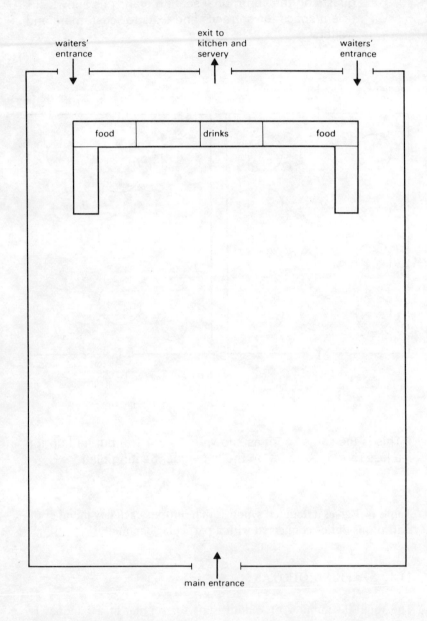

Note: The same banqueting room as shown in Figure 14.1 arranged for a Reception, will hold approximately 200 people comfortably

Fig 14.3 *seating arrangements for a lecture*

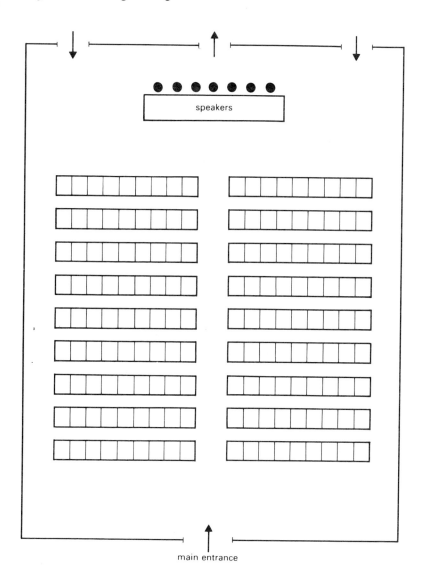

speakers

main entrance

Note: The banqueting room is arranged for a meeting with a central gangway and ample leg-room between the rows of comfortable chairs with arm-rests. It shows the possibility of accommodating the platform with seven speakers and an audience of at least 162 persons

Fig 14.4 *banquet booking form*

Hôtel Ambassador

ℋA

Banquet Booking Form

Function	Dinner and Dance
Date	Wednesday 17ᵗʰ March 1988
Time	7·⁰⁰ for 7⁴⁵ pm
Organiser	Mr James A Johnson
Firm or Society	Grange Lodge Buildings
Address	333 Wentworth Street SW21 6XJ
Number of persons	125
Price	£35·00 p.p. + VAT (£60 gratuities)
Room	Haywork Suite
Menu cards	75 @ £1·10 each
Place cards	we to do
Seating plan	Organiser - top table for 12
Toastmaster	Mr Hamish Grace (he = £25)
Flowers	Button holes for 70
Band	Blue Star Group (£130)
Cabaret	Joan Turner and Micky Finn (£75)
Tombola	They to do
Menu number	N° 7 with extra fish course
Wines	2 cases Bin N° 7 + 2 cases Bin N° 21
Liqueurs	Carvoisier or Green Chartreuse, add to Me
Buffet	8 services each of pasties & sandwiches @ 11·30pm
Reception	10 trays of canapés, nuts etc - cash bar

Table 14.1 *check-list for special functions*

1. Description – e.g. banquet, buffet, wedding breakfast
2. Date and time of the event; times of arrival and departure
3. Name of the organiser and the organisation (bank references)
4. Estimated and guaranteed number of persons
5. Names and titles of any special guests whom the manager should see
6. Room/s allocated for the function
7. Lay-out of the rooms
8. Engagement of toastmaster or master of ceremonies
9. Drinks to be sold in the reception bar
10. Food to be available in the bar for the reception
11. Details of the menu
12. Wine bin numbers and number of bottles authorised
13. Printing of menus and writing of place-cards
14. Lay-up of the cover, including napkin fold
15. Florist's instructions, corsage for each lady, presentation bouquets, table decorations
16. Number of casual waiters required and hours of duty
17. Arrangement for speeches and toasts; public address system
18. After-dinner drinks on sale
19. Service of light refreshments during the dancing
20. Details of cabaret artistes and orchestras
21. Duties of the electrician
22. Time of closure of the bar
23. Time for carriages and name of duty manager
24. Approximate time sequence of the entire function

Copies to:

Head Cellarman	Head Chef
Linen-keeper	Banqueting Manager
Florist	Duty Manager
Night Porter	Hotel Engineer

the same agreed rate per hour or session and are expected to serve up to twelve guests at one table or station. It may be silver service from a large flat onto the customer's plate, or nouvelle cuisine style on separate plates that have to be carried on a salver. They must be capable of clearing the tables afterwards and carry the ten to twelve plates and cutlery out in one go. For some banquets the service is done with two waiters working in tandem to serve two stations, one, the most experienced, serving all the main course, followed by the second with the vegetables and potatoes.

If the ticket for the banquet includes wine, one waiter can serve four stations but if he has to take orders for wine and obtain payment, he will be kept busy dealing with three stations. It is however, the practice on such occasions, to take orders for wine during the reception.

14.5 ARRANGEMENTS FOR SPECIAL FUNCTIONS

The check-list shown in Table 14.1 shows the routine of banqueting work from the arrival of guests to the end of the function, but there are other aspects of organisation that are dealt with by the head banquet waiter as part of his duties. His participation is of great help in the absence of a toastmaster, and when the chairman or organiser of the function is not experienced in the protocol of banquet procedure. The head waiter can help in the following ways:

(a) make the announcement that dinner is served;
(b) conduct the important guests to their places at the top table when the main body of guests have found their seats;
(c) announce Grace;
(d) check that the waiter for the top table is at the head of the line of waiters at the service hotplate ready to lead the way in;
(e) see that waiters enter the room in an orderly fashion;
(f) give the signals for the commencement and clearing of each course;
(g) announce the toasts and speakers;
(h) check that condiments are removed and tables cleared of crumbs before waiters leave the room while the speeches are being given;
(i) ensure that waiters keep quiet outside the room during the speeches;
(j) address any people of note or rank in the correct manner.

Arrangements for specific functions are as follows:

Receptions   These are usually less formal occasions than banquets and the organisation is fairly simple. They are meetings to celebrate or commemorate a particular event such as the introduction to the press of a well-known person, to raise funds for a charity, to make a presentation, or to publicise a product.

There can be a buffet table of food and drink, or waiters who serve it from trays but the only chairs will be for any elderly people who are invited. Suitable food for this kind of function includes sandwiches, cocktail canapés, bouchées, crisps, salted almonds, olives, sausage rolls, all of a size that can be consumed in at most two bites. Drinks can be red or white wines, aperitifs such as sherry, or spirits, including whisky, gin or vodka, mixed with suitable mineral waters.

A *Cocktail Party* is organised on the same lines as a Reception but to be in keeping with the name, there must be cocktails instead of, or in addition to other wines and spirits. It would not be possible to shake individual cocktails so the method is to make stirred cocktails in jugs and to pour and decorate them by the trayful.

Balls These are lively, crowded events given under names such a Hunt Ball, Charity Ball, Military Ball, or Commemoration Ball, as given by a college of a University. The main meal is a fairly formal one, probably of several sittings but there will be a number of cash bars and food kiosks on separate sites in the grounds.

Garden Parties These are afternoon or early evening, summertime functions held in the open air, usually in an elegant marquee in which food is served. The catering is done on the buffet style with plenty of tables and chairs for those who want to sit down to eat but as the food usually consists of dainty sandwiches, filled bridge rolls, fancy cakes and biscuits, it can be consumed while standing up. Sometimes a more substantial meal is served, one that may be eaten by means of a fork and spoon, such as chicken, salmon or lobster mayonnaise followed by fresh fruit salad. Suitable drinks are hot or iced tea, soft drinks, or Pimms No 1 cup. Service would be from a buffet table with staff to assist and others to serve drinks and to clear away the empty plates and cups.

Silver and Golden Weddings These are celebratory functions in the form of a dinner or reception in honour of a long married life, usually booked and paid for by a relation of the happy couple. The theme of the room can be carried out in white and gold or silver and the service will be decided by the style of the meal – either sit-down or buffet-type. There should be a cake to cut and speeches and toasts, often followed by a dance. Ruby and Diamond wedding celebrations follow the same lines as these.

Wedding Breakfasts These are meals partaken after the solemnisa-tion of a marriage by inviting guests to celebrate at a formal meal or reception. The menu for a sit-down meal could be as shown in

Appendix 4. If a buffet meal is served the food should be cut into fairly small pieces to facilitate being eaten with a fork only. The food should be displayed on a central table in order that guests can approach it from several service points. Dishes of cold fish and meat with salads are appropriate.

A formal wedding breakfast requires a top table for seating members of both families and honoured guests in accordance with the plan shown in Figure 14.5. The head waiter may be asked to act as the Master of Ceremonies by regulating the programme from the time of arrival to the toasts and speeches, including the ceremony of cutting the cake.

Medieval Banquets   This kind of function holds great appeal, particularly for visitors from overseas who are happy to participate in the jollifications that make for an evening of fun. It is usual to decorate the banqueting room with artificial tapestries and stained-glass windows and to engage singers and musicians to play tunes of the period. Waiting-staff should be dressed in medieval costumes with some to represent buxom wenches. Jesters, tumblers and other entertainers would provide plenty of amusement throughout the meal which should be plentiful and authentic, as shown in the example in Appendix 4.

Children's Parties   Catering for children is not as easy as it would appear, mainly because of the varying tastes of different age groups; the very young accept all they are offered whereas teenagers require a more sophisticated menu including pizzas, burgers and other savoury foods, in preference to sweet dishes.

The meal must be the highlight of the party and can be arranged on a fashionable theme that is instantly recognised and appreciated. The entertainment can echo the theme, though the traditional features of clowns and magicians are always acceptable. Games with prizes, and a piece of the party cake to take home in a loot bag, can round off the event, though from the age of 9 upwards most children are ready to let down their hair for a disco.

Kosher Catering   This is a highly specialised form of catering that only a few establishments are capable of carrying out correctly. Whenever a group of Jewish people attend an organised banquet it has to be held in an authorised venue which has been approved by Jewish religious officials.

The basic Jewish food law is that milk and meat must not be eaten at the same meal, and that includes any by-products of both foodstuffs. The caterer requires an intimate knowledge of all the

Fig 14.5 *seating plan for top table of 15 persons at a wedding breakfast*

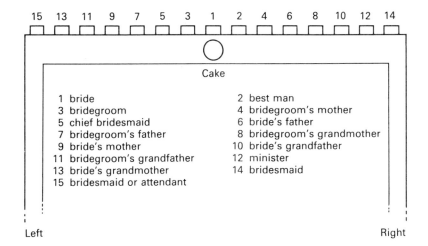

1 bride
3 bridegroom
5 chief bridesmaid
7 bridegroom's father
9 bride's mother
11 bridegroom's grandfather
13 bride's grandmother
15 bridesmaid or attendant

2 best man
4 bridegroom's mother
6 bride's father
8 bridegroom's grandmother
10 bride's grandfather
12 minister
14 bridesmaid

restraints as otherwise he may commit an offence that will cause the supervising rabbi to declare the meal 'non-Kosher', or unclean. The simple answer is to serve fish as the main course which makes it possible to finish other dishes with cream, and to serve milk with the coffee.

In the kitchen and preparation rooms the rabbi may request that stained work surfaces be covered with a tablecloth or that some pans be replaced by clean, new ones.

The presiding religious official then has to sign a card which confirms to the host and hostess that the meal has been prepared according to the biblical laws. There then comes a ritual washing of hands and prayers before the assembled company, prior to the commencement of the meal. Waiting-staff do not have to be Jewish but must be told the nature of the function so they do not unwittingly transgress permitted procedures.

A *Barmitzvah* is a Kosher banquet held to celebrate a Jewish boy's coming-of-age on his thirteenth birthday and is a family affair held after a ceremony in the synagogue. The guests at the meal will wear skull caps at table and there will be a number of presentations and speeches.

Gala Dinners This kind of function takes advantage of the public's wish to celebrate certain days of the year by eating out and enjoying some measure of entertainment, including dancing and a cabaret.

Obvious days during the course of the year include Hogmanay; Burns' Night; St Valentine's Day; Easter Sunday; May Day; St George's Day; Midsummer's Day; Halloween, and Christmas Day, but there are many other events including the Queen's birthday, commemoration of a notable victory, a Centenary or other happenings worthy of being celebrated by a grand Gala dinner and dance. Much thought needs to be given to the arrangement of the theme which should embrace every aspect of the occasion, including the menu, the service, and the cabaret acts.

Gastronomic Meals   One way of bringing in additional restaurant business is by attracting gourmets who wish to further their knowledge of the cookery of a particular country or region. The event should be considered as a serious occasion to which patrons have come to learn about the gastronomic practices of the region.

It is possible to obtain the services of a well-known chef-patron who is willing to leave his own establishment for a few days and come to this country to demonstrate his local specialities to an appreciative band of British gastronomes. Members of staff at the home restaurant also thereby learn from their foreign counterparts about some of the regional dishes of the gourmet area or country.

Conferences   A conference is a combination of business and pleasure held in the banqueting rooms of an hotel for a firm or association that wishes to improve its prospects by an intense examination of its production and sales methods, interspersed by meal and refreshment breaks. The organiser obviously wishes to cover all the aspects of his programme in the available time, yet be able to maintain the momentum during the coffee and tea breaks and during the luncheon meal. Prompt, efficient service by the waiters and attention to such details as the supply of water and minerals, change of ashtrays, clearance of litter, and efficient operation of sound and visual aids, good lighting, and the absence of unwarranted interruptions, all help the smooth-running of the conference.

Breakfast-time conferences are held when business men wish to save valuable time by combining a meal with important discussions, usually early in the morning when the mind is at its most active, so that together with the serving of champagne, inspired thought may bring about significant advancement to the organisation.

A *Convention* is like a conference, open only to invited members directly connected with the organising body.

14.6 OUTDOOR CATERING OPERATIONS

This is one of the most demanding branches of the catering industry for it requires the provision of catering facilities on someone else's property many miles from base, where in all likelihood, the facilities are non-existent, or at best, rather primitive.

It usually involves the erection of marquees to be used as restaurant, kitchen, bar, washing-up room, staff cloakrooms and stores, and the transporting of all the furnishings and equipment necessary to serve meals, either sit-down or buffet-style; or in the case of a show, or trade exhibitions, to serve the general public with refreshments throughout the duration of the event. Then the number of staff, amount of food and equipment has to be able to cope with an unknown demand which may be affected by many things, including the weather. To cope with the problems that can arise in the course of an outdoor catering operation, there must be a comprehensive Organisation Form as shown in Figure 14.6.

14.7 EXAMPLES OF MENUS FOR SPECIAL FUNCTIONS

The writing of menus is one of the most difficult and time-consuming aspects of the job of a catering manager and to save having to keep writing them, he usually produces a set of menus which are ideally suited for banqueting work, being composed of dishes that are out of the ordinary and therefore suitable for a special occasion, yet stay fresh in the hotplate even after two hours or more, which is often the case. One set of menus will be composed for each of the main meals of the day and other sets for the various forms of buffets; they will be priced at various levels according to the number of courses included, so that a person wishing to organise a banquet can decide which price level suits him best and choose the one he thinks his members will prefer.

This system is not so inflexible as it may seem since there could be room for manoeuvre by taking a course from another menu in the same price-range to substitute for the one stated, or by adding a course from another menu, and adding its cost to the stated price. All the menus will be composed of dishes that the kitchen staff can do well and that do not present problems to waiting-staff because of complex garnishes or indeterminate portions. Appendix 4 shows examples of special function menus, as referred to in this chapter.

Fig 14.6 *organisation form for an outdoor catering function*

Name of Organiser	Mr J. G. Grantham
Name of Firm	Grantham Manufacturing PLC
Address of Organiser or Firm	Gable Ends, 7 Forest Row, Summerhayes
Type of Function	Centenary dinner for staff and customers
Site of Event	Firm's Sports Ground at Whitley
Date(s) and Time	Saturday 30.6.88. 3.30 p.m. until 11.30 p.m.
Services available on site	water only
Numbers	600—650 Final confirmation by 9.30 a.m. on 27.6.88.
Setting-up date	Friday 29.6.88.
Dismantling date	Monday 1.7.88.
Marquee Erector	Jewitts of Stoneborough
Furniture	650 chairs, 68 × 4' tables, dais
Equipment	650 covers of crockery and cutlery, 1300 Paris goblets, mobile stoves and boilers, tabling, refrigerators, hot water boilers, hose-pipe, calor-gas, pans
Staff requirements: kitchen –	Arthur plus 10 assistants and 5 porters
dining room –	Angelo plus 35 casuals @ £15 per person
Menu	Seafood Cocktail, Minestrone Soup, Roast Chicken, Buttered Broccoli, Croquette Potatoes, Apple Flan and Cream, Coffee and Mints, Roll and Butter
Wines	8 doz medium sherry, 12 doz bots Liebfraumilch, 12 doz bots Beaujolais
Bar Tariff	spirits 75p lager and light ale 50p per can, mineral waters 40p; all after-dinner drinks on cash sales only
Mileage	46½ miles each way
Transport	3 lorries for equipment on Friday, 2 lorries for food at 9.00 a.m. on Saturday 1 × 45 coach for staff (Comfort Coaches Ltd) pick-up point at 3.00 p.m.
Price	£2.50 p.p. + £500 gratuities
Rubbish Disposal	Grantby UDC — 6 paladins

QUESTIONS

1. What do you understand by the term space utilisation?

2. Discuss the effect of seating arrangements in a banqueting room, using different arrangements.

3. State the main differences between
   (a) a wedding breakfast and
   (b) a cocktail party

4. Outline the requirements of a good cellar.

SERVICE OF LIQUID REFRESHMENT

15.1 THE ROLE OF THE SOMMELIER

The sommelier is the waiter who serves the wines and other drinks at table in the restaurant and a good-class establishment finds it is absolutely essential to employ separate waiters for this important aspect of restaurant service. Restaurateurs realise the need for a person who is very knowledgeable on the subject of wine so as to ensure that sales of this commodity are maximised. A good sommelier can advise on what wine links best with a particular food and so market the products with such mastery, that the sales turnover always produces a high profit.

There is no doubt that the sale of wine adds greatly to the profitability of a restaurant and it can in some cases subsidise the lesser amount of profit that is made on the sale of food. It is not uncommon for a wine to be sold at four or five times the price it cost to purchase, the profit percentage being worked out by the formula:

$$\text{selling price} = \frac{\text{cost price}}{\text{cost price percentage}} \times \frac{100}{I}$$

For example, a restaurateur buys wine at £2.00 per bottle and wishes to make 75 per cent gross profit on each bottle so the calculation is

$$\frac{£2.00}{25} \times \frac{100}{I} = £8.00$$

but this is a high price for what must obviously be an ordinary kind of wine and more bottles might be sold if the mark up or gross profit was lowered to say, 50%

$$\frac{£2.00 \times 100}{50 \quad I} = £4.00 \text{ selling price per bottle.}$$

Of course there are the wages costs of cellarman and sommelier, the purchase of glasses, icebuckets, etc., and incidentals such as the cost of washing-up detergent, to be deducted from the gross profit, so the net profit will be slightly less but nevertheless, this does show how profitable wine can be and why a knowledgeable sommelier must be employed as the person who can encourage customers to drink good quality wine.

15.2 ROUTINE WINE SERVICE

Many factors are involved in the selling and service of wine. First, a wine list is drawn up to show the range of wines kept in stock, together with the various countries and categories. Each wine is listed against a bin number. A section of a wine list is shown in Figure 15.1. Obviously the selection and prices vary considerably between different restaurants and the list has to be compiled to match envisaged demand, at the same time making sure of a constant supply from the wine merchant. A wine list is expected to stay in use over a long period so a lot of care has to be taken in its compilation.

When a customer comes into the restaurant the head waiter shows the menu and takes the order for food and leaves him to look at the wine list. The sommelier comes to take the order for wine and is ready to suggest the most suitable one to link with the food ordered. He writes out an order as shown in Figure 15.2 which the commis wine waiter takes to the cellar or dispense bar to obtain the bottle which he then places in a cradle or bucket of ice.

The commis puts the correct types of glasses on the table and the sommelier shows the customer the unopened bottle, holding it on a folded napkin with the label uppermost. The customer approves it and the bottle is put back in the cradle if red wine, or ice bucket if white wine. The correct serving temperatures for various kinds of wine are given in section 15.14.

15.3 READING THE WINE LABEL

By reading the label on a bottle of wine it is possible to obtain a good idea of what the wine inside will taste like, since the producer will

Fig 15.1 *specimen wine list (carte de vins)*

Red Wines	Vintage	Price	White Wines	Vintage	Price
Bordeaux					
Château Lafite – Rothschild			Bordeaux – Château		
Château Latour			Rieussec		
Château Margaux			Château d'Yquem		
Château Cheval Blanc Conti			Château la Cour Pavillon		
			Château Loudenne		
Burgundy					
Domaine de la Romanée			*Burgundy*		
Gevrey – Chambertin			Bâtard – Montrachet		
Aloxe – Corton			Corton Charlemagne		
			Meursault		
Rhône					
Château Rayas			*Loire*		
Hermitage la Chapelle			Muscadet		
Châteauneuf du Pape			Pouilly Fumé		
Beaujolais			*Chablis*		
Fleurie			Premier Cru Montmains		
Julienas					
			Alsace		
Italy			Gewürztraminer		
Barbera d'Alba			Sylvaner		
Chianti Brolio					
			Germany		
Spain			Rüdesheimer		
Torres Coronas Peñedes			Schloss Bockelheimer		
Marques de Caceres Rioja			Konigsfels		
Portugal			*Italy*		
Dão Caves Velhas			Soave Classico		
			Verdicchio		
Hungary					
Egri Bikaver			*Portugal*		
			Vinho Verde, Verdega		
USA					
Zinfandel, Alexander Valley			*Spain*		
Merlot, Firestone			Torres Gran Vina Sol		
Ridge California Zinfandel			Marques de Riscal		
Australia			*Hungary*		
Shiraz-Cabernet			Tokay Aszu		
Penfolds Grange Hermitage			Tokaji Szamorodni		
Balgownie Cabernet					
Sauvignon			*Yugoslavia*		
			Ljutomer Riesling		
South Africa					
Pinotage, Groot Constantia			*USA*		
KWV Roodeberg, Paarl			Pinot Chardonnay		
			Livermore		
			Chalone Pinot Blanc		

Red Wines	Vintage	Price	White Wines	Vintage	Price
Rosé Wines Mateus Rosé Anjou Rosé			*Australia* Chardonnay, Hunter Valley Petaluma Rhine Riesling *South Africa* Theuniskraal Riesling Tulbagh *UK* Lamberhurst Priory, Adgestone, Isle of Wight		

Champagne: Krug 1975; Louis Roederer Cristal 1978; Bollinger Tradition; Veuve Cliquot; Pol Roger; Lanson Black Label

Sparkling wine: Gratien & Mayer Sparkling Saumur; Club Paradis; Asti Spumante

Sherry: Fino San Patricio; Croft Delicado; La Ina; Tio Pepe; Croft Original Pale Cream

Madeira: Duke of Clarence Malmsey; Old Trinity House Bual; Sercial Eduardo Henriques

Port: Croft Fine Tawny; Delaforce; His Eminence's Choice; Quinta da Noval 1978; Dow 1977; Taylor 1970

SPIRITS:

Scotch Whisky: Catto's Rare Old Scottish Highland; J & B Rare; Glenfiddich Malt; Knockando Single Malt; Peter Dawson

Gin: Gilbeys; Gordons; Beefeater; Bombay

Vodka: Wyborowa; Smirnoff Silver Label; Stolichnaya

Brandy: Hennessey VSOP, Fine Champagne; Hine VSOP; Remy Martin; Armagnac de Montal Brissarc; Janneau Grand Armagnac VSOP

Rum: Dry Cane; Lemon Hart; Ron Bacardi; Carta Blanca; Cardinal Finest Old

Cups and Bitters: Campari; Pimms No 1 and No 2

Liqueurs: Crème de Menthe; Wolfschmidt Kümmel; Tia Maria; Sambuca; Bénédictine; Chartreuse Green; Cointreau

Vermouths and Aperitifs: Martini Rosso; Cinzano Bianco; Chambery Dolin; Carpano Punt e Mes; Dubonnet

Cigars: H. Upmann Petits Coronas; Punch Margaritas; Romeo & Juliet Coronas; Partagas Coronas

Fig 15.2 *wine check*

Hôtel Ambassador

Table No __33__   Covers __6__

1 bot Nº 27

1 bot Nº 29

1 Gin & Tonic

2 Oloroso sherries.

Date __16/3/88__   Signature

---

print sufficient information to authenticate and describe the contents. Figure 15.3 shows examples of labels which include information on (i) country or region of production; (ii) the year it was made; (iii) the name of the wine which may also be the name of the vineyard or château, or the generic name of the wine of an area, or of the grape; it may be a proprietary brand name, or a fanciful one; (iv) the quality of the wine, i.e. if *VDQS, AC, QmP, DOC, DOCG*, etc. (see Glossary); (v) name of the shipper, grower, cooperative, etc. who bought and blended or merely bottled the wine; (vi) where the wine was bottled, e.g. *mise en bouteille au château* (bottled at the vineyard) or where the grapes were grown; (vii) the quantity of liquid contained in the bottle as shown in Table 15.1 (the letter 'e' on the label indicates that the contents are measured to EEC (Common Market) regulations); (viii) the alcohol content expressed as a percentage by volume; this ranges from approx 8 per cent to 12.5 per cent and wines that exceed this upper limit attract additional excise duty.

Fig 15.3 *illustrations of wine labels*

Table 15.1 *bottle sizes and contents*

Name	Metric	Imperial
half bottle	37.5cl	$13\frac{1}{4}$ fl oz
bottle	70cl, 73cl, 75cl	25floz–$26\frac{2}{3}$floz
magnum	1.5 litres	$2\frac{1}{2}$ pints (approx)
litre	100cl	$1\frac{3}{4}$ pints
1.5 litres	150cl	$2\frac{1}{2}$ pints (approx)
2 litres	200cl	$3\frac{1}{2}$ pints
3 litres	300cl	$5\frac{1}{4}$ pints
carafe	1 litre	7–8 glasses
half carafe	0.5 litre	3–4 glasses
jeroboam	3 litres	$\frac{2}{3}$ gallon
rehoboam	4.5 litres	1 gallon
methuselah	5.5 litres	$9\frac{1}{2}$ pints

15.4 USING A CORKSCREW

To avoid any difficulty in drawing a cork it is necessary to have a corkscrew with a wide and open thread that will grip most of the cork. The type normally used by a sommelier is called 'a waiter's friend' and is shaped like a penknife with one blade, the corkscrew, and a lever to rest on the ridge of the bottle to facilitate withdrawing the cork smoothly so avoiding the 'pop' which is an objectionable noise in a restaurant. The gadget folds neatly and fits into the waistcoat pocket.

Other efficient corkscrews include the kind that is screwed into the cork then withdrawn by means of two levers that are folded upwards; the double-handled corkscrew that is screwed in with the bottom handle and withdrawn by turning the top one anticlockwise. To open a bottle of champagne or sparkling wine, remove the wire and the foil cover, press the cork upwards with both thumbs to loosen then hold it in one hand and use the other to turn the bottle against it, taking the cork out rather than allowing it to shoot off with a loud 'pop' as this can be very dangerous since the escaping gas has great force and the cork might hit somebody. If the wine is at the right temperature it will not bubble over and none will be wasted.

A stubborn champagne cork can be removed with a special pincer which can be clamped over the cork so enabling greater pressure to be exerted. Figure 15.4 shows a bottle stopper for use on any sparkling wine to prevent loss of effervescence; the top is spring-loaded and when pressed inward will fit over the top; it has a rubber pad to seal the aperture. The top of the cork on a bottle of wine sometimes gets encrusted and it is necessary to scrape it off and clean the rim of the bottle before starting to open it.

15.5 DECANTING THE WINE

Nearly all red wines improve by 'breathing' for a length of time after being opened, so releasing the bouquet or aroma. Opening a young red wine an hour or more before drinking eliminates the slight bitterness of the first pouring and enables it to recover its natural softness. It is sometimes necessary to decant a rich red wine because of the tannin that is deposited in it when kept for a length of time. The wine is poured very slowly and steadily into a decanter, leaving all the deposit in the bottle. The sommelier must watch closely when pouring so that only clear wine goes into the decanter, and he must

Fig 15.4 *champagne bottle stopper*

know when to stop pouring. A wine cradle may be used but holding an unshaken bottle against a light should ensure an unsullied result. The older and darker the wine, the more difficult the process of decanting.

Vintage and crusted ports keep for fifty years or more and during that time throw a heavy sediment which would spoil the wine when opened unless carefully handled and delicately decanted. It is usual to decant in front of a light so as to see that the wine being poured is unsoiled, and to use a fine strainer to prevent any bits getting into the decanter. Even very ordinary wines can throw a sediment and the wine waiter must be constantly alert to this as it would be very wrong to pour any of it into the customer's glass.

15.6 SERVING RED WINE

Cut around the capsule with the point of the knife – part of the waiter's friend (known as a *limonadier* in France) just below the wide rim and remove it whole. This facilitates pouring the wine and ensures it does not come in contact with the foil which would spoil it. Wipe the top of the bottle with the waiter's cloth then slowly insert the corkscrew into the centre of the cork ensuring that it does not pierce the sides nor go through the bottom as this may cause broken bits of cork to contaminate the wine. Put the lever against the rim and pull the corkscrew steadily against it until the cork comes out cleanly and quietly; there should be no loud popping sound and it should not be necessary to grip the bottle between the knees!

Smell the cork delicately and discreetly to ascertain that it is not contaminated and place in front of the customer, wipe the rim of the bottle using the corner of the waiter's cloth, hold the bottle in the middle using the right hand to cover the label and pour a little into the customer's glass to let him try it before half-filling all the glasses, serving the host last. Wine is served to a party of people in the same order as for food.

After pouring a portion into a glass, twist the bottle slightly to prevent the droplet falling on the tablecloth and wipe the mouth of the bottle against the folded waiter's cloth held in the left hand.

If using a wine cradle, present the bottle in it, on a folded napkin, label uppermost, then place it on a side-table and uncork it gently so that none escapes, then pour the wine, holding the basket across the top with the forefinger to steady the bottle. The cork may be laid on the basket. Some sommeliers carry a *tastevin* or silver cup and use it to taste a wine before serving it.

15.7 SERVING WHITE WINE

Carry in the bottle in a bucket of ice on a stand, or on a plate; take it out, wipe dry and show it to the customer, then replace in the bucket, cut around the capsule and withdraw the cork without letting the screw pierce the sides or bottom so that pieces of cork do not get into the wine. Turn the bottle several times in the ice-bucket then hold it in a cloth, ask the host to approve it, then go around and pour into the glasses.

To serve champagne, bring it in a bucket of ice on a stand with a cloth around the neck of the bottle and draped down each side. Wipe it and present to the customer then untwist and remove the wire and foil covering, push against the cork to loosen it then hold it in the right hand with the cloth, and turn the bottom of the bottle until the cork comes out in the hand. If it is a slightly stubborn cork, dampen the cloth slightly so as to get a better grip on it. Hold the bottle in a folded cloth and pour out to fill the glass, allow the fizzing to subside, and refill; replace in the ice-bucket with the cloth draped across the top.

15.8   SERVING ADDITIONAL WINE

When a customer asks the sommelier to bring another bottle of the same fine wine after the first has been drunk, it is necessary to serve it in clean glasses and not to pour it on top of any of the previous bottle. Although it may be identical to the first bottle, there could be a subtle difference that a discerning customer might notice. It is in order to carry on filling the glasses when two or more of the same wines are ordered at the beginning of the meal. It does not matter so much about changing glasses for a less fine wine.

A skilled wine waiter can pour wine by holding the bottle by the punt at the bottom, doing this dexterously, even with a magnum.

15.9   GRAPES USED FOR MAKING WINE

A good way to recognise the type and quality of a wine is to know something about the variety of grape used to make it. In tasting a wine it helps to put a name to it by identifying the taste of the grape but a lot of practice is necessary to gain this expertise even though there are only six internationally established major grape varieties:

1. *Cabernet Sauvignon* gives a subtle flavour of herbs, berry fruits and certain spices, but is very tannic so it is usually blended with softer red wines. Grown in France, Italy, Spain, Australia and the USA, especially in California. It is one of the finest and most important grapes in Bordeaux.

2. *Chardonnay* is originally from Burgundy in France and now makes the finest dry white wines in the world, of great strength and excellent body. It is used with Pinot in making Champagne and is paramount in the great Californian white wines.

3. *Gewürztraminer* is the grape that gives the wonderful spicy smell and taste to some of the wines of Alsace and also to those of Germany and California; it gives a distinctive aroma of muscat grapes.

4. *Pinot Noir* produces very fine, velvet-smooth red wine that does not require blending. It is used, without immersing the skins, for making Champagne and is a relative of the Gamay grape which is noted for producing Beaujolais wines.

5. *Riesling* is a German grape used for making flowery white wines that range from very dry to very sweet. It is related to the Sylvaner and Müller-Thurgau grapes and is used in producing many of the wines of Austria, Yugoslavia and California.

6. *Sauvignon Blanc* is used to make the white wines of Bordeaux and the Loire which both have its distinctive herby smell and flavour; the wines can range from sour to lusciously sweet and from low to high alcohol content.

Other important grapes in wide cultivation are:

Black

Gamay – light and fragrant wine such as Beaujolais, called Napa Gamay in America

Grenache – strong, mellow and fruity but of pale colour, used for making rosé wines

Merlot – rich and fragrant, used for Pommard and St Emilion

Nebbiolo – very perfumed, used in Italy for Barolo and Barbaresco

Syrah – deep purple, heavy and aromatic, used in Burgundy, Australia and California

Zinfandel – the grape of California, very fruity

White

Chenin Blanc – acid but can be dry or sweet, from the Loire area

Müller-Thurgau – cross between Riesling and Sylvaner, a good sweet wine, low in acid

Muscadet – light and dry

Muscat – perfumed, pungent and sweet

Palomino – makes the finer quality sherries

Pedro Ximenez – for Montilla and Malaga; blended for sherry
Trebbiano – for Chianti, Orvieto and Soave

Wine is the beverage produced from the fermented juice of grapes, the factors that decide the quality of the final product being (i) the vine variety as the above examples; (ii) the climate, which should be warm, fairly dry and with no extremes; (iii) the soil, which should really be poor; and (iv) the pruning and spraying of the vines. At harvest-time the grapes are pressed to yield their juice which is fermented by the yeast that was present on the grape skins. The sugar in the juice is converted into alcohol by the yeast which also causes it to fizz because of the carbon dioxide produced.

15.10   GENERAL RULES OF WINE SERVICE

To carry a large number of glasses in one hand place the stem of the first one between the first and second finger of the left hand, palm upwards, letting it hang between these fingers. Put the next glass between the third and fourth fingers, sliding the base under that of the first glass, then repeat this action, sliding the base of each glass under that of the preceding one, utilising all the fingers. Do not attempt to hold more than twelve in one hand and ensure that they do not bang against each other. This method is used when laying tables; use a tray if customers are seated at table.

Summary of the work of the wine waiter and his staff

To open a bottle of wine, first check that it is the one that was ordered, then cut around below the lip and peel off the foil cover cleanly; wipe the lip and neck and insert a corkscrew into dead centre of the cork until it reaches the end but does not go right through. Pull firmly and smoothly and draw out the cork without letting it go 'pop'. Wipe the inside of the neck of the bottle with the waiter's cloth, ensure the cork is sound and pour a small amount of wine into the host's glass for him to taste and approve then proceed to pour into the ladies' glasses, then those of the gentlemen, and finally the host, doing this from the right-hand side of the customer. The bottle should be opened where the customer can see it being done.

To serve sparkling wine and champagne, peel the foil from the cork, hold the bottle in the left hand, covering the bottom half with the cloth, undo the wire and gently ease out the cork by turning the bottle against the cork. Do not allow it to make a 'pop' and ensure that the cork does not shoot out towards anyone. Pour some into the host's glass before it has a chance to surge out of the bottle.

To pour wine from a bottle, hold it at the side away from the label and tilt it from the wrist until the glass is just over half-full, without letting the bottle rest on the glass; stop pouring by moving the hand upwards from the wrist, turning the bottle slightly to one side so as to prevent any drips falling onto the tablecloth.

To pour wine from a bottle in a wine cradle, hold the outer edges of the basket, place the index finger on the shoulder of the bottle to steady it then pour from the guest's right-hand side by tilting the bottle until the glass is just over half-full. Move the hand upwards to stop the flow and twist the bottle gently to one side to prevent drips.

It is possible to use the specially made drip-collars by placing one just below the rim so that it catches any drips before they soil the tablecloth.

To decant a port of some age or vintage, select a decanter of the right size and shape, insert the funnel and a piece of muslin and filter the wine into it, placing it next to a candle or light. Open the bottle, but try not to disturb the sediment and pour the wine steadily into the decanter looking at the light through the bottle so as to see when the sediment reaches the neck which is the indication to stop pouring. Put the stopper in the decanter for port but not for ordinary wine. Decanting also helps to refresh the port.

Observe customers for any signs that they require your services and go to them immediately, or at least acknowledge that you have seen them and will attend as soon as possible. Avoid being familiar but be tactful and polite to customers even if they are rude to you. Gain the respect of colleagues and superiors by your ability and helpfulness in giving good wine service.

Some customers ask to see the cork taken from their bottle of wine and it is the practice for the sommelier to attach it to the bottle or decanter by means of a rubber band, or placing it in the cradle to help to keep the bottle secure. The cork can be suspended in the foil top cut slightly deeper down the neck and leaving it hanging at one point. When a customer requests a second bottle of the same wine he has been drinking, he must be given some of the new bottle to taste in a clean glass.

On drawing the cork it is usual to examine and smell it, if it smells bad it means the wine is also probably bad because of the cork and another bottle should be obtained from the cellar. A wine in this condition is said to be corked, or corky. The action of smelling the cork should not be done in an obvious manner.

15.11 THE DISPENSE BAR

This department is the place where all the drink for immediate sale in the restaurant is kept. It obtains its supplies from the cellar and makes them ready to be served by the sommelier. Bottles of wine have to be brought to room temperature, or chilled in the refrigerator; cocktails are shaken and dispensed; other mixed drinks are made to order, and draught and bottled beers are dispensed. The dispense barman must be completely familar with every drink on the wine list and bar tariff, and his duties and responsibilities include:

1. ordering the necessary stock to maintain the agreed level so as to be able to meet all orders from customers;
2. adhering to the recognised procedure for ordering and dispensing the drinks, and avoiding any discrepancies in stock levels and stocktaking;
3. keeping the bar in good hygienic order;
4. ensuring that glassware is properly washed-up – glasses should be washed in warm water with detergent, rinsed in clean, warm water, drained and dried with a linen tea-towel;
5. not allowing anyone to smoke in the bar;
6. being honest in ensuring that drinks are served in full measures and are not tampered with, nor adulterated in the bar;
7. possession of a good knowledge of the main cocktails and other mixed drinks;
8. keeping the beer in good condition and avoiding waste.

It is is not usual to take cash at the dispense bar, but every item issued must be authenticated by an official check, as shown in Figure 15.5 made out in triplicate by the sommelier who hands two copies to the dispense barman and one to the restaurant cashier. The barman keeps one copy and puts the flimsy on the tray with the drinks as ordered so that the waiter can check that the order is correct. The wine waiter will price the order and the cashier will ensure that the amount is entered on the customer's bill for payment.

Fig 15.5 *cellar or dispense-bar check*

73027—4

Table No __6__

1 bot Bin N° 12 Chablis
1 bot Bin N°21 Beaujolais

Date __22|7|89__   Signed __M.Tums__

Hôtel Ambassador

15.12 CELLAR ORGANISATION

The cellar of a catering establishment is where stocks of drink are
held in readiness for issue to the dispense bar where it is prepared for
sale to the customer via the sommelier. The cellar should provide
ideal storage conditions for all kinds of beverages so that even after
lengthy storage time, such as for claret and port, it is kept in excellent
condition.

The stock is divided into beer, wine, spirits and mineral waters,
each being housed in that part of the cellar where it will keep in best
condition. The cellar should be kept dim and cool, but well-ventilated
and free from draughts; it should not be damp. Red wine is bottled in
dark green bottles so that its natural colour is not affected by the light
in the cellar which could cause it to turn brown.

Temperature affects the development and maturing process of red
wine so it is important to control this where the stock of claret is kept,

since this may have to lie there for some ten years or more. It is recommended that white wine is stored near to the floor where it is cooler. All wine in bottles is stored horizontally to keep the cork moist so that it can breathe, so helping to keep the wine in good condition. The humidity level should be from 70 to 75 per cent; a higher level could damage the cork and label. No other products should be kept in the cellar as wine can be affected by contact with a strong odour.

Modern methods of beer- and wine-making use the pasteurising process to keep the product stable under all conditions. Both beer and wine are living things but the process of pasteurisation renders them inert so they are not affected by poor cellar conditions. It is usually the keg beers and boxed wines that are pasteurised.

The cellarman must operate his department on a clear control system that gives an accurate record of all movements of stock and ensures exact stock rotation. Each item of stock is given a bin number so as to assist immediate identification and avoid the need to write out the name of an item, some of which are quite long. Cellar control is necessary to ensure that there is always a sufficient stock of every item, to meet known or envisaged demand. When supplies are delivered, the quantity is entered into the stock sheet, under the bin number or name, and every time an issue is made to the bar, it must be entered on the bin card. Cellar documentation can be covered by all or some of the following: order book, goods delivery book, cellar ledger, bin cards, ullage book, and daily issue sheet, as shown in Figures 15.5, 15.6 and 15.7. No stock may be issued unless a duly signed official requisition form is received; it may be necessary to restrict cellar issues to certain times of the day rather than keeping it open all the time. In some establishments, empty bottles, especially of spirits, have to be returned to the cellar before full replacements are issued; the bottles must bear the establishment stamp on the label.

Some of the stock kept in the cellar has a limited shelf-life – for example, white wines do not keep as long as red; most of the light German and Italian white wines should be drunk within three years, good sparkling wines within five years, and champagne within ten years. Ordinary red wines, including Beaujolais should be drunk before they are 5 years old, most red Burgundies and Chianti before they are 10 years, whereas the château-bottled clarets can be kept for fifty years or more while they mature. During prolonged storage, red wines can throw a sediment which means that careful handling is required so as not to disturb it unduly.

Fig 15.6 *bin card*

Bin No 73			Chianti Classico
Date	Received	In hand	Issued
1989 Jan 1		30	12
2	120	138	24
3		114	6
4		108	15
7		93	40
8	60	113	6
9		107	12
12		95	18
		77	20

Fig 15.7 *daily consumption sheet*

Drink	Bin N°	Mon	Tue	Wed	Thur	Fri	Sat	Total

15.13 GLOSSARY OF WINE TERMS

abbocato	word seen on some Italian wine labels such as Orvieto, indicating it is a sweet or semi-sweet wine.
AOC	Appellation d'Origine Contrôlée is a guarantee that the wine is genuinely that of a certain area
ale	old English name for beer, still used as Pale Ale, Mild Ale, etc.
Amontillado	aged fino sherry with a nutty flavour and aroma
Amoroso	very sweet type of sherry of the kind referred to as cream sherry
aperitif	a drink to stimulate the appetite before a meal, such as vermouth, Campari, a cocktail or sherry
Armagnac	quality brandy from a defined area of France; darker and coarser than Cognac
B & B	Bénédictine liqueur mixed with brandy
Barsac	very sweet wine from the southern region of Bordeaux
Beaune	the central area of Burgundy producing fine red and white wines on its many sites
bin	section of a cellar holding a particular drink, controlled by a bin card showing stock and issues; usually numbered to coincide with the wine list
bitters	only a few drops of, for example, Angostura bitters, is used to colour and flavour, for example, gin, but a glassful of Fernet Branca can be drunk as a pick-me-up.
Black Velvet	a drink made of champagne and Guinness stout, in equal quantities
body	a full-flavour in wine that appears to fill the mouth
Buck's Fizz	one third of fresh orange juice with two thirds of champagne and a little grenadine syrup to give it a red hue
Byrrh	bitter sweet aperitif of red wine, quinine and herbs
carafe	glass container, usually of fixed capacity, for serving ordinary wine

cassis	blackcurrant liqueur (see also Kir)
chambré	used to describe the serving temperature for red wine as being room temperature, or 15–18°C
chaptilisation	sugar is added to grape must to assist the fermentation where there is insufficient natural sugar present
charmat	another name for the *cuve close* method of making sparkling wine
château	the castle or house of a French vineyard estate
cider	alcoholic drink made from apples; it can be dry or sweet, still or sparkling, strong or weak
claret	the red wines of Bordeaux, as described in this country
clos	a vineyard area, usually in Burgundy
cocktail	mixed alcoholic drink, such as a Harvey Wallbanger
cognac	quality brandy made in a defined area of France
corked	wine with a musty smell because the cork is bad
coteaux	describes vineyards situated on the slopes of hillsides which can produce better wine than that from the fields
Crémant	lightly sparkling wine
Cru	refers to a vineyard producing a wine of quality; also used to denote the classification of wines
Crusta	long refreshing drink with twists of lemon or orange peel in it
cup	mixed drink such as Pimms, similar to a sling or a punch
cuve clos	sealed vat used to make sparkling wine, ensuring that the CO_2 is maintained during the second fermentation
cuvée	the blending of wines to produce a certain result
Dão	well-known wine region of Portugal producing both white and red wine

decanter	container of glass from which wine or spirit is poured; a bottle of port or wine will need to be decanted into a decanter when it contains a lot of sediment
Diabolo Cassis	mixture of blackcurrant cordial (or Ribena) and fizzy lemonade
DOC	Denominazione di Origine Controllata denotes that the wine is authentic and from the specified region
doux	denotes a sweet champagne
Dubonnet	well known aperitif, either gold or red in colour, made of flavoured wines
Eau-de-vie	French term for brandy or other strong spirit
Fernet Branca	bitter drink used as a reviver or digestive
finings	isinglass, egg-whites, etc., used to clarify beer and wine
fino	the driest type of sherry, light in body and colour but a penetrating aroma; best chilled
flask	straw-coloured round bottle, for example, for Chianti which is not intended to be kept for long as the bottle cannot be laid on its side
flowery	the 'nose' of a wine as it comes from the character of the grapes
flûte	elongated, elegant glass used for champagne and sparkling wines
fortified wines	port, sherry, marsala, etc., wines made with the addition of brandy to bring them to approx 17 per cent alcohol
full-bodied	wine that is heavy with flavour and alcohol, such as a Rhône wine
Gay-Lussac	system of measuring the alcoholic strength of drinks by the percentage method
genever	Dutch gin of fine aroma and flavour
Gomme syrup	high-gravity neutral sugar liquid used for sweetening a cocktail or other mixed drink
Gluhwein	German red wine and spices for heating and serving as warming drink, especially to be drunk après-ski
grappa	spirit produced by distilling the final pressings of skins and pips of grapes

heuriger	German name for a wine bar
highball	long drink, usually of whisky and soda
Hock	general term to describe the German wines from the Rhine area
Hospices de Beaune	old people's home and hospital in Burgundy owning several vineyards, the produce of which is sold annually for their upkeep
hydrometer	an instrument used to measure the density of a wine or other liquid
impériale	name for a very large bottle of claret equal to eight ordinary ones
INAO	stands for the Institut National des Appellations d'Origine Contrôlées which is the organisation that administers the AOC designations
Kabinett	quality German wine, usually sold under the QmP Label as being especially good
keg	metal vessel from which beer is sold under pressure to give a good fizz
kir	drink made by adding blackcurrant liqueur to white wine, which should be Bourgogne Aligoté
Kir Royale	mixture of champagne and blackcurrant liqueur served as an aperitif
lager	light beer made by cold fermentation and a yeast that sinks to the bottom of the vessel; must be served chilled
Liebfraumilch	popular and mild type of German white wine of QbA quality, made only for export
liqueurs	distilled drinks which can be served as an aperitif but more usually after dinner; made in hundreds of flavours and at varying degrees of alcohol
loving cup	two-handled container for sharing a drink between a betrothed couple, or among the members at a ceremonial feast
Madeira	fortified wine made on the island of that name; available as dry, medium and sweet
magnum	large bottle equal to two ordinary bottles, i.e. 1.5 litres capacity
Malmsey	very sweet style of Madeira; usually served as a dessert wine

Manzanilla	a kind of fino sherry matured by the sea, therefore has a salty taste and is dry and fresh
Marc	spirit made by distilling the last pressing from grape-skins, and pips
Marsala	fortified sweet wine from Sicily; also made with egg yolk as Marsala all'Uovo
mead	sweet drink made by fermenting honey
Médoc	district of Bordeaux that produces most of the finest clarets
Montilla	strong but unfortified sherry-style wine made as dry, medium and sweet; cheaper than sherry
mosser	another name of a swizzlestick which is used to destroy the bubbles in champagne
must	juice expressed from grapes for making into wine
negus	hot spicy drink, usually made with port
nog	hot or cold drink made of egg yolks with a spirit or liqueur
nose	combination of the aroma and the bouquet of a wine
ochsle	hydrometer used for testing the specific gravity of grape must, to show by conversion the sugar percentage and amount of pure alcohol
oenology	the subject of wine studied from a scientific angle
OIML	EEC system of determining the proof strength of alcoholic drinks, similar to Gay Lussac in that it is done by a percentage at 20°C
oloroso	very sweet style of sherry that is fairly heavy and dark
optic	measuring device used to dispense spirits
Palo Cortado	sherry that tastes like an oloroso and has a bouquet like an amontillado
Parfait Amour	violet-coloured spirit, very sweet
perry	alcoholic drink made from pears, which can be sparkling or still; Babycham is a perry
pétillant	slightly sparkling wine of about 4 atmospheres as against champagne which has 5

phylloxera	aphid which attacks and destroys roots of vines
Pimms	proprietary brand of sling sold for mixing with lemonade, with borage, cucumber, orange, etc.
plonk	inferior quality wine usually sold under a nondescript label
pony	a 1 fluid ounce measure for brandy, whisky, etc., usually served in a small size tumbler glass
Pousse Café	drink with a rainbow colour effect created by pouring layers of different liqueur on top of each other in a glass, the thickest and heaviest at the bottom
Prairie Oyster	pick-me-up for a hangover, made by placing a whole raw egg yolk in a glass with Worcester sauce, together with seasonings
proof	denotes the strength of alcoholic drinks done under the Sykes system, in which 100° proof is 57% of alcohol by volume
punch	hot or cold mixed drink made in a large bowl, the cold version being made fizzy with lemonade, ginger ale, etc.
punt	the inverted part of the bottom of a bottle into which the sediment is supposed to gather
Pussyfoot Cocktail	non-alcoholic cocktail or mixed drink suitable for teetotallers and children
puttonyos	measure of sweetness added to Tokay, the number of putts of approx 30 litres, from one to five, being stated on the label
QbA	Qualitätswein bestimmer Anbaugebiete, a good quality German wine from a specific area
QmP	Qualitätswein mit Pradikat a German wine of high quality from a defined area, made without added sugar; the base level is Kabinett rising to Tröckenbeerenaüslese
retsina	strong pine flavour, added to white and rosé Greek wines
Rioja	area in north-west Spain renowned for good quality red and white wines

robust	a well-flavoured wine that is weighty by its character
rosé	denotes pink coloured wine usually made by blending red and white wines, drunk young and fresh
rosso	red wine; also denotes red vermouth
saccharometer	instrument for measuring sugar in a liquid
sack	name sometimes given to sherry, probably the dry or seco style
Sauternes	very sweet white wine from Bordeaux made by leaving grapes on the vine until they begin to shrivel up; Château d'Yquem is the finest of these wines
schnapps	unflavoured spirit made from grain, etc., in Austria, Germany and Holland
Schluck	popular Austrian wine that is young and fragrant
Sercial	the driest kind of Madeira, the one that should be served with turtle soup or ox-tail soup
sling	the name of a number of cold long drinks containing a spirit base and a fruit juice with the addition of soda, decorated with fruits
solera	blending and maturing system used in making sherry in which wines of many vintages are gradually blended into the desired type and quality
sommelier	wine waiter who serves all the drinks in a restaurant
Spätlese	wine made in Germany from late-gathered grapes
spirits	distilled drinks including brandy, gin, rum, vodka, whisky and eau-de-vie, sold mainly at 40% alcohol which is 70 degrees proof spirit
stillion	rack on which beer casks are sited ready for beer to be drawn off
stout	dark beer made from coloured malt, for example, Guinness; also called milk stout
Strega	bitter Italian liqueur based on brandy, useful to relieve a headache
sur lie	refers to a wine bottled straight from the cask where it was lying on the lees and

	therefore very fresh; applies mainly to Muscadet
swizzlestick	mosser or stirrer used to destroy the bubbles in champagne
tafelwein	lowest grade of German wine, although there may be some non-German wines mixed with it
tastevin	shallow cup used to taste the quality of wine, sometimes worn on a ribbon round the neck of a sommelier
Tête de Cuvée	a best-quality wine, usually from Burgundy
toddy	hot drink of sugared and spiced whisky and water
Tokay	fine quality Hungarian wine made in several types, bottled in 50cl bottles, the best being Tokay Eszencia and Tokay Aszu which are made in several degrees of sweetness called puttonyos (q.v.)
Trockenbeerenaüslese	type of German wine made from selected shrivelled grapes; very sweet and luscious but expensive
UKBG	United Kingdom Bartender's Guild, the national association of qualified barmen
ullage	beer or wine that is in service with some having been drawn off
VDQS	Vin Délimité de Qualité Supérieure; regional wines, mainly from the south of France of quality nearly as good as AOC
VQPRD	Vins de qualité produits dans les regions determinées, similar to the above
VSOP	implies a Cognac brandy of age and quality but has no legal meaning (very special old pale)
Varietal	wine named after the grape it is made from, usually 85 per cent of the total vat
vat	container in which wine ferments or matures or is blended; made of wood, stainless steel, fibreglass, etc.
vendage	the grape harvest when the grapes are picked for wine-making, or the grapes themselves, or the liquid pressed from the grapes
Verdelho	medium sweet style of Madeira, deep gold, and nutty in flavour

Vermouth	fortified and flavoured wine made with many barks, herbs, flavours and spices; available as dry, sweet, red, rosé and white
viertel	a quarter bottle holding just under 200 ml ($6\frac{1}{2}$ fl.oz)
Vin de Paille	straw wine, made from grapes picked and dried on straw so that the wine is sweet and luscious
vin de pays	ordinary wine slightly better than table wine but not as good as VDQS
Vin Jaune	amber-coloured wine made in the Jura, by maturing it in wood for six years to produce an aperitif-like result
vintage wine	wine of one year bearing the year number when the grapes were gathered; usually allowed to mature in bottle
Zwicker	Alsace wine blended from several varieties of grapes; also called Edelzwicker

15.14 CORRECT SERVING TEMPERATURES

Table 15.2 *correct serving temperatures*

		°C
red	full red wines such as claret, burgundy, Rhône wine	15–18 (chambré)
	medium, e.g. Chianti, Rioja, Mouton Cadet	15 (chambré)
	fresh or young, e.g. Beaujolais, Valpolicella, Valdepeñas	8–10
rosé		6–8 (cool)
white	dry	4.5–6.5
	medium dry – Alsace, Hock, Moselle, Vinho Verde	6.5–9.00
	full-bodied – Burgundy, Rioja, Orvieto	9–13
	very sweet e.g. Monbazillac, Sauternes	5–8
champagne	dry	4
	sweet	2–4
vermouth	dry	6.5–9
	sweet	8–9
sherry	dry	10–12
	sweet	16
port		18–20

To bring a bottle of red wine to room temperature, wrap it in a cloth wrung out in very hot water, or open the bottle and leave in a warm room for several hours. Do not hold it under a hot tap or put in a bain-marie as this can harm the wine irrevocably. A few seconds in a microwave oven will bring it to room temperature.

To reduce the temperature rapidly, place the bottle in a bucket with crushed ice, a little coarse salt and very little water so that it is covered completely up to the neck. Normally sufficient white and rosé wines are kept refrigerated to supply the known or likely demand.

A copper *wine thermometer* as shown in Figure 15.8 may be clipped onto a bottle to give an immediate check that it is at the correct temperature. The wine will be two degrees colder than registered but this allows for the slight rise whilst serving so it should be exactly right for drinking.

Fig 15.8   *copper wine thermometer*

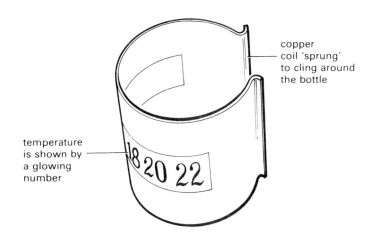

copper
coil 'sprung'
to cling around
the bottle

temperature
is shown by
a glowing
number

15.15   CIGARS AND CIGARETTES

This is usually done by the sommelier who may keep his own stock or draw them to order from the bar; the items will be included on the bill with the food and drink. In some establishments, packets of cigarettes are only sold for cash or obtained from a vending machine.

Cigars require care in storage and serving and unless bought individually in a metal tube or kept in a humidor, they quickly lose their aroma and become dry and crumbly; they do not keep well under damp storage conditions. The price of, say, a hand-rolled Havana cigar is so high that it merits very careful control.

The best known imported cigars include Bolivar, Romeo and Juliet, Montecristo, Partagas, Punch, Ramon Allones, H. Upmann and Henry Clay, and the size ranges from 10 cm to 16 cm, each size having a name, e.g. Corona which is approximately 14cm long. Jamaican, British, Dutch and South American cigars may also be stocked.

To serve a cigar, allow the customer to see the selection and make his choice, take it from him and cut a V-shape piece from the rounded end; remove the band and return it to the customer together with an opened box of cigar smoker's matches which are longer and slower burning than normal to enable the smoker to light his cigar with care and deliberation.

To serve a new packet of cigarettes, remove the top part of the cellophane wrapper, open the lid and pull one or two cigarettes forward; present to the customer on a small plate. A waiter should always be prepared to offer a customer a light, preferably a match but also from a lighter.

To clear a full ash-tray from a table cover it with a clean one, remove to the salver and put the clean one back on the table. Ash-trays must not be left to become overflowing.

15.16 TABLE WATERS

Bottled waters have become very popular thus removing the need to offer customers tap water from a jug. The advantages claimed by the suppliers of mineral water:

1. the quality is scientifically monitored;
2. it is more pure and hygienic because it is sold in a sealed bottle;
3. carries a certain cachet because the water is drawn from a well-known spa;
4. it is more refreshing than water drawn from the tap because it can be kept refrigerated, and some brands are slightly effervescent;
5. it is healthier than tap water because it contains certain mineral salts, although some customers prefer a brand that is low in mineral salts;
6. it is very profitable to the restaurateur.

All the wine waiter has to do is to remove the cap and pour the water into the glasses of those who require it then leave the bottle on the table, bringing another when the first is empty. Some customers prefer to mix a spirit such as whisky with a drop of bottled water, rather than soda from a syphon.

Among the best known brands of what are known as natural mineral waters are Apollinaris, Ashbourne, Badoit, Evian, Highland Spring, Cwm Dale, Contrex, Malvern, San Pellegrino, Ramlosa (Swedish), Perrier, Spa, Volvic, Vichy, and Vittel. A restaurant will keep only one or two of these in stock, usually Perrier because it contains a natural gas that makes it fizzy, which is what British customers seem to prefer.

15.17 PIMMS CUP

Pimms is the basis for a gin sling, sold in concentrated form for mixing with sparkling lemonade. One measure of Pimms is added to two of three measures of lemonade over ice cubes, and garnished with a sprig of borage and a slice of cucumber. Some establishments like to add other ingredients such as slices of apple, orange, lemon, lime, or pear, also cocktail cherries, grapes, cucumber peel or a sprig of mint. It can also be made with tonic water or dry ginger ale, instead of lemonade.

It should be served in a silver tankard or glass mug with a green handle but a tall glass will do. It should be drunk through a straw.

The secret formula for Pimms No 1 gives an alcoholic beverage of 31.4 per cent alcohol which, when sold diluted as a sling or cup, is equal to 11 to 12 per cent alcohol. Pimms No 2 is vodka-based.

QUESTIONS

1. Explain the protocol of wine service throughout a six-course gourmet meal.

2. Give a list of proprietary drinks suitable as (i) aperitifs, (ii) after-dinner drinks.

3. Suggest actual wines to service with (i) oysters, (ii) truite à la meunière, (iii) curried beef, (iv) wiener schnitzel, (v) Stilton cheese, (vi) steak tartare, (vii) ice cream.

4. Outline the operation of a dispense bar and list the duties of the barman.

CHAPTER 16

TRANSPORT CATERING

16.1 INTRODUCTION

Catering for people on the move is a much more demanding job than when doing so in the usual static environment; it is a job that calls for skills and knowledge above and beyond the norm. Doing a job whilst moving at speed or on an undulating floor brings a need not just for good equilibrium but also to be able to cope with a rush of passengers, all of them wanting to be served in a hurry. Above all, it shows the need to be able to keep calm while working under pressure and to be able to show a smiling face although inwardly seething, possibly because of some customer's ill-manners.

It is also the area where there is great dependency on team work and versatility as there is no means of calling up reinforcements during the engagement.

16.2 CATERING ON A CRUISE LINER

This sounds a glamorous way of earning a living but in fact waiters, or stewards as they are called, normally have to serve breakfast, lunch and dinner throughout the voyage to a table of ten to twelve passengers who are encouraged by the company's advertisements, to eat five or six courses plus coffee at every meal. But that is not the end, for in all but the first-class dining-rooms there are normally two sittings at every meal which means having to serve very quickly and even to hurry the first diners out so as to make time to relay the table and stock up the sideboard in time for the second sitting. A typical cruise luncheon menu is shown in Table 16.1.

Shipping companies extol the wonderful dishes they have on offer, cooked to perfection by a brigade of first-class cooks, served skilfully

Table 16.1   *typical luncheon menus on cruise and luxury liners*

(a)   *Cruise liner luncheon menu*

Egg Mayonnaise

Chicken Consommé
Grilled Fillet of Hake Catalan

Curried Chicken with Rice
Chocolate Custard Pudding
Cheese Board
Coffee

(b)   *Luxury liner dinner menu*

Hawaiian Fruit Cup

Old-fashioned Split Pea Soup

Corned Round and Brisket of Beef
Boiled Root Vegetables
Creamed Potatoes

Rhubarb Pie with Custard Sauce
Coffee

by stylish waiters, in superb surroundings, all of it allegedly exceeding the standard of even the best of five-star hotels; in addition there are obeisant wine waiters with a lengthy list of wines to sell. Part of the programme is the captain's champagne reception for all passengers, several parties for various groups travelling together and, at the end, a gala dinner that goes on late into the last night of the voyage. All this keeps the stewards very busy indeed and prevents them from doing anything other than sitting and resting their weary feet during any off-duty breaks.

Most of the service practices are the same as those carried out in restaurants, and most of the dishes are served in the same way. Often however, as the ship visits various locations which have a reputation for different types of food, the chef may offer menus on board which reflect local specialities. It becomes imperative therefore for the steward to familiarise himself fully with international specialities and their methods of presentation.

Many luxury liners offer menus which are the envy of most first-class establishments on shore, but as customers pay extremely high prices for a lengthy cruise it also means that considerable forethought must be given to the customer's needs for variety, of food as well as an opportunity to control one's energy intake.

For example, some shipping companies have introduced a selected menu with a calorie count which means it is essential for the steward to acquire an understanding of nutrition, a knowledge which is not required to the same extent by the food-service worker in an ordinary restaurant. On a cruise liner, the passenger becomes totally dependent on the ship's menus for a balanced diet.

The steward as a member of the crew also has certain responsibilities for the safety of passengers. Even on the stormiest of seas he has to be ready at his place of duty to serve those who wish to eat and must be ready to show his confidence in going down the side during boat drill or in an emergency.

At the end of the voyage there is a great deal of clearing up to be done hurriedly in the turn-around period before the next cruise, which may start within twelve hours of landing. Stewards are kept busy preparing the restaurants in readiness to receive new passengers who are avid to taste the delights of the table and be waited on hand and foot.

Passengers are expected to sit at the same table for all meals throughout the cruise with the same waiter to look after them. His approach, affability and slickness of service will not only make the cruise a pleasurable one for passengers but will also determine how well they reward him.

16.3   CATERING ON A CROSS-CHANNEL FERRY

A cross-channel ferry runs to a timetable by day and night throughout the year, linking various countries by short sea-routes. Some of these ships take freight only but even so lorry-drivers will expect to find facilities for a meal during the crossing. Other ships carry passengers and their cars and coaches, and find it profitable to offer several levels of restaurants as well as bars, therefore, these ships usually employ a number of stewards to serve passengers in the high-class restaurant that operates a silver service.

The quality of food and drink is invariably good and customers expect to be able to choose from an international menu. Service has to be quick so as to complete a three- or four-course meal within the voyage time.

Even on the shortest crossings weather conditions can be such as to make working conditions difficult and at times all equipment has to be battened down to prevent it from falling about, which does of course, make the job of the steward even more fatiguing.

16.4 AIRLINE CATERING

Airline catering for first-class passengers is an entirely different world from the rather indifferent packaged meals issued to people travelling on holiday charter-flights. Yet both meals may be prepared in the same kitchen and by the same staff, which means that the cost of the meal is included in the price of the flight ticket.

Being an airline steward or stewardess, or air hostess as they used to be called, is no sinecure. The working conditions are not entirely congenial as the service areas are small and the aisles are narrow to serve from. Service is constant from take-off to landing and on an ordinary transatlantic flight, two main meals and several snack meals as well as drinks, have to be served to upwards of 200 passengers.

It might be thought that all that is required is to pass a prepared tray of food to each person, serve a drink, then go round to collect the used glasses and crockery. In fact, some of the passengers receive guéridon service and see a hot joint carved in front of them, accompanied with vegetables and the appropriate trimmings. This is complemented with fine wines and a brandy or liqueur to finish a meal, which is equal to that served in the finest hotel anywhere in the world; the service must obviously be at the same high level.

Amongst the passengers on a regular flight there are bound to be those of differing races and religions which means that the steward needs a knowledge of the food laws of the races and nations so as not to cause offence by serving an unacceptable meal. Some of the passengers may have ordered a special menu that is in accordance with their ethnic requirements and others may have requested a special diet meal for health reasons; the steward must see that these passengers receive the meals they ordered.

National airlines obviously like to feature meals of the country they represent so that passengers can sample some of their specialities on the journey there and back, but otherwise the meals served will be of

French derivation, chosen to satisfy a knowledgeable international clientele. Recently a renewed effort has been made by many national airlines to improve their image. One area which can contribute to this marketing effort is the quality of food. British Airways for example, have made great use of a range of products specially created for them by the Roux Brothers. These dishes need to be served with the care and respect their preparation deserves, therefore, only skilled staff should be allowed to distribute them.

Typical airline lunches as served in Club Class and Concorde are shown in Table 16.2.

16.5 CATERING ON A CHARTER AIRLINE

Charter airline catering is the serving of a meal to break the monotony of the journey for people travelling to a foreign holiday resort. It is usually a fairly basic repast that does not demand any skill in serving, consisting as it does of some kind of cold meat with other bought-in items, enclosed in a plastic container from which it is eaten. A hot drink is served, then the empties are collected and the meal service is finished. Disposable knives, forks, spoons, cups and glasses are thrown away on landing. It is a pity however, that charter companies cannot appreciate the value of providing good quality, appetising meals, served by well-mannered and skilled staff, to holidaymakers.

. With the advent of sous-vide and better methods of food production and regeneration, the food standards can now be improved. It is to be hoped that the managers of the airline services understand the need to make the in-flight meal occasion a pleasurable one, and to train staff to do this.

16.6 RAILWAY CATERING

Railway catering takes many forms, from fast-food snack bars in the station concourse to meals served in the first-class dining-car of an inter-city train, or a gourmet meal as on the Orient Express.

Railways have been in the catering business for well over a century, and have always endeavoured to provide a good standard, despite the difficulties that are inherent when dealing with a fluctuating number of passengers going on a journey.

A *buffet* can serve cold and hot snacks over the counter, mainly in disposable containers, so it is easy to clear the buffet car at the end of the journey and to restock for the return trip.

Table 16.2 *typical airline catering*

(a)   *Club class airline lunch*

Hors-d'Oeuvre

Filet de Boeuf au poivre Vert
or
Suprême de Volaille Maryland

Marignan au Rhum

Sélection de Fromages

Café

(b)   *Lunch on board Concorde*

Saumon Fumé d'Ecosse

Délice de Turbot Aïda

Trois Filets Grillés
Chou-fleur Polonaise; Mangetouts au Beurre

Choix de Fromages

Bavarois aux Manges

Café

(c)   *Charter flight – standard lunch*

Fruit juice

Braised beef
peas and carrots
fondante potatoes

Trifle

Coffee

(d)   *Charter flight tea*

Cucumber and ham sandwiches

Scone with butter and jam

Almond slice

Tea or coffee

In the *dining-car* much thought and effort has been given to the improvement of the meals which have been served. British Rail has identified the need for serving a variety of meals for differing markets, including breakfast, lunch, afternoon tea and dinner. Until recently the main meals consisted of:

1. The Inter-City – a two-course meal consisting of a main course with vegetables and potatoes, and a dessert,
2. Main line – a three course table d'hôte meal,
3. Gold star – a four-course meal comparable to a select à la carte menu, with a good selection of wines on popular business routes.

Typical first-class and Orient Express menus are shown in Table 16.3.

Recently much effort has been directed towards providing meal packages similar to those served by airlines, selling them in the carriages without the customer having to go to the dining area. This approach seems to meet customer demand.

16.7 CATERING ON COACHES

Many modern coach companies compete favourably in terms of price and comfort with train catering. Recently a limited buffet service has been introduced to serve sandwiches, snacks and hot drinks en route. This is a pleasant innovation, and it is to be hoped that it will continue and even lead to a more comprehensive service that will require the service of a trained professional food-service worker on all long-distance coaches.

QUESTIONS

1. How does transport catering differ from conventional forms of catering?

2. Outline the nature of cruise catering.

3. What are the problems associated with flight catering?

Table 16.3 *typical first-class and Orient Express menus*

(a) *1st class rail dining car* (selected from the à la carte menu)

Egg Mayonnaise

Fillet of Cod Mornay

Roast Chicken with Bread Sauce
Old Smokey Ham and Tongue and Salad
Garden Peas　　　Glazed Carrots
Lyonnaise and Parsley Potatoes

Lemon Torte

Scotch Woodcock

Coffee

(b)　　　　　　　　*Orient Express Dinner*

Feuilleté de Lotte au Beurre de Nage

Filet de Boeuf Hercule Poirot au Bordeaux

Sélection de Fromages

Alcazar au Chocolat

Mignardises

Café

MULTIPLE-CHOICE

QUESTIONS

These multiple-choice questions are designed to show how examinations are being set by the various examining bodies. You have to choose which of the four answers listed is the correct one and mark it with a tick. The answer you tick will show your knowledge of the subject rather than your ability to write an account of it, as you have had to do in the questions at the end of each chapter.

1. The person in charge of room service in an hotel is called a:

   (a) demi-chef de rang
   (b) chef d'étages
   (c) chef de rang
   (d) station head waiter

2. The person who serves alcoholic beverages in a restaurant is called a:

   (a) commise de rang
   (b) trancheur
   (c) sommelier
   (d) débarrasseur

3. Silverware can be polished using which of the following systems:

   (a) Guéridon
   (b) Helitherm
   (c) Ganymede
   (d) Polivit

4. The main use of a waiter's cloth is for:

   (a) wiping customer's fingers after eating snails
   (b) polishing plates and glasses when laying them on the table
   (c) covering stains on the tablecloth
   (d) wiping spilt food from the carpet

5. If wine is spilt on the tablecloth a waiter should:

    (a) clear the table of everything and sponge the stain with milk
    (b) cover the soiled area with a clean table napkin by unrolling it over the spillage
    (c) ask the customers to wait in the lounge while he fetches a clean cloth
    (d) take the plates of food to the sideboard and change the cloth

6. The correct accompaniments for roast grouse are:

    (a) bacon rolls, meat balls, jus lié, heart-shape croûtons spread with duxelles
    (b) gravy, bread sauce, fried breadcrumbs, game chips, watercress
    (c) redcurrant jelly, grapes, slices of kiwi-fruit, horseradish sauce
    (d) cranberry sauce, chestnuts, thyme and parsley stuffing, chipolatas

7. The main accompaniments for curried chicken, apart from rice, are:

    (a) plain boiled potatoes, quenelles, matignon of vegetables
    (b) mangos, stuffed tomatoes, château potatoes
    (c) fried onion-rings, chou-paste gnocchi, turned mushrooms
    (d) poppadums, sambals, Bombay ducks

8. Horseradish sauce should be offered when serving:

    (a) smoked mackerel
    (b) wiener schnitzel
    (c) fried whitebait
    (d) roast leg of lamb

9. The correct accompaniments for a grilled steak are:

    (a) grilled mushrooms and tomatoes, anchovy butter
    (b) straw potatoes, watercress, parsley butter
    (c) fried onion-rings, streaky bacon, picked parsley
    (d) fried egg, slice of truffle, horseradish sauce

10. A customer who orders Coeur de Filet would expect it to be:

    (a) braised lambs heart
    (b) stewed ox-tail
    (c) fried calf's liver
    (d) fillet of beef

11. Grissini is another name for:

    (a) small brioches
    (b) Melba toast
    (c) thin bread sticks
    (d) slices of French bread

12. State which of the following dishes is eaten raw:

    (a) contrefilet bouquetière
    (b) entrecôte minute
    (c) steak tartare
    (d) tournedos Rossini

13. Sorbet is a:

    (a) mild herb used in making stuffings
    (b) refreshing water ice served midway through a banquet
    (c) cold sauce served with globe artichokes
    (d) continental smoked sausage

14. A Chateaubriand is a:

    (a) porterhouse steak
    (b) thick rump steak
    (c) thick salmon steak
    (d) double- or treble-size fillet steak

15. Canard à la Presse is:

    (a) roast wild duck finished by the waiter
    (b) pot-roasted Aylesbury duckling with herbs
    (c) duck liver pâté flavoured with Armagnac
    (d) conserve of duck and goose with calvados

16. A Mixed Grill consists of:

    (a) pork chop, veal kidney, button mushrooms, pineapple ring, chips
    (b) lamb cutlet and kidney, chipolata, bacon, tomato, mushroom, straw potatoes
    (c) thin sirloin steak, fried onion-rings, slice of liver, fried egg, sausage, cress
    (d) mutton chop, slice of black pudding, scrambled egg, fried bread, tomato

17. The liqueurs used to prepare Crêpes Suzette should be:

    (a) Kirsch and Maraschino
    (b) Curaçao and Grand Marnier
    (c) Tia Maria and Bénédictine
    (d) Glayva and Marnique

18. A guéridon is a:

    (a) moveable sideboard
    (b) mobile table for doing lampwork
    (c) cigar and liqueur handcart
    (d) trolley for taking used crockery and cutlery to the wash-up

19. State which of the following selections represents the ideal cheese-board:

   (a) Cheddar, Camembert, Stilton, demi-sel, Wensleydale
   (b) Gruyère, sbrinz, Emmenthal, Parmesan, bel paese
   (c) Edam, Gouda, processed, quark, mozzarella
   (d) Gorgonzola, Stilton, Rocquefort, Mycella, danablu

20. The main accompaniments for caviar are:

   (a) ratafia biscuits, quarters of lemon, grated Parmesan
   (b) fingers of hot toast, melted butter, quarter of lemon
   (c) brown bread and butter, oriental salt
   (d) Melba toast, mayonnaise, French mustard

21. When serving gulls' eggs the accompaniments should be:

   (a) horseradish, acidulated cream, game chips, spiced salt
   (b) chopped capers and gherkins, vinaigrette dressing, cayenne
   (c) chilli vinegar, oriental salt, mustard and cress, walnut oil
   (d) sieved yolk and white of hard-boiled egg, tabasco, peppermill, lemon

22. Decide which of the following items require a finger bowl:

   (a) avocado pear, shrimp cocktail, smoked salmon
   (b) fruit basket, fresh asparagus, artichaut vinaigrette
   (c) cantaloup melon, pâté maison, potted shrimps
   (d) caviar, foie gras, corn on the cob, half grapefruit

23. The best way to deal with a customer who complains about poor service is to:

   (a) apologise
   (b) offer him a free drink
   (c) inform the head waiter
   (d) try to make excuses

24. Which of the following groups does not contain a liqueur:

   (a) Campari, Cherry Brandy, Grande Champagne, Goldwasser
   (b) Grappa, Schnapps, Bacardi, Pernod
   (c) Drambuie, Glayva, Grand Marnier, Drambuie
   (d) Bénédictine, Crème de Menthe, Kahlúa, Cointreau

25. A humidor is a box in which:

   (a) a hydrometer for measuring density of liquids is kept
   (b) all the gratuities given by customers are pooled
   (c) waiter's checks are placed whilst waiting for the food
   (d) cigars are kept in perfect condition

26. The abbreviation 'B and B' means:

 (a) a bartender's beaker
 (b) Bénédictine liqueur and brandy
 (c) a barbecue for spit-roasting foods outdoors
 (d) Babycham and Bacardi

27. The Gay-Lussac system of measuring alcoholic strength shows Scotch whisky to be:

 (a) 75° degrees under proof
 (b) neutral grain spirit
 (c) 25° over proof
 (d) 40% by volume

28. Which well-known cocktail is made of vodka and tomato juice:

 (a) Bloody Mary
 (b) Harvey Wallbanger
 (c) Manhattan
 (d) White Lady

29. A table d'hôte is a:

 (a) meal comprised of main dish and sweet
 (b) set menu, sold at an inclusive price
 (c) list of all the available dishes each individually priced
 (d) sequence of dishes in categories from soup to sweet

30. The term à la carte means:

 (a) a set menu without any alternatives or beverages
 (b) a carte du jour menu inclusive of coffee and service charge
 (c) a series of dishes as chosen by a customer and cooked to order
 (d) a prix-fixe menu with several choices on each course

31. Which of the following is the best source of Vitamin C in the daily diet:

 (a) baked beans on toast
 (b) new potatoes sprinkled with parsley
 (c) oatmeal porridge with gold syrup
 (d) hot beef essence such as Bovril

32. Which of the following groups are all single hors-d'oeuvre:

 (a) potato salad, stuffed celery, asparagus vinaigrette, salade niçoise
 (b) tunny fish, sardines, Russian salad, Japanese salad
 (c) Florida cocktail, seafood cocktail, smoked trout, foie gras
 (d) cauliflower à la grecque, coleslaw, stuffed tomatoes, oysters

33. In which line are all items farinaceous:

   (a) tagliatelle, gnocchi romaine, carolines, cromeskis
   (b) canneloni, macaroni, fritto misto, piroquis
   (c) ravioli, risotto, pilaff of rice, lasagne verdi
   (d) vermicelli, polenta, zampino, pignatelli

34. Match the sauces to the main dishes:

   (a) tartare   (a) calf's head
   (b) tomato   (b) poached river trout
   (c) tortue   (c) filets de sole frits à l'Orly
   (d) tarragon   (d) deep fried fillet of plaice

35. The correct sequence of lay-out on a cafeteria counter is:

   (a) main course, sweet, cash till, cutlery, paper napkins
   (b) cold dish, soup, main dish, sweet, sundries, beverages
   (c) snacks, vending machine, microwave oven, tray stand
   (d) cutlery, trays, condiments, called order, cash till, water font

36. Which of the following groups of nuts is correct for dessert?

   (a) chestnuts, coconuts, pecans
   (b) pistachios, macadamia, pine kernels
   (c) almonds, walnuts, brazils
   (d) peanuts, filberts, cashews

37. Decide which menu is the best composed:

   (a) Egg mayonnaise, Chicken Pancake Mornay, mashed potato, carrots, steamed chocolate pudding
   (b) Melon Cocktail, Curried Beef and Rice, Brussels sprouts, boiled potatoes, bread and butter pudding
   (c) Cream of Tomato Soup, Chicken Chasseur, Vichy carrots, Rissolée potatoes, Strawberry Flan
   (d) Cream of Leek Soup, Blanquette of Lamb, cauliflower, new potatoes, Vanilla mousse

38. Which line is comprised only of sherries?

   (a) tarragona, montilla, bual, ratafia, campari
   (b) muscatel, alto douro, sercial, mead, schnapps
   (c) Malmsey, Marsala, Malaga, Madeira, Verdelho
   (d) fino, manzanilla, amontillado, sack, oloroso

39. The cover laid for an à la carte meal consists of:

   (a) teacup, saucer and teaspoon, ash-tray, cone-shape serviette
   (b) fish-knife and fork, side-plate and knife, centre plate with a napkin on it
   (c) joint-knife and fork, soup spoon, side-knife, glass
   (d) complete accoutrement of cutlery, crockery and glasses

40. Serving a room service meal, a waiter should

   (a) knock on the door loudly and announce his presence:
   (b) look through the keyhole and if he sees the guest is up, go straight inside
   (c) carry the tray at waist level and enter the room
   (d) carry the tray shoulder-high in his left hand, knock and wait until told to enter

41. Decide which group consists of natural mineral waters only:

   (a) Tonic water, Cola, Soda water syphon, Bath Spa
   (b) Perrier, Malvern water, Vichy, Spa
   (c) Chartreuse, ginger ale, citronelle, bitter lemon
   (d) Grenadine, cordial, cona, perry

42. A rognonnade is a:

   (a) loin of veal cooked with the kidney in it
   (b) hard roe of the sturgeon
   (c) stew of lamb kidney, chipolata and mushrooms
   (d) mixture of cockscombs and kidneys

43. Say what steps you would take if you accidentally spilt sauce on a customer's jacket:

   (a) offer to have it cleaned if you cannot remove it with warm water
   (b) dab it with some detergent and hot water
   (c) go and tell the head waiter what happened
   (d) fetch a damp cloth and wipe the stain off quickly

44. Tick the line of foods which are most closely associated with Scotland:

   (a) succotash, angel-food cake, clam chowder, chicken à la king
   (b) truffles, frog's legs, foie gras, glacé cherries
   (c) garlic, salami, pastasciutta, pizza, olive oil
   (d) haggis, arbroath smokies, finnan haddock, smoked salmon

45. Which of the following is the correct lay-up for use with the famous French dish, bouillabaisse:

   (a) hot joint-plate, finger-bowl and soup-spoon
   (b) soup-spoon and soup-plate, fish-knife and fork
   (c) tureen and ladle, large fork and lobster crackers
   (d) large plate, dessert spoon, lobster-pick and tongs

46. Which is the correct liqueur for making Café Calypso?

   (a) Kahlùa
   (b) Curaçao
   (c) Tia Maria
   (d) Ron Bacardi

47. The definition of amontillado sherry is:

    (a) rather fragrant and slightly sweet
    (b) mellow but medium-dry and nutty
    (c) very dry and crisp
    (d) darkish coloured and medium sweet

48. From which of the following areas does Nuits Saint-Georges come:

    (a) the Côtes du Rhône
    (b) the Côte d'Or of France
    (c) The Rioja of Spain
    (d) the Médoc region of Bordeaux

49. Say how many bottles and of which of the following are required to serve 180 customers with an aperitif each:

    (a) 2 dozen Dubonnet
    (b) 7 bottles of Campari
    (c) 6 dozen litres of vermouth
    (d) 15 bottles of Manzanilla

50. In which form of food service does the customer help himself from the dish held by a waiter:

    (a) à la carte
    (b) family
    (c) à la Russe
    (d) banquet

51. Petits fours are served:

    (a) with the coffee
    (b) with the aperitif before a meal
    (c) with the soup
    (d) halfway through a meal, with the sorbet

52. A bisque soup is made of:

    (a) scallops, sturgeon or clams
    (b) lobster, crab or prawns
    (c) mussels, oysters and cockles
    (d) potted shrimps, squid and scampi

53. The staff of the still-room are responsible for the preparation of:

    (a) fruit baskets
    (b) porridge, boiled eggs, hot beverages, Melba toast
    (c) salads, the cheese board and cold buffet
    (d) breakfast cereals, hot sandwiches

54. Decaffeinated coffee may be defined as:

    (a)   strong because it contains chicory
    (b)   flavoured with figs in the Turkish style
    (c)   continental high roast made in a Cona machine
    (d)   having the stimulant caffeine removed

55. Real pâté de foie gras is made from:

    (a)   fattened goose liver
    (b)   best quality calf's liver
    (c)   duck livers in a pastry crust
    (d)   venison flesh and salt pork fat

56. The term 'Ménage' on the duty list refers to:

    (a)   slicing and buttering brown bread
    (b)   filling the cruets, preparing the lamps
    (c)   polishing cutlery and glassware
    (d)   making butter pats and Melba toast

57. Which of the following is the most junior member of the brigade:

    (a)   a chef d'étage
    (b)   a dumb waiter
    (c)   the demi-chef de rang
    (d)   the commis débarrasseur

58. Which one of the following items requires a finger bowl:

    (a)   melon with Parma ham
    (b)   oysters in the half shell
    (c)   grapefruit cocktail
    (d)   hors-d'oeuvre variés

59. Under which circumstances should a waiter write an 'en place' check?

    (a)   when a customer changes his mind and asks for something else
    (b)   to obtain the customer's coat from the cloakroom
    (c)   if a customer asks for a double brandy with his coffee
    (d)   if a customer finds he cannot afford the prices

60. The traditional sequence of courses for an elaborate dinner is

    (a)   soup, egg, fish, entrée, savoury, cheese
    (b)   hors-d'oeuvre, soup, fish, meat, sweet
    (c)   fish, entrée, relevé, cheese, sweet, coffee
    (d)   soup, farinaceous, meat, cheese, dessert

ANSWERS TO MULTIPLE-CHOICE QUESTIONS

1 (b); 2 (c); 3 (d); 4 (b); 5 (b); 6 (b); 7 (d); 8 (a); 9 (b);
10 (d); 11 (c); 12 (c); 13 (b); 14 (d); 15 (a); 16 (b); 17 (b);

18 (b); 19 (a); 20 (c); 21 (c); 22 (b); 23 (c); 24 (b); 25 (d);
26 (b); 27 (d); 28 (a); 29 (b); 30 (c); 31 (b); 32 (c); 33 (c);
34 (a & b)(b & c)(c & a)(d & b); 35 (b); 36 (c); 37 (b); 38 (d);
39 (b); 40 (d); 41 (b); 42 (a); 43 (d); 44 (d); 45 (b); 46 (c);
47 (b); 48 (b); 49 (d); 50 (b); 51 (a); 52 (b); 53 (b); 54 (d);
55 (a); 56 (b); 57 (d); 58 (b); 59 (a); 60 (b).

MODEL ANSWERS TO QUESTIONS AT END OF CHAPTERS

1. The evolution of restaurant service

1. The word 'service' at present may be taken to mean the provision of a special kind of attention to a person or organisation. In the specific context of restaurant operation the word 'service' also means a group of dishes as a specific component part of a meal, c.f. entrée or relevé.

2. Within the context of 'service', the first provision of dishes, or the first main course, was called an *entrée*, derived from a French word meaning 'the food that was on the table when the diners entered the room'. The empty dishes and surplus food of this course, which may have consisted of some 16–24 items, were then removed while guests circulated to stretch their legs and then sat down again to the next course called the *relevé*, which contained more substantial dishes than the first course.

3. Table presentation received considerable importance in the Renaissance period but it reached its zenith of artistic presentation in late Regency and early Victorian times mainly through the work of a great French chef named Marie-Antoin Carême (1784–1833). He was a person who took great pride in presenting his dishes in classical architectural styles reflecting the ornamental styles of ancient Greece and Rome, whilst at the same time he also gave due importance to the newly emerging style of far eastern architecture.

2. The origins of restaurants

1. The separation into seven levels of food service is somewhat arbitrary, as by necessity one style may be fused into another. The levels are however clearly distinguisable by the following characteristics:

(a) *Self-service*: where the customer collects his own food from a long counter, containing hot and cold courses.
(b) *Counter service*: where the customer sits on a stool and is handed his food from an operative who may also have cooked it in front of him.
(c) *Plate service*: where the customer, sitting at the table, is handed his food by the waiting-staff.

(d) *Buffet service*: where a certain amount of carving and plate presentation is carried out from behind the counter, at the customer's request.

(e) *Silver service*: where the waiter serves the customer at the table, taking food from a salver using a spoon and fork.

(f) *Family service*: a fairly complex and misunderstood form of service, where the customer helps himself, with the use of a spoon and fork, from a salver containing pre-portioned food, neatly presented.

(g) *Guéridon service*: where the carving and finishing of food is carried out at the table in front of the customer.

2. The reputation of most hotels rests on their Restaurants and the quality of food and service provided therein.

3. The word 'restorative' was originally used to define a health-giving soup and later applied to places where such soups were offered for sale, hence 'Restaurant'. The first were established in Paris early in the eighteenth century and the first restaurant as we know it today was opened in 1782.

4. The contributing factors to the ambience of the restaurant are; the shape and size of the room, the colour combinations, the level of illumination, the level of noise and background music, the temperature, and the age and dress of staff and customers, plus any music or other entertainment.

5. The presentation of food is very important because it elicits the initial consumer reaction to its acceptance or rejection; we eat first with our eyes, then with the nose and finally with the mouth.

3 Restaurant lay-out, furniture and equipment

1. Price has a direct influence on customers' expectations in terms of food quality. The higher the price charged the higher the perception of quality promised. For this reason extreme care must be taken to ensure that pricing is balanced with the real quality of the product, thus avoiding dissonance in the customer's mind.

2.

Level of service	*Allowance per person* (in m^2)
(a) Self-Service	0.8
(b) Counter-Service	1.4
(c) Plate	1.2
(d) Buffet-style (help-yourself)	0.5
(e) Silver	1.5
(f) Family	1.5
(g) Guéridon	1.8

3. The following are the most important reasons for variations in the methods of service:

(a) the style of the operation;
(b) the need and purpose of the customer;
(c) the time of the day when the food is consumed;
(d) the price charged; .

(e) the nature of the occasion at which the food is consumed – formal or informal;

(f). the type of menu offered;

(g) the socioeconomic status of the customer.

4. The menu in a restaurant is the 'modus operandi' or the outward expression of the total catering operation. It defines what is available for the customer, how to organise its production, and preparation for its service. It further dictates how the order should be taken. For à la carte, this requires that each item is separately listed and separately priced.

4 Restaurant staff

1.   (i) *Restaurant Manager*: in overall charge of the restaurant.

   (ii) *First Head Waiter*: in direct charge of the restaurant brigade and deputy to the manager.

   (iii) *Second Head Waiter*: responsible for the reservation system and a customer-profile index.

   (iv)' *Head Wine Waiter*: responsible for all the non-alcoholic and alcoholic beverage service in the restaurant.

   (v) *Station Head Waiter*: in charge of a section of the restaurant.

   (vi) *The Carver* (trancheur): responsible for the carving done at the buffet table and on the carving trolley.

   (vii) *The Station Waiter*: responsible for the service of approximately five to nine tables.

   (viii) *The Commis Waiter*: an assistant waiter, who fetches and carries food from the kitchen to the restaurant.

   (ix) *The Clearer* (débarrasseur): is responsible for clearing dirty plates and keeps the working sideboard in order.

2. *Social skills* are required for efficient interaction with the customer; they include stance, voice intonation, and body language. *Technical skills* are demonstrable skills of a technical nature; they include manipulation of serving spoon and fork, carving, filleting and the knowledge required to serve each dish correctly and with the appropriate accompaniments.

3. A food service worker requires a number of attributes in order to discharge his duties and responsibilities effectively; for some these may be innate abilities, but others may need to cultivate and develop them. These attributes include: (i) a good memory for names and faces and for descriptions of dishes; (ii) an ability to attend to details; (iii) a capacity for organising one's own work sequentially; (iv) an inbuilt curiosity and a desire for knowledge leading to good conversation, and (v) a tactful manner.

4. Personal care refers in this context to an ability through proper care of one's general appearance to project an image of personal cleanliness and orderliness and, in consequence, to assure the customer that he is in safe hands. Personal hygiene is concerned with keeping one's body healthy, through sober habits and personal cleanliness.

5 The menu

1. An à la carte menu is a list of individual dishes each having its own price printed next to it; the menu is laid out in the usual form of the sequence of courses of a meal. The customer can choose just one or as many of these dishes as he likes, although there may be the proviso that a minimum charge will be made. Each dish on the menu will be cooked to order which means that the customer may have to wait while it is being prepared. The head chef has to ensure that every item on the à la carte menu is kept in readiness for cooking to order. This kind of menu is usually dearer than a table d'hôte menu.

A table d'hôte menu is a set list of dishes, usually in the form of a three- or four-course menu which is cooked in readiness for immediate service; it is usually sold at a set price. There may be alternatives on each course and if there is some difference in the quality of the main dish, this may decide the overall price.

2. The principles of menu composition must be based on the consumer's needs, and expectations, and the kind of meal; the following factors need to be taken into consideration: type of menu – table d'hôte, à la carte, banquet, fast food, etc.; sequence of courses; colour balance of the meal; texture of the dishes; flavour of the dishes; aroma of the meal; selection of garnishes and accompaniments; ingredients available according to season; ability of cooking- and waiting-staff to produce and serve the meal; kind of large and small equipment in the establishment; nutritional aspects; the language in which the menu is to be written; range of wines on the wine list.

3. Nutrition is the supplying of food of a beneficial nature to life and health so that the human body has energy to keep it functioning, can grow from birth, and can renew its body tissues. The body is like a machine which needs fuel to make it work, the fuel being the intake of food.

Foods contain various nutrients which are classed as: *protein* which provides growth, repair and maintenance; *carbohydrate* which provides energy; *fat* which gives heat and energy to the body; *vitamins* which are essential chemical substances found in food that assist in maintaining good health; and *mineral salts* found in many forms of plant life and assist in several ways such as bone formation and repair, functioning of glands and the nervous system, etc. *Water* is also a nutrient and is the one that acts as a lubricant.

The ideal diet should contain foods from each of these sections and those engaged in the catering trade should try to memorise the list of important suppliers of each and what quantity of the nutrient is contained in each portion of food.

4. One of the principles of menu composition is that foodstuffs should be made a special feature when they first come into season. At first, these foods may be expensive to purchase but become cheaper as they become available in greater quantities, for example, Jersey new potatoes can cost 90p per lb in April before gradually reducing to approximately 15p in June.

Every season has its special foods, including salmon in the spring and game during autumn and winter. The weather has an impact on menus because it is well-known that customers prefer substantial dishes during cold weather and salads with cold meats during summer.

6 Restaurant organisation

1. The number of wine waiters employed by a restaurant is much less than that of ordinary waiters so that at very busy times the food waiter should be prepared to assist his wine service colleague. In any event, an ordinary waiter could be detailed as wine commis at short notice so although not having an expert knowledge of the subject, every waiter can benefit from a study of wine, even if it is only to know something about each of the main wine-growing areas of the world and the qualities and characteristics of the major ones.

2. Accompaniments and condiments can contribute a lot to the enjoyment of a dish, by adding an extra dimension to what the chef has prepared. Many of these items are essential to a dish – e.g. English or French mustard with grilled steak – while others are optional and perhaps no great loss is felt if they are not offered. In all cases, these things must be compatible and there should be a reason for offering them as they may help the digestion, add an aroma, or extra pungency. All the various kinds of salt such as sea salt, coarse salt from a mill, seasoned salt, etc., and the various peppers such as chilli, cayenne, peppercorns, are included; there are dozens of different kinds of mustard, each having its own peculiar characteristic; flavoured vinegars, various kinds of oil such as walnut, hazelnut, and olive; flavouring sauces such as Tabasco and Worcester; lemon juice; verjuice and flavoured butters; proprietary brands of pickle, chutney and bottled sauce – all these and many others have a part to play in meal service at the table.

3. The term 'mise en place' means the preparation of things in readiness for serving food, in advance of the customers' arrival. It means preparing the restaurant by cleaning it, laying the tables, putting on uniforms, and being briefed on the day's menu, so that when the doors are opened, the restaurant looks immaculate and everything is ready to begin serving. The jobs of cleaning the room, filling cruets, fetching linen, polishing silver and glass-ware, fetching iced water, bread rolls and butter pats, etc., will have been allocated to certain members of the restaurant brigade and these must be finished in good time for waiters to have their meal and get dressed in uniform before the customers start to arrive.

4. Customers must be put at ease as soon as they enter a restaurant and must be given helpful and attentive service throughout the meal; this must continue until the customers get up to leave, when their custom should be shown to have been much appreciated. A waiter needs to be skilful in the art of food service but, in addition, he must be socially skilled which means the way he relates to customers, over and above the service he provides.

His appearance, stance, attitude, interest in his job, deference of approach, pleasing manner of speech, all make an impression on customers, and if it adds up to a pleasant personality allied to a craftsman, then customers will leave at the end of the meal with a feeling of great satisfaction as though they had undergone an uplifting experience.

7 Service procedures

1. A guéridon is a movable table or trolley that makes it possible to carry out certain aspects of service in close proximity to the customer at table. Sometimes a lighted spirit lamp is kept on it so that a dish of food can be kept hot while being served onto the plate; at other times the lamp is used to cook an item of food and finish it by flaming with e.g. brandy.

Guéridon service is reckoned to be the most personal method of service and ranks high as being an advanced form, although it is really easier than doing silver service.

2. The role of the still-room is to prepare and serve to waiters, against a check, with non-alcoholic beverages including coffee, tea, fruit juices, hot proprietary beverages, milk and cream; toast, butter brown bread, rolls, croissants and brioches; porridge and breakfast cereals; butter pats, fruit baskets and sometimes, the cheese-board; also boiled eggs for breafast.

The duty of the still-room maid is to have all these items ready to serve without delay and to brew fresh coffee several times during the day so that stale coffee is not served. She will make tea by the pot to order, this also applies to herbal teas and other infusions for drinking as beverages.

3. Family service is a form of silver service whereby a waiter presents a dish of food to a guest who then takes the serving-spoon and fork and helps himself to the amount of food he wants, transferring it onto this plate which is already in front of him. This takes more time to do than if the waiter did the serving and there is a risk of the dish of food becoming cold before all the guests have taken their choice.

Family service used to be used for serving school meals whereby a group of children around a table were given a dish of food which one child was detailed to serve evenly onto the plates and pass one to each child.

Silver service is the way in which a waiter serves food from a serving-dish onto a guest's plate with a serving-spoon and fork. For a main course, he places the portion of meat at the 6 o'clock position, places the garnish, if any, on top or around, then spoons some sauce or gravy immediately by it; he then brings the dish of vegetables and uses separate spoons to serve each kind, placing them neatly around the meat in a neat and colourful pattern.

Plate-cum-silver is 'where the main item only of a meal is served by the waiter onto the customer's plate, the dish of vegetables being placed on the table for the customer to help himself, using the serving-spoon and fork provided. Thus this is a quicker form of service than full silver service.

8 Service procedures for hors-d'oeuvre

1. An *hors-d'oeuvre varié* is a mixture of several kinds of items displayed on a tray or trolley. The waiter takes spoonfuls of these to customers' choice, arranging them neatly on a cold side-plate or fish plate. There are usually at least a dozen kinds, the most popular salads being Russian, potato, tomato, beetroot and tomato, plus egg mayonnaise, anchovy fillets, sardines, tunny fish, olives, gherkins, radishes and salami.

Charcuterie is served as a first course, usually as a single hors-d'oeuvre because several of the items that comprise it are so expensive to purchase. It can include two kinds of salami, garlic sausage, liver sausage, coppa, mortadella, brawn and Parma ham, cut in very thin slices and served garnished with gherkins and radicchio.

2. Buttered brown bread, made with Hovis, wholemeal or wheatgerm bread is cut thinly and served overlapping in triangular-shaped pieces with several single hors-d'oeuvre, both cold and hot. These include smoked eel, trout and salmon, seafood cocktails, snails, fried whitebait and potted shrimps.

3. Ripe melon is a popular starter course in all the different kinds such as Charentais, Galia, Ogen, Cantaloupe and Honeydew. A *honeydew melon* is cut in half lengthways, the seeds discarded and each half cut into two or more sections. After levelling the skin so that the slice stays upright, it can be served with caster sugar and ground ginger, or cut across into slices or cubes, leaving it on the outer skin. Suitable decorations include maraschino cherries, orange segments, slices of kiwi-fruit, pineapple cubes, etc. It can be dressed on crushed ice in a soup plate or plain with a dessert-spoon and fork. Sometimes melon is served with a thin slice of Parma ham.

To make *Melon Oporto*, cut a small melon in half, remove the seeds and pour in a measure of any kind of port, or cut off the top in zig-zag fashion, discard the seeds, then scrape the flesh from inside, add some port and keep in the refrigerator until the melon becomes port-flavoured. Serve spoonfuls in a glass dish.

4. The names of some of the most popular single hors-d'oeuvre are as given in model answers 8(1), (2) and (3), plus caviar, oysters, foie gras, gull's eggs, pâté maison, grapefruit, avocado pear, rollmops, coupe miami, quail's eggs and cold asparagus. Hot hors-d'oeuvre include snails, frog's legs, fried whitebait, hot asparagus, globe artichoke, chicken tartlets, quichelette, attereaux, fritters.

9 Service procedures for soups, eggs, farinaceous and fish dishes

1. These are all thin, clear soups. *Petite Marmite* is served in an individual earthenware soup marmite, covered with a lid; it is put on a d'oyley on a small under-plate and the lid is removed. The customer drinks it with a dessert spoon and is offered grated cheese to sprinkle over, and toasted slices of French bread known as croûtes de flûte. Sometimes there is a slice of bone marrow floating on top of this soup which is also garnished with pieces of vegetables, chicken and beef. *Consommé* is usually served in a two- handled cup which is placed on a saucer which in turn is placed on a side-plate; a dessert-spoon is used to drink it; the cup should be hot. *Clear turtle soup* is made like a consommé so is served in the same way as that kind of soup, very often a small measure of dry sherry is added at table and it is usual to offer a quarter of lemon and a dish of cheese straws.

2. Fortified wines can be added to certain kinds of soup to enhance the flavour and aroma of the soup without altering its character. Both thick and clear soups derive benefit from the addition of either sherry, Madeira or port, for example, a portion of thick oxtail soup is much tastier if a small

measure of dry Madeira is added just before serving and clear or thick turtle soups are greatly enhanced by the addition of some dry sherry.

Brandy is also used to provide a luxury finishing touch to soup, adding it at the point of service rather than during the cooking; the bisque kind of soups also benefit from this.

3. An *oeuf en cocotte* is meant to be eaten from the dish on which it was cooked, placed on a d'oyley on a side-plate. It is eaten with a teaspoon and the peppermill may be offered.

4. A single omelette is made in a matter of seconds yet because of the fierce heat on which it is cooked, and its final state, the thin ends could get dry, which is why it has always been the habit to trim off the two ends before serving. This tradition is not really necessary and is not always done, in fact it is only possible to carry it out if the omelette is served on a silver dish; if on a plate it should be served as it is.

5. Pastas such as elbow macaroni, ravioli and gnocchi are easy to pick up between a serving-spoon and fork to transfer from serving dish to plate but very long ones such as spaghetti need to be curled into a bunch to prevent loose strands falling onto the table. The customer uses a similar technique to eat long pastas, curling it around the prongs of his fork in the bowl of a dessert-spoon so as to obtain an easily manoeuvered mouthful. Grated Parmesan and extra sauce may be offered.

10 Service of poultry, game and meat dishes

1. *Roast chicken* is served with game chips, a sprig of watercress, roast gravy and bread sauce; some chefs add a rasher of streaky bacon, one or two chipolata sausages and a spoonful of parsley and thyme stuffing.

Roast duck and *goose* are served with game chips and watercress, roast gravy, apple sauce and sage and onion stuffing; there is also a sauce called sage and onion sauce which is a moist version of the stuffing.

Roast turkey can be served with chestnut and/or sausage-meat stuffing, roast gravy, chipolatas and either bread sauce or cranberry sauce.

Roast game birds are served on a fried bread croûton, cut to the size of the bird and spread with liver forcemeat, roast gravy, bread sauce and fried breadcrumbs. Game chips and watercress are on the dish with the bird as are the strips of bacon or salt pork fat which were placed over the breast of the bird during cooking.

2. Game animals include the various kinds of deer, hare and rabbit; wild boar and bear are available in some countries. Game animals of the deer family are referred to as venison; a saddle of venison can be marinated and roasted with a garnish of chestnuts, pears or braised fennel and poivrade sauce. Small cuts of venison can be sautéd in butter and served with many of the classical garnishes associated with beef such as mushrooms, foie gras, celery, croquette potatoes, and various fruits.

The best known dish using hare is jugged hare, called Civet de Lièvre in French. It can be garnished with bread croûtons, braised chestnuts, mushrooms, bacon, forcemeat balls, etc. The saddle of hare is often roasted on its own and served with a classical garnish.

Rabbit can be made into a pie, stew, pâté, or roasted whole.

Juniper berries are often used to flavour game animals and redcurrant jelly or Cumberland sauce are the usual accompaniments.

3. *English mustard* is best made with cold water and allowed to stand for ten minutes, so as to develop the pungent taste. If mixed with vinegar it becomes bitter and the use of boiling water makes it taste mild. It is best made fresh daily and portioned into the small containers. If purchased ready-made it should be used fairly soon after opening the jar although a little acetic acid and modified starch is added to preserve it.

French mustard is either the pale-coloured Dijon or the darker Bordeaux mustard. The Dijon style is light, sharp, salty and its clean taste does not mask the steak with which it is served, whereas the Bordeaux style tends to mask the taste of the meat. *German mustard* has a sweet-and-sour taste and is flavoured with herbs and spices.

To serve mustard from jars, place two or three kinds on a plate, ask the customers which kind he wants, then serve it with a mustard-spoon onto the rim of the plate.

11 Service of desserts, fruits, savouries, cheese and coffee

1. A slice of gâteau must be presented on a sweet plate with the pointed section placed directly in front of the customer with the dessertspoon and fork, as shown. Cream may be offered.

Fig Q.1 *serving a slice of gâteau*

2.   Classification of cheeses vary, but in general they may be divided into (i) hard; (ii) blue vein; (iii) soft; (iv) semi-hard; (v) fresh cream; (vi) flavoured cream, and (vii) goats' or ewes' milk cheese. Their flavours may be subdivided into mild, medium and strong. The main sources of cheese are cows', goats' and ewes' milk.

3.   The accompaniments for savouries normally consists of salt and pepper, peppermill, cayenne pepper and Worcester sauce. For savouries which contain chicken liver or bacon, French and English mustards are also offered. In some instances – e.g. for savouries such as angels on horseback – Tabasco may also be made available.

12   Lamp work

1.   A naked flame in a public room is always a source of danger, and the ignition of alcohol in a crowded room can be a further source of danger. The precautions that should be taken include:

(a)   ensuring that staff doing flambé work have received proper training and are either experienced or use the lamp under supervision;
(b)   flambé preparation must take place away from inflammable materials such as curtains, and at least 1 metre distant from any customer;
(c)   always transfer the spirit to be ignited to a sauceboat so as to avoid 'bottle blow-back'.

2.   The principal characteristics of all the meat flambé dishes is that such dishes are normally composed of meat thinly sliced so that appropriate cooking can take place in less than five minutes. Further, all the meat cuts should be of a tender nature and as such should be capable of being prepared in the shortest space of time; tough meat cuts are not suitable for this purpose.

3.   In ideal conditions flambé dishes should be served while the spirit is still flaming. However, silk, light clothing and hair lacquer can easily ignite, and the waiter must ensure that he is well clear of the customer before approaching with the flaming dish.

4.   The spirit used for flaming a particular dish should be complementary to the basic characteristic of the main ingredients. For this reason one should follow time-honoured recipes rather than risking such a contrast of flavours which could be nauseous to the customer.

13   Service of breakfast, afternoon tea and supper

1.   For room service all the meal courses are served simultaneously, unless special arrangements have been made. Therefore the room tray or room trolley should be presented complete with all the items ordered, the only exception being coffee.

2.   The service procedure for afternoon tea involves the service of the requested type of tea, with the appropriate sandwiches, cakes, biscuits and fruit, as ordered by the customer. Particular care is taken to ensure that all the correct items are placed on the table as conventions decree (see 13.6).

3.   Room service for breakfast is extremely convenient, particularly for late risers. It is organised in the floor pantry and each customer is given a complete tray containing each item as ordered. In the dining-room this would involve a sequential preparation and separate service of the various courses.

4.   Supper dishes are items which are appropriate late at night, with more emphasis being placed on savouries, such as mushrooms or sardines on toast. For the complete selection see Table 13.6.

14   Function catering

Space must be used so that it produces a return that adds to the profitability of a company, and every cubic metre should contribute its share. Each public room of an establishment is only producing its right return when it is filled with customers buying food and drink. Public rooms must have fire exits clearly marked and the local fire officer suggests the maximum number of people that can be safely accommodated.

Seating arrangements affect the number of tables and chairs it is possible to set up in a given area, allowing for vacant space around the entrance and exit, including that to the servery and pantry. The width of aisles must be adequate and space given for the required number of sideboards. The remaining space is then divided according to the size and shape of tables and whether there is to be banquette seating around the walls or in the divisions, then each square metre can be said to represent one customer in the restaurant.

2.   The way in which a banqueting room is furnished decides the number of customers that can be accommodated. Using the communal seating plan, $1–1.3$ m^2 per person is possible. Using round tables of several sizes, the allowance is 1.75 m^2 per person; for a stand-up reception, only 0.75 m^2 per person is necessary.

A *wedding breakfast* can be organised as a sit-down meal, or as a buffet reception, according to whether a formal or informal event is requested. Food can be a carved cold buffet with salmon, turkey, ham, beef and salads, or bite-size snack items such as bouchées and tartlets, chipolatas, scampi, sandwiches, trifles, mousses and cakes.

A *cocktail party* menu includes such food as crisps, salted nuts, olives, assorted cocktail canapés, sandwiches, chipolatas, sausage rolls, bridge rolls and cheese straws. The drinks can include sherry, stirred cocktails, whisky and ginger ale, gin and tonic water, vermouth and some non-alcoholic drinks.

4.   The cellar is the storeroom for alcoholic drinks and adjuncts such as lemonade and mineral waters. The stock is valuable and great security must be maintained. The cellarman arranges the stock in bin numbers as they correspond to the wine numbers on the wine list, keeping white wine in the coolest part and red wine where it is warmer. Wine bottles are stored horizontally or upside down so the contents are always touching the corks which might otherwise dry out and allow air to enter so spoiling the wine.

The cellar must not be brightly lit, there should not be any hot water pipes running through it and no vibration from passing traffic. It must be draught proof.

15 Service of liquid refreshment

1. A gastronomic dinner of six courses is likely to be booked in advance and the menu and wines discussed with the organiser or host. The protocol for wine service is to start with a light one, proceed to heavier ones, then on to a dessert wine with the sweet, port with cheese, and brandy or a liqueur with the coffee and cigars. It is usual to serve white before red, dry before sweet, and full-bodied with red meat and game.

An experienced sommelier will be able to suggest exact names and vintages of wines to match each one of the six courses as soon as he sees the chosen menu.

2. The most popular aperitifs are: Byrrh; Campari; Dubonnet; Kir; Lillet; Pastis; Pernod; Ricard; St Raphaël; sherry and vermouth, which are meant to stimulate the appetite in anticipation of a good meal. Dry white wine is also suitable.

It is usual to drink either brandy or a liqueur at the end of the meal, with the coffee. Among the many flavours of the liqueurs, most of which are sweet, are Amaretto; Apricot brandy; Atholl Brose; Bénédictine; Calisay; Chartreuse – green or yellow; Cherry brandy; Cointreau; Drambuie; Glayva; Grand Marnier; Irish Velvet; Kahlùa; Kümmel; Millefiore; Pulque; Sambuca; Southern Comfort; Tequila; Tia Maria, and Van der Hum.

When serving brandy it is not necessary to heat the balloon glass on the lamp, which is supposed to render the smell of the brandy more pronounced. A good brandy balloon is made of thin, high-quality glass so that by holding it in the palm of the hand, the customer will warm it sufficiently to bring out the 'nose' so as to savour the aroma. This can also be done with the various brands of malt whisky which some customers ask for in preference to brandy.

3. The traditional wines for drinking with oysters are champagne, Chablis, Muscadet, or Entre-Deux-Mers. Trout can be accompanied by an Alsace Gewürztraminer, a Moselle, or an Australian dry white, from say, the Hunter Valley. Curried beef does not really go with wine, and lager is quite suitable; a medium-sweet wine such as Yugoslav Traminer is in order but it should be well-chilled. For wiener schnitzel, a light red is appropriate, whilst for a raw Steak Tartare a full-bodied wine is most suitable. It is not appropriate to serve any kind of wine with ice cream, whether it contains fruit or not.

4. A dispense bar is the place where drinks are held in readiness for serving to customers in the restaurant, and only wine waiters are allowed to use it. It is kept supplied by the cellar so as to ensure it can meet anticipated orders for all kinds of drinks – cocktails, mixed drinks, beer, spirits, and bottles of wine. The barman must have a wide experience and good knowledge of the subject of drink so as to fulfil orders quickly and correctly. He must be completely honest so as not to be tempted into any malpractices. He will only issue drink against an official check signed by the sommelier, and ensure that his stock is always accurate.

16 Transport catering

1. Transport catering does not mean a restaurant approved by the 'Les Routiers' organisation, nor a 'good pull-up for car-men' in a lay-by on a trunk road. The term covers all forms of transport by land, sea, and air, where there is a need to feed people during a long journey.

Most forms of catering establishment are in a static situation where it is easier to function than on a fast-moving vehicle where there is a great risk of spilling food and where the demand is never known exactly.

The food is taken aboard at the departure depot, and prepared and served whilst the vehicle is moving at some speed. In some cases it is taken to the customer but usually the customer has to go to the point of service.

2. A cruise is a luxury holiday on board what is really a floating hotel that travels to places of interest and allows a period for sightseeing. Apart from the leisurely voyage, the main features are the food and drink, and shipping companies usually place much more emphasis on its high standard of food than on the cabin.

Stewards are on duty throughout the cruise to serve breakfast, lunch and dinner to a table of ten to twelve passengers, although some ships have two sittings for each meal. Passengers like to avail themselves of as many as six courses at each and every meal, simple because the brochure says they can have them but this can overwhelm the steward so delaying the speed of service.

3. In-flight catering is the provision of meals for passengers flying in an aeroplane; it differs from the catering done in airport restaurants by being packed into individual trays, ready to be reheated and served, with the minimum amount of fuss. Only first-class passenger will be given a choice of menu; and only those who notified the airline in advance that they can eat only an ethnic or a diet meal will be sure of getting this.

The price of the meal is included in the air ticket and some airlines provide guéridon service for first-class passengers. Fine wines are carried and there is a good choice of drink. Charter passengers flying on holiday will be offered either a snack or a full meal, according to the time of day and flying-time to the destination. It will be a hot or cold portioned meal with a hot beverage, just sufficient to alleviate the monotony of the journey rather than to satisfy a gourmets' appetite.

GLOSSARY OF TECHNICAL
TERMS

aïgo	simple Provence soup of garlic broth, served poured over sliced crusty bread
aiguillette	long thin strip cut in a slice from a breast of poultry, especially duck
aïoli	garlic-flavoured sauce made like mayonnaise; usually served with fish, salad, or snails
amuses-gueule	another name for petits fours, assorted canapés or other dainty titbits
andouille	sausage made from pig's chitterling, bought ready-made for frying
antipasto	Italian term for hors-d'oeuvre, embracing both mixed and single ones
assiette anglaise	dish of cold cuts of meat including roast beef, ham, ox-tongue and other similar joints
attereaux	small items of meat, fish, vegetables on a skewer, dipped into a sauce, coated with breadcrumbs and deep-fried; served as a hot hors-d'oeuvre
avocat	avocado pear, much used as a single hors-d'oeuvre, often with a filling and dressing
baba	light yeast-cake soaked in rum syrup, brushed with apricot jam and decorated with cream
baguette	small-length French loaf with an open texture and thick golden brown crust
ballotine	boned and stuffed chicken leg cooked by braising and served with, e.g. vegetables or rice garnish; or any boned and stuffed joint
banquet	formal meal for a number of persons, all seated and served with the same meal at the same time
Bar-le-Duc	French town famous for its quality jam and other preserves which bear the name on the label
barquette	small boat-shape pastry case; can also be shaped from other foods, e.g. cucumber
batavia	a salad vegetable also known as escarole or broad leaf endive
bâton	French loaf made in the shape of a long thin stick
baveuse	technical term used to denote a soft-centre omelette

beluga	second-best quality of caviar, with large grey grains and about 5 per cent salt; the best quality caviar is called Malossol
bisque	cream soup made of shellfish such as crab, lobster or prawns
bitocke	round flat shape of minced raw beef or chicken, usually mixed with cream or butter and fried
blancmange	cold sweet made of milk and cornflour set in a mould, then turned out
blanquette	white stew of chicken, lamb, rabbit or veal, garnished with mushrooms, onions and croûtons
blinis	yeast pancake, 10cm diameter × 1.5cm thick, made with buckwheat flour for serving hot with caviar, instead of toast
bombe	mould shaped like a bomb; filled with several flavours of ice cream, turned out and cut into portions
bortsch	broth-type soup flavoured with beetroot and duck, a speciality of Poland and Russia; served with sour cream
bouillabaisse	fish stew-cum-soup; a broth-type mixture of several kinds of fish with saffron, vegetables and garlic
bouillon	clear but not clarified stock, usually served as a soup but can also be made into a sauce
brandade	purée of cooked salt cod, usually served as Lenten dish
Brie	large flat round soft cheese from France, one of the most popular cheeses
brioche	light yeast cake made in a large or small mould, the small ones being served as part of a continental breakfast
café-complet	service of coffee with sugar, milk and cream, all in separate jugs, a croissant or brioche and jam or other preserve
calamaio, or calamari	the squid or inkfish
Camembert	soft French cheese, 12 cm diameter by 2.5 cm high; one of the most popular cheeses
canapé	small shape of toast or biscuit covered with egg, fish, meat, etc., neatly decorated and often glazed with aspic
cappuccino	cup of frothy milk coffee made with one part expresso coffee to two parts hot milk
carbonnade	thin slices of beef cooked in beer with onions; a Belgian dish
Caroline	small chou-pastry bun filled with a savoury filling and glazed with chaudfroid, as part of a hors-d'oeuvre selection
casserole	saucepan or cooking vessel made of metal or earthenware
cassolette	small china dish

cassoulet	kind of stew usually of goose or pork and haricot beans, cooked and served in an earthenware dish
cayenne	very strong kind of pepper which must be used sparingly; often offered with oysters
cèpe	thick, spongy kind of wild mushroom
Charlotte	large-size mould used for making, e.g. Apple Charlotte, Bavarois
Chartreuse	a moulded stew, usually made with game birds and cabbage; or a moulded sweet of jelly, fruit and bavarois
chaudfroid	cold dish of fish, chicken, etc., coated with sauce and set in aspic jelly; sauce used for coating cold foods
chef d'étages	the head floor waiter responsible for food and beverage service in the rooms of an hotel
chevreuil	a roebuck, the most common form of venison; usually cooked as a joint by roasting or braising
chiffonade	finely shredded items of food used to garnish or decorate a dish
civet	stew of hare; the French name for jugged hare
cloche	bell-shaped glass cover used for cooking suprêmes of chicken, mushrooms, etc., in cream
cocotte	earthenware or metal vessel with a lid; used for cooking and serving; usually oval or round in shape
condé	sweetened rice entremet, usually garnished with a fruit and coated with sauce
consommé	very clear soup made by clarifying a stock and adding a garnish
cornet	cone-shaped slice of ham, salmon, tongue, etc.; as a garnish, it may be filled with a suitable item, e.g. smoked salmon with prawns
coulibiac	large pie filled with pieces of salmon, hard-boiled egg, rice, vésiga, etc., served hot; of Russian origin
coulis	concentrated essence made by prolonged cookery for eventual use in an extended form; made from shellfish, game, ham, vegetables, etc.
coupe	glass or silver stemmed dish for serving ice cream, stewed fruit, etc.
courgette	baby marrow used mainly as a vegetable; the flower also may be served stuffed and cooked
couvert	the accoutrements for laying a place at table for one person, done in accordance with the expected choice of menu; abbreviated to cvt
cover	the same as couvert; can also be the term used to denote one customer in the restaurant
croissant	crescent-shape flaky roll served for breakfast; made of yeast dough rolled out like puff pastry
croquette	mixture of finely chopped fish or meat, etc., bound with sauce, moulded into a sausage shape, breadcrumbed and deep fried

croûton	(a) small diced fried pieces of bread for a thick soup
	(b) heart-shape slice of bread as garnish in a stew
	(c) thick square or oblong of bread for roast game birds
crudités	pieces of crisp raw celery, cucumber, carrot, green and red pimento, radishes, etc., served with dips as an appetiser
darne	slice, approximately 2 cm thick, cut through a whole round fish, such as cod or salmon
demi-tasse	smallest size cup, used for after-dinner coffee
dessert	the sweet course at the end of a meal; can also refer to the fresh fruit and nuts served in this country at the end of a meal
dips	cold sauces of various flavours usually based on mayonnaise or salad dressing, in which bread, biscuits, pieces of vegetables, etc., can be dipped; used at receptions
dumb waiter	food-lift between the kitchen and dining-room; also used to denote the waiter's sideboard
duxelles	stuffing made of finely chopped mushrooms, breadcrumbs, etc.
entremets	nowadays the French name for the sweet course on a menu; this used to be the name of the entrée course
escargots	edible snails; usually served hot in the shells as a first course
espresso	strong black coffee made under steam pressure and served in a small cup
flambé work	cooking carried out in front of a customer in which a spirit or liqueur is added and set alight
flat	a flat silver plated or stainless steel tray used for service
fleuron	crescent-shape piece of baked puff pastry to garnish, e.g., a fish dish
flûte	long thin French loaf, often used with broth soups. Also a glass for the service of sparkling wine
fondue	cheese melted with white wine and kirsch, into which cubes of bread are dipped and eaten
friandises	a term used to denote petits fours as a dish of several different kinds, served with the coffee
fricassée	white stew of chicken, veal, etc.; slightly richer than a blanquette
frog's legs	the hind legs only are served as a fish course, cooked by boiling or frying
fruits de mer	term to cover a mixture of shellfish including crab, lobster, mussels, prawns, shrimps, etc.
galantine	sausage-shaped chicken or veal forcemeat, decorated and glazed as a cold buffet dish
gamba	large prawn, also called crevette rose
garçon	general French term for a waiter especially in a café where all are of the same rank

gâteau	elaborately decorated sponge cake for cutting into wedge-shaped portions; often served as a sweet in this country
gibier	collective term for game; gibier à plumes means game birds and gibier à poil means hares, deer, wild boar, etc.
gnocchi	small dumplings made of chou pastry, potato or semolina, etc., served in a sauce as a farinaceous course
goujons	small strips of fillets of fish approx 7 cm × 0.5 cm thick, usually fried and served in a bunch
gourmet	a person who is very knowledgeable about wine and food and who enjoys savouring it
guéridon	the trolley from which final preparations to a dish are performed
hachis	dish of finely chopped cooked meat, chicken, etc., bound with a sauce and served in a border of duchesse potato
hâtelet	ornamental skewer used on large joints, particular cold ones on a buffet display
hors-d'oeuvre	first course of a menu, usually a selection of small items of egg, fish, meat and vegetables in pungent dressings
jambon	a ham such as a fine cooked York ham or a smoked Parma ham, cut into thin slices
jus	thin gravy as made from the drippings of a roast joint, or a thickened sauce known as jus lié
kebab	small pieces of fish or meat, with onion, tomato, bay-leaf, etc., threaded on a skewer and grilled; another name for brochette
kedgeree	a mixture of flaked smoked haddock, hard-boiled egg, rice, etc. served as a breakfast or supper dish; sometimes served with curry sauce
kipper	smoked opened herring, served as a breakfast or supper dish
langoustine	the Dublin Bay prawn, an orange-pink crustacean that stays the same colour when cooked
langue de chat	dry biscuit shaped like a long tongue, served with ice cream, stewed fruit, etc.
lasagne	thin broad ribbon strips of pasta, cooked and served as for spaghetti
MP	seen next to seasonal items on a menu to indicate that the price to be charged will be according to that paid at market
macédoine	diced carrot and turnip mixed with peas and diamonds of French beans, as a vegetable garnish
magret	the breast of duck that was fattened for its liver; usually cooked rare in that it has little fat
maigre	lean in that it has little or no fat; or Lenten, meaning a dish suitable for eating during Lent
Maître d'Hôtel	a head waiter or restaurant manager

mange-tout	the snow or sugar pea, grown to be cooked and eaten whole in the pod
marinade	flavouring and tenderising liquid of wine, vinegar, herbs and spices; used for tough meat and for certain vegetables and fish
marron glacé	whole candied chestnut often served as a part of a petits fours selection
matelote	fish stew made with cider or red or white wine
mayonnaise	thick cold basic sauce made of egg yolks, oil and vinegar, for serving with cold eggs, fish, vegetables, etc.
médaillon	thin round escalope of fish or meat
menu	the list of dishes on offer in a restaurant; those ready prepared are on the table d'hôte side, those cooked to order, on the à la carte side
meringue	light sweet made of whisked egg-whites and sugar and dried until crisp
mesclin	a mixture of salads grown together including cress, dandelion, chervil, chicory, fennel and lamb's lettuce
meurette	stew of fish in red wine with onion, bacon, mushroom, etc.
millefeuille	flaky gâteau of layers of puff pastry, jam and cream, covered and feathered with fondant icing
mise en place	preparations that have to be carried out before the restaurant is opened, e.g. filling cruets, laying tables
Mont Blanc	sweet made of sieved dry chestnut purée and cream
morille	a species of wild mushroom with a pitted, conical shape cap (morel)
mousse	savoury or sweet moulded item, set or cooked in a mould; very light and aerated
mousseron	small wild mushroom, called the St George
mustard	the three main kinds are English – strong, French – milder, and German – spiced with herbs; also coarse or fine, made with red wine, cider or vinegar, thus there are dozens from which to choose
mustard and cress	very delicate salad vegetable used mainly as a garnish with cold food
nage	e.g. homard à la nage, or lobster boiled and served 'swimming' in some of its cooking liquid
natives	name given to oysters reared in beds such as at Colchester
navarin	rich stew made with cheap cuts of mutton, usually garnished with potatoes and spring vegetables
nouilles	thin strips of noodle paste, plain-boiled and usually tossed in hot butter and served with grated Parmesan cheese
nuts	almonds, brazils, pecans, walnuts, etc., served as a dessert
oil	several kinds of oil are used to make salad dressing, e.g. olive, peanut, sunflower, walnut, grapeseed

okras	also called 'lady's fingers' or gombos; a pale green, elongated and hollow vegetable pod
orgeat	sweet cold drink made of barley, almonds and orange-flower water
ormer	the abalone – a large ear-shaped shellfish sometimes caught off the Channel Islands
ortanique	citrus fruit, a cross between an orange and a tangerine
oursin	seafood with a spiky cover, known as a sea urchin
paillettes	refers to cheese straws as served with some soups, such as turtle soup
palmier	biscuit made of puff pastry in the form of a palm leaf
papillote	an item finished to cook in a paper case so that it expands and turns brown in the oven
parfait	light rich mixture such as foie gras, ice cream, etc.
parma ham	cured ham eaten raw as an hors-d'oeuvre, when cut into wafer thin slices
Parmesan	very hard cheese with a sharp flavour, nearly always used grated for sprinkling over pasta dishes
pâté	hot or cold pie, with or without a crust, with any kind of filling; or a paste as pâté de foie – liver paste baked in a mould
paupiette	long fillet of fish or meat, spread with forcemeat and rolled up and cooked (a beef olive can be made as a paupiette)
Pavlova	cake made of meringue with cream and fruit filling; of Australasian origin
. petits fours	variety of small dainty biscuits, iced cakes, chocolates, glazed fruits, marzipan, etc.
piroquis	meat or fish mixture moulded into crescent shapes, crumbed and fried; served as an appetiser or hot hors-d'oeuvre
poêlé	the French equivalent of pot-roasting – cooking an item with butter and aromates in a closely-lidded container
pojarski	finely chopped chicken, veal, salmon, etc., with milk, breadcrumbs and cream, moulded into cutlet shapes and shallow-fried
Polenta	Italian type of dumpling made of cornmeal and water, stamped out as flat round cakes
potage	the general name for all soups, but more specifically as a thick purée soup made of pulse or vegetables
pouding	the French word for an English pudding, such as steak and kidney, steamed sponge pudding, etc.
poularde	a young but large tender chicken of 2–2.5 kg in weight
pousse café	spirit or liqueur served with the coffee after a meal; it can be either brandy, kirsch, Cointreau, Bénédictine, Chartreuse, etc. Also a cocktail of several layers of liqueurs poured in a rainbow effect

primeurs	early vegetables such as baby carrots and turnips and the first-grown peas and beans
profiteroles	buns baked from chou pastry and filled with cream, foie gras, etc., as a sweet or as a garnish
prosciutto	the Italian name for cured ham, served raw and cut in very thin slices, often served with melon or a pear
quail	very small game bird, now mainly reared on farms
quenelle	moulded forcemeat of chicken, veal, fish, etc., poached in stock; can be a main dish or used as a garnish
quiche	open flan usually filled with egg custard mix, cheese, ham, bacon, mushrooms, etc.
râble	saddle of hare, the part from just above the legs up to the ribs
ragoût	rich stew of beef
ramequin	cheese-flavoured pastry tartlet
ratatouille	sliced onion, egg-plant, baby marrow, tomatoes, pimentoes, etc., stewed together as a vegetable dish
ravioli	small stuffed pieces of noodle paste, poached and served with a sauce
réchaud	the hotplate on a waiter's sideboard for keeping food, plates, etc., warm
rechauffé	a reheated or made-up dish; usually appears on a table d'hôte lunch menu
risotto	braised rice; large-grain rice cooked in stock
rissole	cooked fish or meat filling enclosed in a pastry turnover and deep-fried
rosette	a round slice of meat, e.g. lamb, shallow-fried and garnished
SG	menu abbreviation to indicate that the price of a seasonal or luxury item will be charged according to its size (sélon grosseur)
sambals	side dishes served as accompaniments with curried meat
salmis	game stew, usually made with cooked game birds in a rich sauce
salpicon	a mixture of sweet or savoury items cut into small dice and bound with a sauce, for use as a filling
sauté	quick method of cookery by shallow-frying tender items, or by tossing them over and over in the pan
savarin	light yeast-cake, baked in a ring-mould then soaked in rum syrup and served as a sweet
Sea salt	coarse salt also known as freezing salt, often requested by people who prefer natural foods
serviette	a linen table-napkin or waiter's cloth
shishkebab	skewered and grilled meats with vegetables; often abbreviated to kebab
sorbet	light kind of water-ice made in many flavours, for serving midway through a long banquet meal
soufflé	very light, well-aerated sweet or savoury dish that has to be served immediately it comes from the oven

späetzle	very small dumplings made by pouring a batter through a colander into boiling water; a farinaceous dish
subric	purée of, e.g. a vegetable mixed with béchamel and eggs, shallow-fried in spoonfuls
suprême	a quality piece of fish or meat, e.g. suprême de volaille is a breast of chicken
tabasco	very pungent pepper-sauce sold in small bottles; used mainly to flavour a sauce or cocktail
table d'hôte	set menu consisting of a number of courses, charged at an inclusive price
tagliatelli	thin strips of pasta
terrine	earthenware dish in which items, e.g. liver pâté can be cooked and served
tilleuil	herbal tea made of lime tree flowers
tisane	herbal tea with barley or other flavour; useful to cure a headache or other mild ill-health
torten	large round continental sponge cake, flavoured with liqueurs and elaborately decorated
tourte	large round savoury or sweet tart with pastry top
tournedos	round piece 4·5 cm thick cut from the centre part of a fillet of beef; usually shallow-fried and served with a garnish
tronc	container for all the gratuities received by waiters, which are shared out weekly according to rank
tronçon	slice cut on the bone from a flat fish such as turbot
truffle	very black subterranean fungus used mainly cut into slices as a decoration; Italian truffles are pale cream in colour
turban	slices of fish or meat and forcemeat moulded and cooked in a ring-mould
tuxedo	name given to a short dinner-jacket, known in France as 'le smoking'
vacherin	sweet made of meringue in the form of a nest filled with cream, etc.
velouté	thin white sauce or soup made with veal or chicken stock
venison	flesh of a deer, served as a grilled steak or roasted joint
verjus	juice pressed from sour unripe grapes or crab apples, used instead of vinegar in salad dressings
vinaigrette	salad-dressing, sauce made of oil, vinegar and seasonings
voiture	a trolley such as used for hors-d'oeuvre, sweets, carving, and for lamp work
walnut oil	one of the many kinds of oil used in salad dressings
waterzoi	Belgian and Dutch fish stew made with several kinds of fish
whitebait	tiny fish of up to 5cm, served deep-fried
Xérès	the French name for sherry, e.g. sauce au Xérès

zabaglione	eggs, sugar and wine whisked until thick, for serving as a sweet dish
zeste	thinly pared lemon or orange rind, used in drinks or grated in various dishes
zakouskis	appetisers eaten before a meal to stimulate the appetite; they may consist of small items of fish, meat, vegetables and cheese
zucchini	the Italian (and US) name for baby marrows

APPENDIX 1

SYSTEMATIC CATERING

INTRODUCTION

Systematic catering is a concept in which an operation, from a single establishment to a large chain of restaurants, operates to a planned programme from which no deviation is possible. The systematic approach adopted will have analysed each aspect of the operation, no matter how simple or complex, and drawn up a description of it in the form of a manual of instruction to inform staff exactly how that particular aspect must be done.

The ideal is that the implementation of the system will ensure that every single customer gets treated alike, thus ensuring that he will be satisfied with the food and service and have no cause for complaint. No malpractices are possible as the system is foolproof and it is virtually impossible for an employee or a piece of equipment to spoil the product or cause anything to go wrong.

The firm sets its menu prices to yield the desired gross profit and can put a cost on each section of the food production operation to ensure that it makes a contribution to the profitability of the enterprise. The gross profit forecast should neither rise nor fall once the system is installed and in operation.

The result will be that customers are sure of receiving a reliable meal every time they go there and know how much it will cost and will be sure of receiving value for money.

There are two main forms of systems catering, one of which is concerned with food service, the other being mainly the concern of cooks because it is a kitchen system that produces meals for chilling or freezing. To implement a system of food service it is possible to select any kind of catering operation, to identify the salient operational factors and draw up a system that will control the whole enterprise, be it in one or many branches, each operating on exactly the same lines as the others, to a simplified and standardised restaurant system.

CONVENIENCE FOODS

These foods usually play a big part in any systematic catering operation because they can streamline the process of the food production-line. The definition of a convenience food is that it is one in which the degree of preparation has been taken to an advanced stage so as to make it labour-saving in terms of kitchen staff. In other words, a manufacturer has done much of the preliminary preparation so there is not as much to be done to it as there would be to the raw commodity.

There are various degrees of preparedness – fully prepared raw products such as portion-control cutlets, steaks, and chicken breasts, boned joints, filleted fish, peeled and turned potatoes, cut and washed vegetables, soup powders, instant sauces, instant mixes for making sponge cakes, pastry, cheesecake and many other gâteaux. Another is the range of canned and bottled meats, fruits, vegetables, soups and stews, dried foods such as fruit and vegetables, frozen foods in both raw and cooked forms which enable a caterer to serve foods regardless of seasonal availability. The list of convenience foods is lengthy.

Standardised recipes exert total control over food production and are an integral part of systems catering. A recipe will list the exact amounts of necessary ingredients and the method to be used in cooking them so as to produce a dish of uniform quality of an exact portion, and with the desired amount of profit. A recipe has to be drawn up for every dish on the menu, even though it may be only a grilled hamburger and it must be tried out as regards consumer acceptance, cooking time, oven temperature, size of portion, method of service, equipment used, before being pronounced fit for sale to customers.

Standardisation starts when purchasing specifications are drawn up to determine the exact quality of commodities required for a dish so that the supplier knows precisely what he must send, thus avoiding the use of a substandard item. This applies to all goods – convenience foods, perishables and non-perishables.

Automatic vending is the sale of food through slot machines, as found in cafeterias, factories, hospitals, kiosks, leisure centres, offices, sports halls, stores, takeaways, waiting rooms and so on. It is possible to run a catering establishment solely by means of vending machines and those establishments which cannot afford to operate a full meal service – possibly because of a small clientele or insufficient space – may decide to install a bank of automatic machines as catering amenities.

The items on sale will be snack items such as crisps, chocolate, filled rolls, and cold pies – bought in ready to put into the machine – and hot and cold beverages made in the machine. The food is constantly available but many machines cannot deal with a large number of customers without causing a queue. A member of staff is instructed on the filling and cleaning of the machines and a technician can be summoned in the event of a breakdown.

Micro-vending is a system that enables an establishment to offer hot meals at all times by means of a vending machine and a microwave oven sited close together. Chilled meals are placed in the refrigerated machine, the customer chooses the one he wants, inserts the correct money, which allows the slot to be opened and the plated meal removed. The meal has a time-token attached to it which when inserted into the mechanism operates the oven into which the meal has been placed, for the correct length of time; it then opens the door again when the food is hot. Together with a beverage vending-machine the system offers a good service for a small number of people especially if they have a meal break at staggered intervals.

The person who portions the food onto the plates must ensure that it does not exceed 5cm in depth and is arranged evenly, as otherwise, the regeneration may be uneven, leaving cold spots. The vending cabinet must be maintained at 3°C and any meal not sold within three days of production has to be discarded.

MICROWAVE COOKERY

This is not a new method but is gaining in popularity. The oven is an item of equipment that gives off electromagnetic waves that penetrate food causing the molecules to oscillate, thereby generating heat in the food and causing it to be cooked. It is a very fast method when applied to small items of up to 5 cm in thickness but does not colour food unless it is either painted with brown food colour, or a browning plate is inserted in the oven, or if it is a combined infra-red and microwave cooker.

Glass and ceramic dishes must be used as metal causes the microwaves to arc. Even the gold band or badge on a plate may be destroyed. At one time dishes of food were 'flashed' under salamander grill for half a minute or so to ensure they were hot before being passed to the waiter but the microwave oven is now frequently used to do this. Thus it is an ideal item of equipment for reheating food and regenerating chilled and frozen food, but only in small amounts.

Mealstream is the name given to a catering system based on a microwave oven that combines infra-red and hot air as found in an ordinary oven. The two powers usually work in combination to give quick results but can be operated separately; and metal pans can be used in this kind of oven.

As the system consists of oven and stove it can serve a table d'hôte menu and some à la carte dishes to order, using a minimum number of staff, and in a closely confined space. A stove is not absolutely essential as the oven will cook the vegetables and sauté chops, steaks and escalopes rapidly but a deep fryer for chips and any other deep-fried food is necessary.

Sous-vide is a method of cooking food under vacuum by placing the raw item into an impermeable pouch, removing the air by vacuum, sealing it then cooking at between 65°–85° for a specific period of time. It is then chilled to 0°C and stored at 3°C for up to six days. When required for serving it is regenerated in the pouch, opened and arranged on the dish. This is an advance on boil-in-the-bag portions of food which need to be kept deep-frozen.

It may seem a paradox to suggest that a refrigerator can also be used to cook food but such a system does exist; the *ReconPlus oven* was developed for serving hot meals to passengers travelling in jumbo jet airplanes and the same equipment is also used in large-scale catering establishments on land. Food is stored in the oven which is switched to cold until a timer is activated to turn it to cook, which is done by infra-red tubes and forced air. All kinds of fresh food can be grilled, poached, baked and roasted, and frozen meals are quickly regenerated.

The *Frigofour* is a combined refrigerator and regenerating oven into which chilled portioned meals are packed and the timer programmed to reheat them to the right temperature at a particular time; a separate section is given to each kind of food so that it receives the correct temperature.

There are several well-established systems of food service designed for large-scale catering operations, such·as Ganymede, Regithermic, Helither-mic for service purposes, and Chaudfroid, and Cuisson froid, in which large numbers of portions of food are cooked then chilled or blast-frozen for regeneration and distribution at a later date.

Most of these systems are designed to supply individual meals as chosen by the consumers, who are usually patients in hospital or elderly or disabled homebound people receiving meals-on-wheels. The meals are kept at the right temperature and in the best condition so as to stimulate the appetite.

Other systems are being developed and the reader should endeavour to keep up to date with methods of systematic cooking and serving.

The *cafeteria counter service* and layout for large-scale catering establishments and fast-food restaurants has to make the best possible use of available space, using sufficient length to accommodate every item available on the menu. Customers come to these counters to receive their meal and to collect cutlery, drinks and adjuncts on their way to the cash register; there must be sufficient circulatory space between the service-counter and seating-area to accommodate these other facilities.

A *refectory* that offers a single menu with few choices can operate from one small service-counter but for larger numbers and greater choice a longer length of counter is necessary as otherwise a long queue will cause customers frustration.

It is better to have a counter for each menu rather than one counter for main dishes, one for sweets and another for starters, because customers will then have to go from one counter to the other in order to obtain a full meal. If possible the lay-out should be in sequence from meal-counter to beverage-point, to the sundry-counter, to cash desk, to cutlery-counter and thence into the dining-area.

The area taken up by self-service counters amounts to some 25 per cent of the total refectory or dining-room area and since the need is to provide sufficient eating-space it may be advisable to site the serving-counters in echelon style at an angle of 45°, so allowing a greater length of counter-run in less space.

The servery must be adjacent to the kitchen so that fresh supplies of food can be quickly obtained. It is possible to use hot and cold mobile servery counters of various sizes, which can be fitted together as required.

Modular service is a system that uses only standardised items of equipment throughout the kitchen and restaurant. It applies equally to large items of equipment such as ovens, steamers, refrigerators and service counters as it does to trolleys, trays and dishes. The dishes used for cooking foods will fit oven shelves, refrigeration racks and trolleys, and will slot into the bain-marie on a service-counter; all are based on a module of 527 mm × 324 mm in halves, quarters and other fractions and of several depths. Being made of stainless steel, plastic or aluminium, they are light in weight and hygienic, are very versatile and even the lids can be used for cooking, and for displaying foods. Each size holds a given amount of food and definite number of portions.

Gastronorm is the name given to these food-service containers which are made and used in many countries including Switzerland, where they were first launched in 1964. Many equipment manufacturers now base the sizes of the equipment they make on this system.

A *Carousel* is a merry-go-round and some years ago a French catering equipment firm developed a system of food service under that name in the form of a rotating circular servery. It was sited in the dividing wall between kitchen and restaurant so that one half was always on view to customers who could select their meal from a wide range of food and drink as the counter slowly rotated. As necessary, the cook behind the scenes, replenished the trays, which were arranged in different levels on the turntable which took approximately one minute to go full-circle. Crockery and cutlery were kept on a separate table; Figure A.1 shows this system.

Fig A.1 *diagram of a carousel food service system*

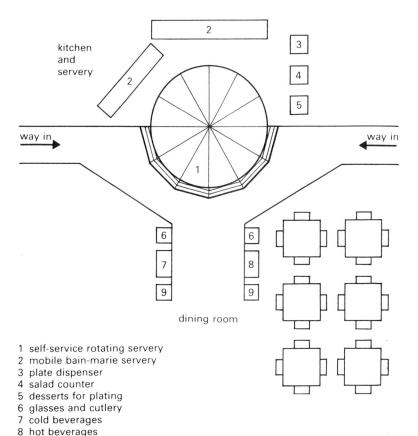

1 self-service rotating servery
2 mobile bain-marie servery
3 plate dispenser
4 salad counter
5 desserts for plating
6 glasses and cutlery
7 cold beverages
8 hot beverages
9 cash desk

DISHWASHING SYSTEM

The servery is also the place where the waiter obtains his supply of hot plates, taking them from a heated cupboard at the same time as he receives the food he has ordered. An efficient arrangement for the supply of clean crockery and cutlery makes the waiter's job much easier and the amount available must be adequate, as otherwise the waiter may be forced to dip dirty cutlery into a bucket of greasy water then wipe it dry on his cloth ready for use.

The siting of the plate-room where dirty cutlery, crockery and silverware is deposited and from where clean utensils are easily obtained, is crucial to the efficiency of the catering operation. It has to be close to the exit from the restaurant but not so close that the noise and steam seep into the restaurant.

The operational feature of this department is first the stripping-down area which waiters can facilitate by separating the dirty items when clearing the table; then the plateman puts the dirty cutlery into baskets, the glasses and cups into trays, and stacks the plates in readiness to put between the pegs on the dishwasher conveyor-belt. Another plateman takes them off at the other end in a clean and dry condition ready for re-use.

Some items may need soaking before being put through the dish-washing machine and each item should be checked as it is emitted to ensure it is perfectly clean.

Conveyor-belt dish-washing systems have revolutionised the operating of the dish-washing area by speeding up the process and giving improved working conditions to the staff; much of the reputation of a restaurant stems from the shine on the cutlery, glassware and crockery, and waiting-staff appreciate the support service provided by the factotums of plate-room and silver-room.

FAST FOOD OPERATION

Fast-food systems and takeaways meet a consumer need by offering simple food of a consistent quality at an affordable price, especially for people on a low income who like to eat out occasionally. These establishments are totally standardised and operate to a formula that ensures both customer satisfaction and maximum profitability.

There are many multinational firms in the fast-food business, some being run by the firm itself while others are franchised to an operator who must run his place exactly to company formula, with the same décor, menu and prices, and has to obtain most of his food from nominated suppliers. He pays a percentage of the takings as the royalty for holding the franchise.

A fast-food operation does not conjure an image of an exciting eating occasion because the customer–staff contact is fleeting and as in a supermarket, the experience can be alienating. People patronise a cafe for the sociability of the occasion, exchanging gossip and making acquaintances but though the smile may be fixed on the face of the fast-food server, there can be no real communication, apart from the sometimes frenetic activity of a restaurant full of customers.

Takeaway food service plays a big part in the eating patterns of many millions of people in this country and although it does not usually require the service of a waiter, it is sometimes the offshoot of a traditional restaurant or fast-food shop.

Takeaway is available in many forms, the most popular being fish and chips, followed by Chinese foods, pizzas, hamburgers, baked potatoes, Indian foods, and foods from kebab houses. Some customers prefer takeaway meals because of their convenience and cost; also it saves them having to cook for themselves and they may dislike cookery or have no facilities. Some takeaways offer a delivery service and for a small delivery fee, will accept a telephone order and send a hot meal with minimum delay.

Takeaway meal service fulfils a modern need and is likely to expand in the future; some of the items are already provided on a franchise basis and these have set a standard for all takeaway establishments.

A *steak house* usually has a traditional décor and a sedate pace of operation; the formula for the system is that which suits the menu desired by a particular clientele. The waiter may introduce himself by name or wear a name badge, and should greet his customers with a smile.

THE NON-PROFIT SECTOR

This is the section of the catering industry which includes Institutional and Welfare Catering and all the non-profit making establishments, run mostly by local Councils and government agencies, such as hospitals, and also factory and office canteens where meals are served at cost or are subsidised as a service to employees. In most of these institutions the catering has to be done on a large scale which precludes any individual finishing touches as practised in restaurant catering. Food service is done by a pre-plated system or by a counter self-service system, and in most of them – as in college and university catering services – must operate so that all costs are met by the income received from customers.

The Social Services departments of local authorities send meals-on-wheels to the elderly and to housebound people, usually by means of the Women's Royal Voluntary Service (WRVS). The meal may be a frozen one prepared by a commercial firm, which is regenerated and taken in insulated boxes from a Day Centre direct to the recipients' house. Day Centres also serve a midday meal to people attending there. Some of these establishments may have their own cooks but these are being replaced by the use of prepared chilled or frozen meals.

A *cook–freeze* or *cook–chill* system is very cost-effective since semi-skilled operatives in one kitchen can produce thousands of meals for distribution to a large number of sites.

Industrial catering

This can mean the serving of meals to staff employed in, for example, a factory. It may be cooked by catering employees of that firm, or a service carried out under contract by a firm of industrial caterers who will operate the kitchen for the firm at a fee.

Working as a caterer in a factory or office is not an inferior grade of job and most firms are proud of the standard of food and service they offer to their employees and although the trend is towards one canteen for all grades of staff, irrespective of status, there is always a requirement for high-class meals for prospective customers as well as for staff parties and various celebrations.

There are some very good jobs in this sector of the industry, where the pay and conditions of waiting staff are equivalent to or better than those in the commercial world, in addition to which the hours of duty and working conditions may be more congenial.

APPENDIX 2

CALENDAR OF SEASONS

This list shows the month when home-grown foods first come into season and are at their best as regards quality, freshness and price. The novelty of their first appearance makes them eminently suitable to be featured as the speciality of the day and as an à la carte item. Despite modern transport which can bring exotic foods from across the world, there is a lot of interest for the freshly-gathered local item, as soon as it makes its appearance on the market and is featured prominently on the menu.

Many items of meat, fish and vegetables are available all the year because they do not have seasons; only those which make an impact on menus are included here:

January	scallops, forced rhubarb, Jerusalem artichokes
February	Brussels tops, whitebait, salmon, sprats
March	watercress, radishes, spring onions, spring greens, spinach
April	asparagus, mackerel, smelts, new carrots and turnips, globe artichokes, new potatoes, corn salad
May	salmon-trout, eel, broccoli, courgettes, peas, turnips, strawberries
June	Melons, gooseberries, broad beans, French beans, carp, pike
July	aubergines, field mushrooms, sweetcorn, mange-touts, blackcurrants, cherries, peaches, greengages, raspberries
August	grouse, snipe, roebuck, fallow deer, wood pigeon, runner beans, plums, pears, damsons
September	oysters, turbot, John Dory, partridge, wild duck, cèpes, apples, parsnips, pumpkin, salsify, swede, endive, walnuts
October	Brussels sprouts, sea-kale, filberts, chestnuts, red cabbage, pheasant, woodcock

APPENDIX 3

COURSES AND

EXAMINATIONS

The possession of certificates or other proof of competence and knowledge can be an advantage when applying for a job, or requesting a promotion. These pieces of paper show the subject taken and the level attained and, in the case of the *City and Guilds* as an examining body, states the examination number and the date taken. For example, the examination in Food and Beverage Service is CG707 and covers the theory and practice of the job of a waiter – a course that can be taken on a full or part-time basis at a catering college. There are also a number of on-the-job courses with skills tests including CG7003 for Food Service Assistant, 7004 for Counter Service, and 7005 for Bar Service Staff. There is also the CG717 course on Alcoholic Beverages.

The *Wine and Spirits Education Trust* offers short courses on the subject of drink, the sequence being the Certificate, Higher Certificate, and Diploma. Courses are held at technical colleges as well as at the Trust's offices.

The *Guild of Sommeliers* has branches all over the country which hold regular meetings on the subject of wine service. The *United Kingdom Bartender's Guild* has many branches which hold meetings and organise competitions on the subject of cocktail-making, among other similar topics. Some firms hold wine-tastings and specialist travel agents organise visits to, and courses at, well-known vineyards in many countries.

APPENDIX 4

EXAMPLES OF MENUS FOR

SPECIAL FUNCTIONS

(a) Banquet – 4 course lunch

Consommé Madrilène

☆ ☆ ☆

Truite de Rivière Belle
Meunière

☆ ☆ ☆

Poulet en Casserole Bonne Femme
Petits Pois à la Française
Pommes Marquise

☆ ☆ ☆

Coupe Montmorency

☆ ☆ ☆

Café

(b) Banquet – Dinner

La Terrine de Lapereau

☆ ☆ ☆

Le Bisque de Homard

☆ ☆ ☆

Les Quenelles de Brochet Lyonnaise

☆ ☆ ☆

La Selle d'Agneau de Lait Cadmos

Les Primeurs du Marché

Les Pommes Sarladaise

☆ ☆ ☆

Le Parfait Glacé aux Kiwis

☆ ☆ ☆

Les Petits Fours
Le Café

(c) Cocktail Party

Canapés à la Russe

Petits Pains de Windsor

Sandwiches de Langue, Poulet, et
Saumon Fumé

Chipolatas; Paillettes au Parmesan

Sausage rolls; Bouchées Forestière; Quichelettes Lorraine

Olives; Amandes Salées; Céleris Farcis

(d)   Hunt Ball

Saumon froid en Bellevue

Mayonnaise de Homard

Suprême de Volaille Jeannette

Aiguillette de Caneton en Chaudfroid

Selle d'Agneau Bouquetière

Côte de Boeuf   Langue Ecarlate

Pâté de Gibier   Jambon de York

Salades Variées

Macédoine de Fruit   Fraises Chantilly

Poire Impératrice   Croquembouche

Thé   Café   Chocolat

(e)   Medieval-type Banquet of 5 courses

A Smokie Mackrel wythe Ye Horse-raddish

Ye Slurpe of Friar Tuck

Ye Soal Dressed Finely Fryed

Ye Baron of Beefe from ye Spit

Earthe Apples of ye Endies

Colewurtes wythe Chesten Nuttes

☆ ☆ ☆

A Slice of Mistress Rowbottom's
Apple Tarte wythe ye Cheshire Cheesie

☆ ☆ ☆

Ye Tasse of Brewed Brazil Beanes

(f)   Garden Party

Mayonnaise de Saumon

Canapés Moscovite

Sandwiches de Concombre, Tomate, et Foie gras

Carolines de Volaille: Bouchées de Homard

Gâteaux-Chocolat, Printanière, Moccha

Fraises Melba; Pâtisseries Françaises

Hock Cup

(g) Wedding Anniversary

Avocat Pasadena

☆ ☆ ☆

Crème Portugaise

☆ ☆ ☆

Filets de Plie Caprice

☆ ☆ ☆

Jambon Braisé Port-Maillot
Subrics d'Epinard; Pommes Persillées

☆ ☆ ☆

Gâteau Nougatine

☆ ☆ ☆

Corbeille de Fruits
Café

(h) Christmas Day Menu

Coupe de la Terrine-Sainte

☆ ☆ ☆

Potage des Trois Mages

☆ ☆ ☆

Berceau de Sole Cherubin

☆ ☆ ☆

Dinde de Norfolk Rôtie
Choux de Bruxelles Limousine
Pommes Château

☆ ☆ ☆

Pouding de Noël au Feu de Joie

☆ ☆ ☆

Délice du Bon Pasteur

Mendiants
Café

(i) Wedding Breakfast (formal sit-down)

Coupe Miami

☆ ☆ ☆

Consommé Célestine

☆ ☆ ☆

Rosettes d'Agneau
Haricots Verts au Beurre
Pommes Dauphine

☆ ☆ ☆

Savarin aux Fruits

☆ ☆ ☆

Café

(j) Kosher Menu (non-milk)

Hors-d'oeuvre Riche aux Cornets de Saumon Fumé

☆ ☆ ☆

Bortsch Polonaise Cachère

☆ ☆ ☆

Gefilltefisch Galilénne

☆ ☆ ☆

Poussin Rôti farci au Matzos
Carottes et Petits Pois Etuvées

☆ ☆ ☆

Apfelstrüdel

☆ ☆ ☆

Café Noir

(k) Gala Dinner of 6 courses

Le Caviar de Beluga aux Blinis

☆ ☆ ☆

La Tortue Claire au Xérès

☆ ☆ ☆

Les Délices de Sole Clarence

☆ ☆ ☆

La Suprême de Pintadeau Epicurienne
Les Mangetouts au Beurre
Le Panier de Pommes Berny

☆ ☆ ☆

Le Zéphyr de Foie Gras Oporto
La Salade Lorette

☆ ☆ ☆

Le Soufflé Rothschild

☆ ☆ ☆

Les Mignardises
Le Café Moccha

Gala Dinner of 8 courses

Le Parfait de Foie Gras au Porto

☆ ☆ ☆

Le Velouté Doria

☆ ☆ ☆

La Suprême de Truite-saumonée Florentine

☆ ☆ ☆

Le Coeur de Filet de Boeuf en Croûte
Les Céleris Braisés à la Moelle
Les Pommes Nouvelles de Jersey au Beurre

☆ ☆ ☆

Les Asperges Froides, Sauce Vinaigrette

☆ ☆ ☆

Le Bombe Alexandra
Les Friandises

☆ ☆ ☆

Le Canapé Menelik

☆ ☆ ☆

La Corbeille de Fruits
Le Café

Menus for Outdoor Catering Functions

Pheasant and Brandy Pâté
Melba Toast

☆ ☆ ☆

Cream of Asparagus Soup

☆ ☆ ☆

Contrefilet of Beef Chasseur
Braised Celery
French Beans
New Potatoes

☆ ☆ ☆

Fresh Fruit Salad and Cream

Cheese Board

Coffee

Wines: Niersteiner Domtal
Château La Tour Canon

Cocktail de Fruits de Mer

☆ ☆ ☆

Saumon froid en Bellevue
Sauce Verte

☆ ☆ ☆

Poularde Poêlée Forestière
Petits Pois au Beurre
Pommes Nouvelles Rissolées

☆ ☆ ☆

Crème Impératrice

☆ ☆ ☆

Petits Fours

Café

Gourmet Dinner

Le Zephyr de Foie Gras à la Gelée au Porto
Les Petites Brioches Chaudes

☆ ☆ ☆

Le Suprême de Turbot Braisé Amphytrion

☆ ☆ ☆

La Caille Fourrée à la Façon du Grand-Vatel

☆ ☆ ☆

Le Neige au Champagne

☆ ☆ ☆

Le Coeur de Contrefilet de Boeuf Epicurienne

☆ ☆ ☆

Le Turban de Comices Lucullus

☆ ☆ ☆

Le Coffret Fleuri de Frivolités

L'Extrait de Moccha

New Year's Eve Dinner

Les Huîtres Royales Perlées au Citron
Le Foie Gras en Croûte Strasbourgeoise
Le Rosé d'Ecosse au Pain Bis

☆ ☆ ☆

Le Bisque de Homard à l'Armagnac
La Tasse de Consommé Madrilène

☆ ☆ ☆

La Paupiette de Sole Grand-duc

☆ ☆ ☆

Le Coeur de Filet Reveillon
Le Fond d'Artichaut Marie-Louise
Les Pommes Lorette

☆ ☆ ☆

Le Parfait Grand Marnier

☆ ☆ ☆

La Tranche d'Ananas Bonne Année

La Corbeille de Friandises

Le Café

BIBLIOGRAPHY

Further insight into the many different aspects of restaurant service may be obtained from these books.

Challenor-Chadwick, A., *A Foot in Front* (Old Rectory (Denton) Ltd, 1985) a humorous account of a provincial hotel by its very down-to-earth patron who ran the kitchen and restaurant in a style all of his own.

Contarini, P., *The Savoy was my Oyster* (London: Robert Hale, 1976) the story of a waiter who rose to become the banqueting manager and subsequently joint-manager of the Savoy Hotel in London.

Cracknell, H. and Nobis, G., *Practical Professional Gastronomy* (London: Macmillan, 1985) an encyclopaedic book on the factors which create the enjoyment of food and drink.

Deghy, G., *Paradise in the Strand* (London: Richards Press, 1958) the history of Romano's Restaurant in the Strand with portraits of its notable staff and customers from 1875 until its closure shortly after the Second World War.

Fuller, J. and Currie, A., *The Waiter*, 3rd edn (London: Barrie & Rockliff, 1967) one of the first complete texts on waiting.

Gallati, M., *Mario of the Caprice* (London: Hutchinson, 1960) the life story of a great head waiter who rose from humble general assistant at the age of 10 in Milan, to become the proud owner of the most fashionable restaurant in London.

Ginder, S. J., *A Guide to Napkin Folding* (Tunbridge Wells: Costello, 1985) shows dozens of different ways of folding table napkins.

Hasler, G. F., *Wine Service in Restaurants* (London: Wine and Spirits Publications, 1968) a very good though brief treatise on all aspects of the service of drink in a good-class restaurant.

Johnson, R. H., *Running your own Restaurant* (London: Hutchinson, 1982) first hand account of the problems and pleasures of owning a good-class restaurant.

Julyan, B., *Multiple-choice Questions on Food Service* (London: Heinemann, 1980) a useful guide to the type of questions as set by the City and Guilds Institute, with 500 examples.

Ritz, M. L., *César Ritz – Host to the World* (London: Harrap, 1938) describes in detail how a young Swiss waiter went on to become the greatest hotelier in the world.

Tuor, C., *Wine and Food Handbook* (London: Hodder & Stoughton, 1984) a good guide to the art of serving wine and food.

INDEX